TICONDEROGA'S MAJOR RACES

1936 – 1967

1936	Jeffrey's Ledge	First to Finish
1938	Jeffrey's Ledge	First to Finish
	New London/Marblehead	First to Finish/Set Record
	Boston Lightship	First to Finish/Set Record
1940	Miami/Nassau	First to Finish/Set Record
1947	Marblehead/Halifax	First to Finish/Set Record
1949	Ft. Lauderdale/Cat Cay	First to Finish
1950	Lipton Cup	First to Finish
	Governor's Cup	First to Finish
	St. Pete/Havana	First to Finish
1951	Lipton Cup	First to Finish/Set Record
	Miami/Nassau	First to Finish
	Nassau Cup	First to Finish
	St. Pete/Havana	First to Finish
1952	Nassau Cup	First to Finish/Set Record
	St. Pete/Havana	First to Finish/Set Record
	Bermuda/Halifax	First to Finish/Set Record
	Monhegan Island	First to Finish/Set Record
1953	Cornfield Light	First to Finish/Set Record
1954	St. Pete/Havana	First to Finish
1960	Miami/Nassau	First to Finish
	Nassau Cup	First to Finish
1962	St. Pete/Ft. Lauderdale	First to Finish/Set Record
1963	Los Angeles/Honolulu	First to Finish
1964	Los Angeles/Papeete	First to Finish/Set Record
1965	St. Pete/Venice	First to Finish/Set Record
	St. Pete/Ft. Lauderdale	First to Finish
	Miami/West End	First to Finish
	Lauderdale YC Trophy	First to Finish
	Miami/Montego Bay	First to Finish/Set Record
	Los Angeles/Honolulu	First to Finish/Set Record
1966	Bermuda/Copenhagen	First to Finish
	Skaw Race	First to Finish/Set Record
1967	Miami/Montego Bay	First to Finish

TICONDEROGA

Tales Of An Enchanted Yacht

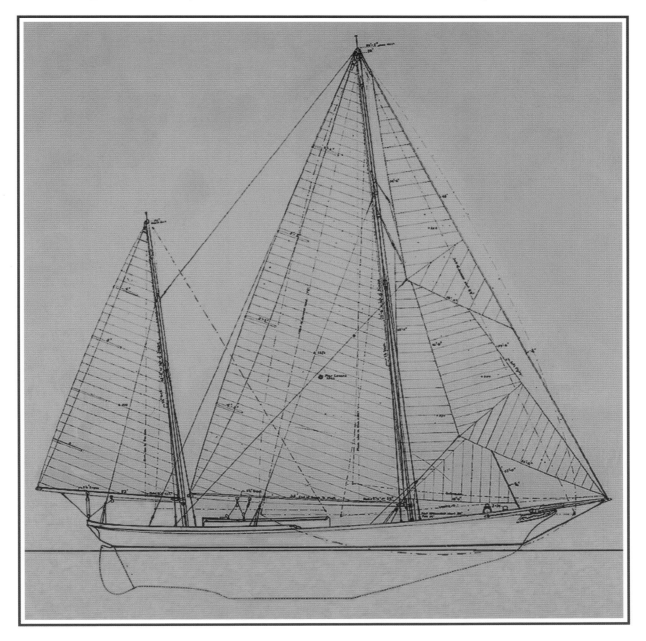

Jack A. Somer

A MYSTIC SEAPORT MUSEUM BOOK

PRODUCED BY CONCEPTS PUBLISHING INC.
DISTRIBUTED BY W.W. NORTON & COMPANY

For my beloved parents, Pauline and David, who set the course;
and the owners, captains, crews, and many friends
who sailed *Ticonderoga* into history.

Other books by Jack A. Somer:

Juliet: The Creation of a Masterpiece
M/Y Izanami
Ocean Giants

First Edition 1997

Library of Congress Cataloging-in-Publication Data

Somer, Jack A., 1935–
      Ticonderoga : tales of an enchanted yacht / by Jack A. Somer.
         p. cm.— (A Mystic Seaport Museum book)
      ISBN 0-393-04613-3
       1. Ticonderoga (Ketch)   2. Yachts — United States.   I. Title.
  II. Series.
  VM331.S66 1997
  797.1'4—dc21
                                             97-16311
                                           CIP

ISBN 0-393-04613-3

Design: Bonnie Atwater, Atwater Design
Design Consultant: Dana Jinkins, Concepts Publishing Inc.
Color Separations: John Matthews, Graphic Services
Typeset in Centaur with Benguiat and Belwe as display faces.

Printed in Canada

Mystic Seaport Museum, Inc.
75 Greenmanville Avenue
Mystic, CT 06355-0990

CONTENTS

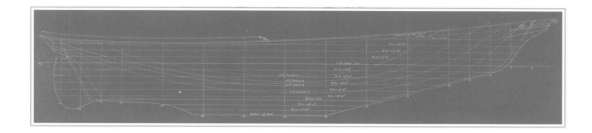

PREFACE

THE SCHOONER *AMERICA* (which, sadly, was destroyed by a crush of snow in early 1942) gained global fame by winning only one 60-mile race around the Isle of Wight (albeit against a fleet of aggressively sailed British yachts). As a result of that singular event, in 1851, the 101-foot yacht gave her name forever to the most vigorous sailing competition and embattled trophy the world has known: The America's Cup.

By contrast, the 72-ketch *Ticonderoga* (stronger, more vigorous, and as fast today as when she was launched in 1936) won her continuing global fame on the basis of an extended series of extraordinary racing victories—spanning six decades and taking place on two magnificent oceans, several stormy seas, and along the coasts of three continents. In her first 37 racing starts (in major and minor events between 1936 and 1951), *Ticonderoga* was first to finish 24 times. Beginning with her first major record-breaking performance, in the 1938 New London to Marblehead Race, she set a blazing pace of winning never again to be equalled. During her most productive ocean racing years—from the end of World War II until the spring of 1967—she was first to finish countless more times, and she broke dozens of more records. At one time this gold-and-white beauty held more than 30 elapsed-time records—including both Transpac Races, the Transatlantic Race, and all the events in the SORC. Many of these records still stand today, despite the subsequent launching of several new generations of more modern racing machines.

Yet *Ticonderoga* was not designed for racing. Despite her continued racing success (she had the best cumulative elapsed time in Antigua Classic Week, in April 1997) there is more to *Ticonderoga's* sixty-year story than just her astonishing and unique collection of silver. She is deemed to be one of the most graceful yachts ever designed, and she has given pleasure to a dozen owners and a thousand sailors who have contributed to her speed and her mythology.

What follows here is the complete and (I feel compelled to add) fascinating story of *Ticonderoga*—one yacht among many, perhaps, but possibly the most important, probably the most handsome, and surely the most inspiring sailing yacht ever to leave her wake across a stormy ocean or windswept sea. J.A.S.

VINTAGE WINE
In Several New Bottles

1923–1934

I N THE WIDE-RANGING EBB and flood of America's turbulent history the 1920s stand out for their effervescent revelry, sparkling animation, and torrential change. The American 1920s were the equivalent of a national adolescence for a population awakened to its global role by the brutality of World War I, but not yet matured into fulfilling that role by the exigencies of World War II. Still, those complex years between the end of the Great War and the beginning of the Great Depression witnessed momentous currents in American society.

A large portion of an unworldly population found itself shifting from Spartan rural farms to industrialized urban centers, where it was duly baffled by flappers, speakeasies, the whirling Charleston, and the whizzing Model T. The period was the heyday of such lustrous flesh-and-blood creators as Ben Hecht, e.e. cummings, W.C. Fields, Ellington, Valentino, Hemingway, and the Gershwin brothers. And it gave birth to such

The clipper-bowed schooner America.
(Mystic Seaport Museum, Inc.)

magnificent American creations as *The Great Gatsby, The Gold Rush, The New Yorker,* "Star Dust," Faulkner's first novel, Calder's first mobile, and Mickey Mouse's debut as Steamboat Willie.

To add to the rush and roar of the 1920s this relatively unfledged nation had to simultaneously take in stride the tumultuous and often unsettling effects of rural electrification, women's suffrage, capricious stock markets, soaring skyscrapers, regular airmail, the eerie sound of the theremin, the patent miracle of Cellophane, and a golden statue called "Oscar." It was indeed an era of flux, jazz, and innovation.

Yet, as if to counter America's post-war mania, the 1920s were also a troubled time, one that gave raw and long-lasting notoriety to such haunting emblems as Sacco and Vanzetti, Leopold and Loeb, and the Scopes Monkey Trial. And to add to the decade's complexity, a deepening conservatism and growing isolationism gripped the nation's psyche: the Quota Act defended Americans against immigrants; high tariffs defended Americans against foreign competitors; and

Prohibition defended Americans against themselves. Indeed, with president Warren G. Harding's heartfelt promise of "normalcy" to a people weary from war, the nation's political life from 1920 to the end of the decade was so unspeakably dull that even the Teapot Dome oil-leasing scandal could not fully resuscitate it. As a result, in the topsy-turvy milieu of the 1920s ordinary Americans by the millions chose to stay at home to delight in an almost carnal affair with electricity and its endless progeny: toasters, irons, vacuum cleaners, refrigerators, ranges and, above all, superheterodyne amplitude-modulation radios from which they could learn of Babe Ruth's homers, Bill Tilden's backhand, Jack Dempsey's knockouts, Notre Dame's "Four Horsemen," and Man O' War retiring to stud.

But the stultifying blanket of "normalcy" spread by Washington also permitted the centers of leveraged power to shift away from government into the hands of canny industrialists and aggressive entrepreneurs— Fords, Rockefellers, Morgans, Astors, and Vanderbilts—whose talents for management and persuasion overpowered the government's and ultimately ruled the day. Spurred by an unprecedented accumulation of wealth and leisure time, the 1920s inevitably saw a renewal in the gentlemanly sport of yachting, ushering in a golden age of mahogany speedboats, dashing commuters, luxurious diesel yachts, and a proliferation of classic gold-leaf decorations. For less speed-conscious yachtsmen, a new breed of sailing yachts was created, with still-illustrious names such as *Niña*, *Elena*, *Zodiac*, and a series of *Malabars*.

At the same time (like the yacht-design revolution of the 1840s, which culminated in George Steers' singular schooner *America*) there were tectonic shifts in the American yachting marketplace. Edward Burgess, one of the titans of American yacht design, was long dead. Nathanael Greene Herreshoff, the craggy "Wizard of Bristol"—who, with his almost supernatural sense of proportion, had single-handedly moved the epicenter of yacht design from the great seafaring capitals of Europe to modest Bristol, Rhode Island—was in his seventies and essentially retired. The family-held stock of the Herreshoff Manufacturing Company, a leading American boatbuilder, had been sold during World War I to a syndicate of detached yachtsmen. And a new generation of postwar designers was at work, zealously improving upon the Herreshoff legacies of speed, grace, and economy of design, to satisfy a new generation of postwar clients with disposable postwar wealth seeking greater pleasure on the water.

A modern yacht style was emerging. Refined hullforms and rigs were coming into vogue, in large part in response to the compelling new science of aerodynamics. Growing directly out of aviation's explosive impact on war and transport, new understandings of the sailboat's unique behavior in two fluids—water and air—directed naval architects toward the greater possibilities of reducing a yacht's resistance in both. Beginning with William Froude's pioneering work in the 1870s, the towing tank had already

John Alden's Malabar IV, *the semifisherman schooner that won the 1923 Bermuda Race.*
(Mystic Seaport Museum, Inc./Rosenfeld Collection)

proven its great value in transfiguring hullforms. Now the wind tunnel was increasingly being applied as a tool to cultivate better sails and rigs.

Traditional European science was finding welcome application to yacht design, which in the 1920s evolved in new directions. With new understanding of how wind passing over a sail's surface develops power more efficiently as the ratio of the sail's height to width increases, naval architects began to cast off

the primordial gaff-headed rig in favor of the more effective jib-headed, or Marconi, rig, prescribing ever-taller masts, shorter booms, and lesser bowsprits. (The 1920 America's Cup sailed by *Resolute* and *Shamrock IV* would be the last ever contested in those mammoth gaff-rigged sloops, which were replaced in 1930 by more efficient, aerodynamic J-Class yachts designed to the International Rule.) Under aviation's burgeoning influence, sailmakers refined the airfoil shape of sails through new-style panel cuts that more close-ly emulated the long foils of aircraft wings (themselves inspired by the uncannily efficient wings of birds). The new generation of jib-headed yachts climbed into the wind as none had done before, changing the nature of casual sailing and gallant racing for all time.

This technical revolution was popularized on both sides of the Atlantic by Manfred Curry, an American sailor/scientist living in Germany, whose aesthetic visions, keen observations, and practical experiments inspired him to write *Yacht Racing*, the first widely read, if not altogether credible, twentieth-century scientific treatise on sailing theory and practice. Curry's graphic two-color illustrations of bird wings, sails, wind-tunnel tests, and polar plots were subtly instructive to a new generation of international sportsmen seeking to apply science to the more practical and artistic aspects of sailing.

In 1923—the year *Aeroflot* was created, *Bambi* was published, Adolf Hitler wrote *Mein Kampf*, and Wamsutta introduced duck sailcloth—yachting took another bold step forward on America's shores. After a thir-teen-year hiatus brought on by war and apathy, the Bermuda Race was reborn at the assertive urging of *Yachting's* colorful editor, Herbert L. Stone. Stone recognized that American yachtsmen were once more aching for robust ocean competition and shoreside fellowship. Stone organized the Bermuda Race primarily around sturdy semifisherman-type schooners, which, despite their soon-to-be outdated gaff rigs, were snug, stable, and highly suitable for the blustery reaching that often typifies conditions along the Bermuda Race rhumbline. Stone and a band of gaff-loving friends (without an American yacht club to back them but with the accommodating patronage of The Royal Bermuda Yacht Club) enlisted a mixed fleet of 22 yachts—many designed by Alden, Hand, Mower, and Winslow—to race from New London, Connecticut, to St. David's Head, Bermuda. In a not-unexpected heavy-weather thrash, John G. Alden, on his schooner *Malabar IV*, won the Bermuda Trophy, and Robert N.

Bavier won Class "B" in his *Memory*. The biennial Bermuda Race remains one of the international circuit's most imposing challenges, particularly to navigators who relish weighing the weather's eternal vagaries against the Gulf Stream's churning eddies and snaking meanders. (In 1923, one of Stone's writers quoted a Furness Line skipper, who called the Stream "the most variable river on earth." He was quite correct.)

In view of this reawakening of yachting in America, many Brahmins of industry and finance sought new sailing yachts for quiet family diversion and vigorous manly racing. It was more than apposite, therefore, that sometime in 1923 Waldo Hayward Brown, a young, energetic, and very bright yachtsman with some spare equity at his disposal, elected to build himself and his growing family a new boat. Waldo "Brownie" Brown (from a family whose men, for many generations, were mostly sea captains or boatbuilders) was

descended directly from Paul Brown, a mariner active during the American Revolution. But Brown could, with confidence, trace his American roots as far back as the Englishman William Brown, a physician who arrived on these shores in 1620 on that most famous of historic little ships, the *Mayflower*. (The name Brown is encountered frequently throughout America's history, maritime or otherwise. In 1801 the minuscule Herreshoff clan was united with a branch of the more prolific Brown clan when Carl Friedric Herreshoff, Nathanael Herreshoff's great-grandfather, married Sarah Brown, daughter of John Brown, who is best remembered for burning the British war schooner *Gaspée* in Narragansett Bay, four years before the out-break of the revolution.)

Waldo Brown's father, Harry Hosmer Brown, was one of the few men in the long Brown line to break from the tradition of the sea: instead of becoming a ship captain or

A youthful Waldo H. Brown behind the wheel of his sporty Gray roadster.

(Courtesy of John Noble Brown)

shipbuilder, he studied accounting and mastered the art of commerce and numbers. He eventually founded H.H. Brown & Co., a Boston-based cotton brokerage. As a result of his success in cotton trading, Harry Brown created a safe and secure estate in which to raise his children, among them Waldo, born in Salem in 1896. Though Harry Brown, like the majority of his contemporaries, was inclined toward the pleasures of motoryachts, Waldo began sailing as a child on a little catboat, *Ann*, which Harry had bought for him. Out on the water, sometimes alone and surrounded by larger boats, young Waldo had a perfect opportunity to appreciate the shapes of fine craft. As he matured, he decided he wanted to study naval architecture.

Waldo Brown graduated from Andover Academy at the top of his class, was awarded the prize in chemistry, and was offered a job at the Du Pont chemical company. But he chose, in about 1915, to enter MIT and pursue his dream of designing ships and yachts. At MIT Brown studied marine engineering, ship mechanics, woodworking, modelmaking, drafting, and naval architecture, and was rated by his professors as one of the best students in the discipline. With the United States preparing to enter World War I, Brown also enrolled in MIT's Naval ROTC program to avoid being drafted into the army and to secure the rank of officer when his time came to serve. It soon did.

Instead of accepting a commission to go to sea on the deck of a warship, which would be expected of this would-be naval architect, the romance of flying momentarily tugged more strongly at Waldo Brown's imagination and led him to choose an aviation specialty. He was soon ranked among the first elite group of 500 pilots ever commissioned to fly for the U.S. Navy. Brown took his flight training at Pensacola Naval Air Station, in Florida, where he became known affectionately as "Coconut" Brown, because—inspired by his wicked sense of humor—he managed to bomb the airstrip at Key West with a planeload of coconuts. (Because the country needed every pilot, his punishment

was limited to cleaning up the mess.) After Pensacola, Brown was assigned to patrol duty along the Massachusetts coast, out of Chatham Air Base. His group's mission was to spot and attack German submarines. Brown flew hundreds of hours during the war, becoming an expert pilot. But he gained his greatest notoriety, and a citation, from one incident only. On patrol one day he came upon an audacious German submarine shelling a barge-towing tug and the town of Orleans, on Cape Cod. He dutifully unloaded his full cache of bombs on it. Though none of the ordnance exploded, the sub's commander took the gesture in the spirit with which it was intended; he submerged. In his last patrol of the war, out of Chatham, Brown's engine failed and he had to ditch his aircraft at sea. He was rescued after a three-day search by several destroyers. Both his crewmen died from exposure. Brown contracted pneumonia and was hospitalized, but he survived. Waldo Brown had an angel looking over his shoulder—he was forever outspoken in his determination never to die in an airplane crash.

Toward the end of the war, Brown—a debonair, high-spirited, handsome, and blonde presence in or out of uniform—was among elite Chatham pilots invited to a garden party given in their honor at the Harwich Port summer home of Mr. and Mrs. Paul Robert Gray, of Grosse Pointe, Michigan. (Paul Gray was a son of John Simpson Gray, one of the founders of the Ford Motor Company; he and his siblings had jointly inherited one-third of Ford's outstanding stock. On his own, Paul Gray became a versatile Detroit industrialist, founder of the Gray Motor Company and manufacturer of the well-known Graymarine boat engine. The Grays were, it can safely be said, well off.) During that afternoon tea, Waldo fell in love with his hosts' exquisite young daughter, Frances.

At war's end Brown was discharged from active duty and in 1919 he and Frances, still just twenty-two and seventeen years old, were married; they settled into a house in an

upper-class Boston suburb. Yes, despite the Gray's enormous wealth, and his own family's comfortable circumstances, Waldo Brown felt compelled by manly custom to earn his living independently: he still had his mind set on being a naval architect. Unfortunately, the MIT program he had enrolled in before the war (and didn't complete) hadn't offered the requisite curriculum for a specialty in yacht design. So around 1920 Brown accepted an apprenticeship at the Boston office of Burgess, Swasey & Paine, naval architects. Brown chose his training ground well.

The firm's three partners constituted a constellation of stars in the American yacht-design firmament. W. Starling Burgess was the son of Edward Burgess, the prodigious creator of the America's Cup defenders *Puritan, Volunteer,* and *Mayflower.* Equal distinction lay ahead for Starling, who would also design three cup defenders—*Enterprise, Rainbow,* and (with Olin Stephens) *Ranger*—for syndicates headed by Harold S. Vanderbilt. The second partner, powerboat specialist A. Loring Swasey, was a man of equally comprehensive talent. Recently he had been forced to leave the Herreshoff Manufacturing Company, along with other loyal employees, by a severe downturn in orders. The third partner, Frank C. Paine, a no-less-gifted designer of sailing craft, was later to draw the comely J-Class sloop *Yankee* and the 62-foot *Highland Light,* which would hold the Newport to Bermuda Race course record for twenty-four years.

Brown set to work at BS&P and by 1923 he had grown sufficiently in stature and ability to begin work on designing a small gaff-rigged schooner for a most unusual client: himself. For some time, it seems, Brown had been thinking of developing a yacht modeled on a 325-ton pilot boat designed by his grandfather, Joshua Brown, and built in 1856 at Joshua's shipyard, Turner & Brown, in Salem, Massachusetts. Waldo had lived vicariously with that pilot boat, the *Clarence Barclay,* in the form of an oil painting that had been passed down to him from his father. In spite of the determined march toward

Francis Herreshoff's mentor Starling Burgess, and an exemplary cutter of his design.
(Mystic Seaport Museum, Inc.)

modernism that surrounded him elsewhere, Waldo Brown saw himself sailing a relatively old-fashioned, clipper-bowed, gaff-rigged schooner.

With this distinctive combination of technical insight, assertive persona, and a classic nineteenth-century painting for inspiration, Waldo Brown was not a run-of-the-mill yacht client, not even to himself. But Brown apparently had the wisdom (and lack of ego) not to take on the design alone. He asked for, and received, some collaborative help from another, more experienced, young designer at Burgess, Swasey & Paine. It was a providential meeting for the two men, as both Brown and his colleague were of an experimental frame of mind. More to the point, they were willing to ignore the current trend toward modernism, and use the *Clarence Barclay* as a base to create a yacht that in most respects was a throwback. As a result of their similar world views, Brown and his colleague became close friends: long after each had left Burgess, Swasey & Paine, and Brown had abandoned his career in naval architecture for more profitable enterprises, he would return to this good friend to commission several more designs.

But perhaps it is best to allow that other designer to briefly pick up the story here, and to relate his own recollection of his collaboration with Waldo Brown, as he did rather prosaically, thirty years later, in a letter to an inquisitive sailor:

[A] young man, Waldo Brown, came to me with an oil painting of a boat his grandfather had had built in Salem in about 1850. She was a very nice looking boat that was used for a pilot boat, and he asked me if a modern [yacht] of that type would be practical. I told him that she would not only be practical, but better than the usual boat of that time that was designed to fit some of the measurement rules, and he gave me an order to design that boat, which was a schooner named *Joann,* 50' on deck.

That designer was thirty-five-year-old Lewis Francis Herreshoff, fifth child of the Wizard of Bristol, Nathanael G. Herreshoff. An artist of consummate skill and passion, Francis Herreshoff was destined to become one of America's most beloved yacht designers. It will seem odd to the reader, therefore, that in this letter Herreshoff fails to credit Waldo Brown with anything more than presenting him with the *Clarence Barclay* painting, giving the clear but erroneous impression that he, Herreshoff, designed *Joann* alone. But this was, as we shall see, typical of another of Herreshoff's many well-developed talents, the art of self-promotion, a facet of the man that would both advance

Francis Herreshoff (seen here in his workshop in 1923) carves a model of Waldo Brown's Joann.

His father, Nathanael, stands in the back row left, in this Herreshoff family portrait.
(Mystic Seaport Museum, Inc.)

his career and engender disdain among more than one of his peers and competitors.

Francis Herreshoff had joined Burgess, Swasey & Paine in 1921, sometime after being mustered out of the Navy Reserve, having served during World War I as a skipper and ship designer. Though he was apparently qualified as a naval architect by virtue of his wartime work, it had been no impediment to his hiring at Burgess, Swasey & Paine that the Herreshoff and Burgess families were distantly related and often closely allied in business. (Part of the agreement between the two was that Burgess would instruct Herreshoff in matters of importance. On the evening of Herreshoff's first work day Burgess gave him a book to study. Herreshoff of course expected it to be a formula-filled treatise on the intricacies of naval architecture and ship design; it was Henry David Thoreau's *Cape Cod*. Burgess sensed that even a son of Nat Herreshoff might need some broadening to his outlook.)

Surely, coming from such a lineage, and with "Captain Nat" as his father, one might assume that Francis Herreshoff was ordained from birth (or likely earlier) to be a naval architect. (The Herreshoffs, in America since 1787, seemed to have an almost genetic penchant for bringing forth accomplished inventors, tinkerers, engineers, and designers.) But, oddly, as a youth Francis found laboring on the family's Bristol Neck farm more compelling. He was accustomed to seeing chickens and pigs killed by the time he was six; by eighteen he was running the farm and doing the butchery himself. He continued working the farm on and off for nearly ten years. Assessing his son's skill and devotion to the animals, Captain Nat had even planned to have him take over the farm, and after Francis completed high school Nathanael packed him off to a land-grant agricultural school (today the University of Rhode Island).

But the techniques of farms and farming (fortunately for the world of yachts and yachting) were not all that Lewis Francis Herreshoff absorbed as a youth. As he later wrote:

Until I was 27 my bedroom was next to the rooms my father used for drawing, model making and experimenting. On the walls were models which represented nearly all the history of American yachting since the eighteen-sixties. . . . When [I was] quite young . . . my father used to take me by the hand to inspect the work at the yacht yard. . . . Here he deposited me in the row-boat shop. . . . Soon I was running errands to the stock room, holding the weight for riveting, etc., and by six years of age was under pay working after school and on Saturdays. As the years went by I was riveting, bending frames, planing. At ten I knew all the woods by sight, and was a good judge of timber for bending. Later I served my time . . . in the pattern shop, the foundry, the blacksmith shop, machine shop, boiler shop, mold loft, sail loft, rigging loft, the steel construction shop, drafting room and the office.

Pigs and chickens notwithstanding, growing up surrounded by models and full-size vessels helped Francis soak up his father's genius and style, and hone a unique set of yacht-design instincts. These early experiences would run as powerful undercurrents throughout his life, becoming the foundation for his view that *building* boats was an essential prerequisite to *designing* them. But, while Captain Nat's Prussian austerity had led him toward an emphasis on engineering precision, Francis' more intuitive soul would lead him along a more aesthetic path: he was destined, perhaps inwardly determined, to be the consummate artist among yacht designers. As a result, he believed all his life that the solutions to the knottiest technical compromises of yacht design could only be arrived at through art. (This deep-rooted difference in their views was one compelling element in a lifelong coolness between father and son, which Francis often expressed in his letters. He once wrote that every time he picked up the mooring for his 24-foot sailboat, under his father's window, he felt as though he were

"a soldier standing inspection," and that his father would occasionally row out to the boat to see that everything was in its proper place, "not so much for looks but for its proper use and function." The tension between Francis and Nathanael lasted until the old man's death on June 2, 1938, at the age of ninety.)

For Waldo Brown, who also had a distinctly artistic outlook, the accident of his meeting Herreshoff would prove a perfect synergy. Taking the *Clarence Barclay* painting as an architectonic guide, they drew a perfectly charming auxiliary schooner, Design No. 257 in the BS&P catalogue. She was 49 feet 11 inches on deck; 43 feet on the water; 13 feet 2 inches in maximum beam; 4 feet 8 inches in draft; with a design displacement of 22.3 tons. They gave her a rather full but graceful clipper bow, with a slight hollow at the waterline, and an easy run culminating in a fetching wine-glass stern. They prescribed a cast-iron ballast, running the full length of her keel, which provided the requisite stability to offset her relatively shoal draft. Her well-raked schooner sailplan—set on equal-height masts—consisted of a flying jib set on a hefty bowsprit, a club-footed jib, a boomless gaff foresail with brails, and a gaff mainsail with lazy jacks. Her standing rigging featured traditional deadeyes and lanyards. She was without doubt a child of *Clarence Barclay*.

By any standard *Joann* was a pretty, balanced, easily handled, and genteel family cruiser—not a prime contender for racing silver. But she was not entirely unique for her day—the clipper bow was still somewhat in vogue in the early 1920s and a commentator in a 1923 issue of *Yachting* found the type to have "a very pleasing profile and weatherly qualities (when properly designed)." Early in 1924, once the Britt Brothers yard in Boston had won the contract to build *Joann*, Waldo Brown drafted the final plans, and signed them. *Joann* was a true collaboration between two exceptional young men.

Neither Herreshoff nor Brown, however, could have known when they collaborated in 1923, that *Joann* would prove so attractive

The pilot schooner Clarence Barclay: *the inspiration for Waldo Brown's concept of* Joann.

(Courtesy of John Noble Brown)

that she would soon propel Herreshoff into designing a series of clipper-bowed boats. Nor could either of these exceptional men have known that six years after he left Starling Burgess' gentle tutorship, and had found his own clear artistic voice, Francis Herreshoff would culminate the series in one clipper-bowed beauty that would rewrite the history of ocean racing.

When Francis Herreshoff wrote that *Joann* was better than boats made "to fit some of the measurement rules," he was staking out another lifelong position: a yacht can be shaped below the waterline for speed and above the waterline for beauty purely by the architect's skill and intuition, not according to the dictates of current rating rules. In breaking with that common "design-by-rule" philosophy, which unquestionably has produced many outstanding yachts, Herreshoff was bucking a tide that yacht designers had been swept up in for well over a century— the mandate to shape a yacht to satisfy (or evade) a formula that handicaps diverse yachts for equitable racing.

Though there is today a glut of such international design formulae (and countless national, regional, club, and local rules as well), these have their origins not in the world of twentieth-century yacht racing but in the universe of eighteenth-century British trade. It was in 1773 that Parliament required that commercial vessels be measured to determine their liability for port fees and other taxes. The taxation formula, based plainly on a ship's length and beam, was then adopted by English shipyards as a convenient method of fleshing out the cost per ton of building a vessel. This landed version of the rule became known as "The Builders' Old Measurement." The Royal Thames Yacht Club, recognizing the formula's elegance, then adopted it to handicap yachts for racing, the first time such a rule was developed for the sport. But by 1855 the club's race committee noticed that some devious designers (yes, even then) had found a loophole in the

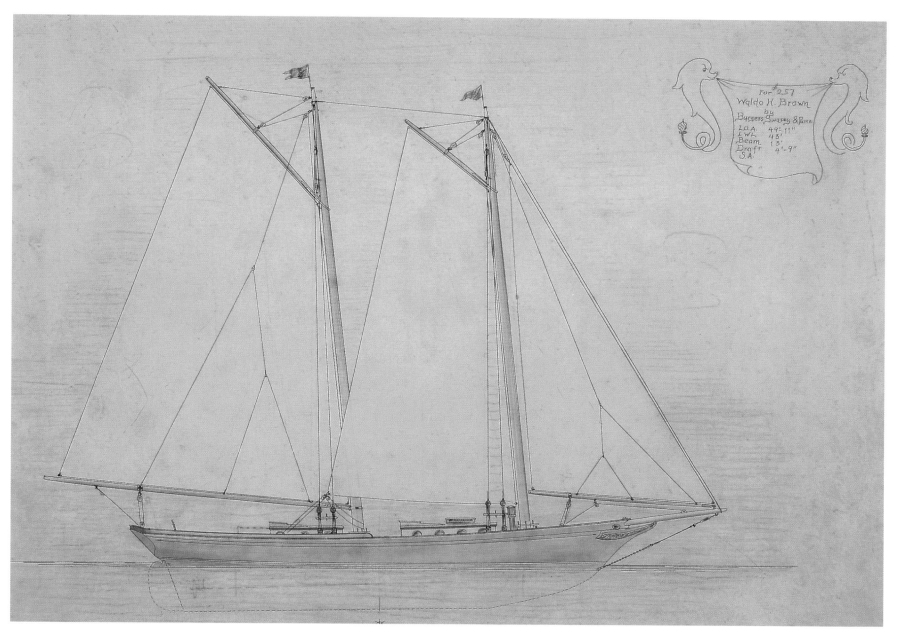

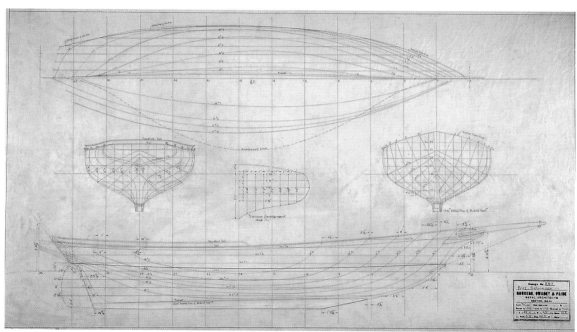

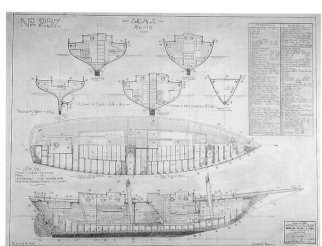

Joann's *design drawings, completed by Waldo Brown,*
included a hand-colored profile by Herreshoff.

(Mystic Seaport Museum, Inc.)

(TOP) *Joann's foresail boom was added later.* (ABOVE) *Brown inspects* Joann, *his first custom yacht.*
(Top: Mystic Seaport Museum, Inc./Above: Courtesy of John Noble Brown)

formula to avoid a heavy beam penalty: they narrowed the hull, deepened the keel and increased ballast, leading to the typical plank-on-end British yacht of the day. Club officials, fearing a proliferation of unseaworthy craft, reduced the beam penalty to encourage safer yachts. Such machinations led to more sophisticated rating rules, culminating in the Universal and International Rules of the late nineteenth century and early twentieth.

American yacht designs of the nineteenth century, however, were generally beamy and shallow and, as *America* proved in 1851, fast. In fact, those yachts were modeled after working craft: fishing or pilot boats. Fishing boats, naturally, were designed to go to sea and work in the worst of weather; their sturdy type spawned yachts with good seakeeping character (like those that sailed the 1923 Bermuda Race). But pilot boats were designed to sprint out of a harbor, meet an incoming ship and put a pilot aboard; they had to be agile and fast. Thus, a typical American pilot boat had a shallow, somewhat flat hull with low freeboards, and a long shoal keel or centerboard. To maximize the spread of canvas, designers gave them a long bowsprit or a main boom extending well over the transom; they added beam to provide sufficient stability to carry the canvas (except in very brisk weather, when a quick reef was necessary, or a quick capsize was possible).

Among the most famous (and beautiful) of nineteenth-century American yachts whose forms followed the pilot-boat pattern were *Sappho, Magic,* and, of course, *America,* designed by George Steers, who based her shape on a swift 1849 pilot boat, *Mary Taylor.* In modeling *Joann* after vessels like *America,* Brown and Herreshoff were simply extending that proven lineage at a time when newer concepts were being popularized by other designers obeying the beat of a more modern drum.

Waldo Brown left Burgess, Swasey & Paine about the time his schooner *Joann* was being built in 1924. He then plunged into several years of restless engagement in a variety of business ventures, most of them only marginally successful. He opened an office in Boston with a letterhead proclaiming himself "Naval Architect" and "Marine Engineer," but apparently accomplished little in the field. He worked for his father-in-law for several years, running the Boston dealership of Gray automobiles, until the unscrupulous manipulations of Henry Ford forced the company into bankruptcy. From his knowledge of electricity, acquired at MIT, he secured a job under the tutelage of the brilliant engineer and inventor Vannevar Bush at the Raytheon Corporation, but it didn't last long. He tried his hand at building a large dredge, offering his services to local harbor authorities. From his connections in aviation he became president of Colonial Airways, a position that soon dissolved when Colonial merged with American Airlines. Waldo Brown had Promethean talents and Protean interests, but he seemed to lack the luck that business success so often demands.

Francis Herreshoff's luck at the time wasn't much better. He continued his education at Burgess, Swasey & Paine, but elected to leave that haven in 1929 (on the eve of the stock market crash) to establish his own practice in Marblehead. The Great Depression that followed Herreshoff's declaration of independence was a bad time for yacht designers, young or established, as the shortage of ready cash to build new yachts was pervasive. In that light, Herreshoff's maintenance of his autonomy after the crash must be deemed a remarkable act of courage.

But fortunately for Francis Herreshoff, Waldo Brown and his family did not suffer from the crash. In fact, Frances' father died in 1929 and left his daughter the bulk of his multi-million dollar estate. She arranged for Waldo to receive a generous allowance, while she enjoyed the fruits of her inheritance to the fullest, buying extravagant luxuries, throwing parties, relishing the privileged life. Waldo became an active sportsman, hunter, racquet-club regular, distinguished Massachusetts Bay yachtsman, and respected member of the Stone Horse Yacht Club in

Harwich Port. Together, depression or not, the Browns continued to enjoy their mansions, their limousines, their high-society life in Massachusetts and Michigan, and their friends in high places, as though time and money would never run out.

By the third summer of the Great Depression, the Browns had produced five children, four boys and a girl; they needed more space at sea, as well as at home. So after six years of delight with *Joann*, Brown put her on the market and returned to his good friend Francis Herreshoff for a larger yacht, the second significant design in their clipper-bowed series. (Years later *Joann*, under the name *Brigadoon*, came into the hands of that electrifying movie figure, Sterling Hayden.) Brown named his new yacht after another vessel his grandfather had designed (and built in 1881): a 63-foot schooner named *Tioga*. (The name, according to the mythology that has been handed down by historians and other blunderers, is an American Indian word meaning "Beautiful Wife.")

Tioga, like *Joann*, was a close collaboration between Brown and Herreshoff. Brown, who had much to say about her hull lines, pre-

scribed his needs with verbal clarity and Herreshoff did the graphic work in his Marblehead studio. Brown, as a result of their cooperation, would visit Herreshoff often, sometimes bringing along one of his sons, John Noble, who was born the year *Joann* was designed and was eight years old during the year of *Tioga*'s design. As an occasional reward for the lad's patience and good behavior, while the grownups talked, Herreshoff would whittle a small wooden boat for "Johnny." The friendship between Brown and Herreshoff was deep and genuine.

As Herreshoff finally put her lines on paper, *Tioga* was 57 feet 6 inches on deck with a 50-foot waterline. In his underwater search for greater speed, Herreshoff reduced the fullness of *Tioga*'s bows, compared to *Joann*'s, by deepening the hollows in the waterlines forward, and he pinched the waterlines aft. Both features were intended to ease water flow around the underbody. Above the waterline, like *Joann*, Herreshoff modeled *Tioga*'s hull sweetly, with no inharmonious edges or acute corners. With her after-sheer raised, *Tioga* had an even

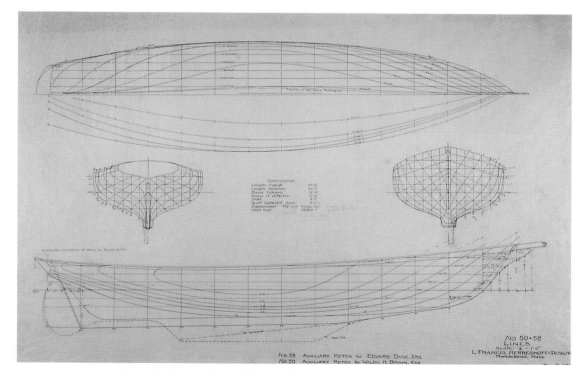

Herreshoff' lines plan of Tioga of Boston, *a clear refinement of* Joann.
(Mystic Seaport Museum, Inc.)

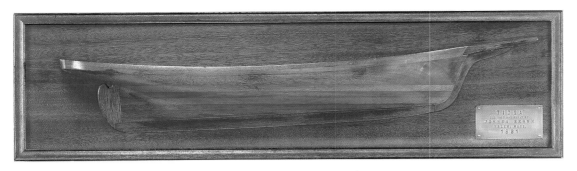

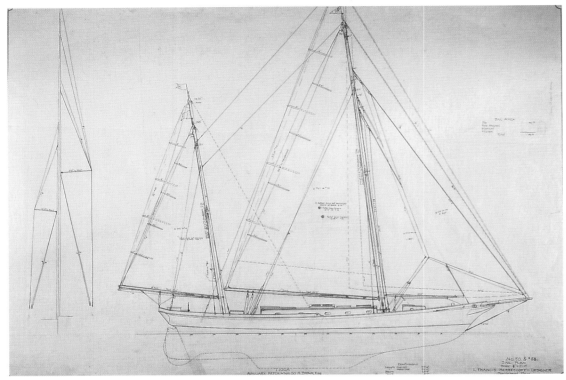

Tioga's sailplan and half model, with (TOP) a half model of her 1881 namesake.
(Models: Courtesy of John Noble Brown/Center: Mystic Seaport Museum, Inc.)

anchor with sails furled and their crew below-decks. Each boat took its handicap at the start (small boats starting first, largest last); each skipper could choose to sail the course either clockwise or anti-clockwise. To Waldo Brown's surprise (and Francis Herreshoff's delight) *Tioga* won the race not just in her debut year of 1932 but in the subsequent two years as well. In Massachusetts Bay that is almost equivalent to the Boston Red Sox winning the pennant: it just never happens.

One year after Brown launched *Tioga*, Herreshoff put the finishing touches on a sistership, *Bounty*, for another Massachusetts Bay client, Edward Dane. In drawing *Bounty* Herreshoff reverted to the full keel and gave her 1,519 square feet of sail, nearly 200 more than *Tioga*, set on a taller, thus prettier rig. He gave *Bounty* a slightly shorter water-line by floating her higher forward. Otherwise the two were identical. Edward Dane spent around $20,000 to build *Bounty*; *Tioga* cost Waldo Brown about $22,000. Each included a 60-hp gasoline engine and a set of working sails. Herreshoff was quite pleased with both yachts, as well he should have been, as they were splendid vessels, with rakish bows, optimal sheerlines, and sweet curves everywhere. In January 1935, in a de-served state of pride, Herreshoff wrote to his longtime friend and colleague, Uffa Fox, the English yacht designer, intellect, and author, that *Tioga* and *Bounty* were surpris-ingly fast and very easy to handle. He con-cluded his letter by saying that *Tioga* "is a great favorite of the sailor men as she is not at all tiresome to look at."

Not at all tiresome to look at. The capacity for admirable understatement was a Herre-shoff gift. Yet he was absolutely correct in this unassuming opinion. The new hulls he was creating were all beautifully sculpted, more in tune with the organic fluidity of nineteenth-century art nouveau, than the more industri-alized geometry of twentieth-century art deco. With these beautiful shapes and rea-sonable prices, Herreshoff was clearly onto something good. Today, he might be seen as having created a "niche" market. And he was

saucier grace than did *Joann*. Unlike *Joann's* long ballast keel, Herreshoff gave *Tioga* a shoal keel and centerboard, to further reduce her draft. Unlike the gaff-rigged *Joann*, he gave *Tioga* a more modern Marconi ketch rig, but with rather short masts and low-aspect sails; he didn't want her to be overpowered in a breeze (or reefed, for that matter) because he believed her hullform to be so easily dri-ven and stable.

Tioga turned out to be just that: easily dri-ven and stable. Brown, who had become a capable sailor with *Joann* and enjoyed occa-sional competition, put *Tioga* in the water for the 1932 racing season. She cleaned up, win-ning just about every race she entered. Among them was the annual Jeffrey's Ledge Race, an unusually nonchalant regatta for cruising yachts that ran from Manchester, to Peaked Hill Bar, to Jeffrey's Ledge, and back to Manchester, a distance of 138 nautical miles. The rules required the fleet to start at

Joann *still sails today, under the name* Brigadoon.
(Benjamin Mendlowitz)

not hesitant to exploit that market. As a means of keeping his cash flow up, Herreshoff sold copies of his yacht plans to all comers: a set of *Joann* plans cost seventy-five dollars; *Tioga/Bounty* one hundred. Though most of the plan purchasers did not follow through and build boats, a few later did with the resulting launch of such handsome contemporary craft as *Charade, Circe,* and *Dianbola.* (When Brown sold *Joann* to build *Tioga,* her new owners wrote Herreshoff asking for her plans as well; he charged them the princely sum of one dollar to cover his printing and mailing costs. The

discount was no doubt his quaint way of wishing Godspeed to one of his very favorite designs.)

But, as his innate sense of perfection would dictate, Francis Herreshoff was not completely satisfied with these yachts. In regard to *Tioga,* particularly, he later expressed a wish that he had been able to convince Waldo Brown to build her *without* an auxiliary engine, to simplify her construction and reduce her cost. The space made available by eliminating the engine room, Herreshoff felt, could have been better used by Brown and his big family for stowing cruising gear.

Then, while sailing the boat, he asserted, "the land would be the only thing to fear while the grub lasts." Apparently, Herreshoff had a peculiar disdain for engines, which, in combination with an equally eccentric touch of misogyny ("I am not particularly fond of the ladies," he once wrote), inspired him also to equate engines to women: He found them "not all bad." But he preferred "the simple, clean, reliable ones." He admired "the economical ones." And he almost loved "the quiet ones that are small and don't smell."

Lewis Francis Herreshoff remained a bachelor all his life.

TIOGA OF MARBLEHEAD

1934–1940

THE NOYES FAMILY, like the ubiquitous Browns, are among the true founders of American society, sailing to these shores in the wake of the *Mayflower.* In the early 1620s, the Reverend James Noyes and his wife Sarah came across from England on the good ship *Mary and John,* settling in Newburyport, Massachusetts, north of Boston. The family flourished and succeeding generations produced such distinguished progeny as Eliot Noyes, the celebrated designer and architect, and John Humphrey Noyes, a social reformer and maverick theologian. The Noyes family tree, though eminently fruitful, remained pretty much rooted in New England, where many of its descendants live today, between Cape Cod and New Hampshire.

In 1906 one of those descendants, Harry K. Noyes, sensed the future American hunger for that newfangled contraption, the "horseless carriage," and obtained a Buick automobile dealership in Lowell, Massachusetts. At the time there were fewer than one hundred

Harry Edward Noyes. (Courtesy of Bradley Noyes)

thousand registered autos in all of the forty-five United States, and many of the more timorous pundits of the day were convinced that the number was not destined to grow much larger. Yet Harry Noyes, a believer in the future, was so locally successful that his Buick sales surpassed two million dollars that first year. By 1915 he was appointed head of the main regional dealership in Boston, with a much larger market and forty-five employees within his command.

In a few years Noyes had expanded that market so well that he bought out the parent company's interests and became the sole Buick distributor for New England, with more than a hundred dealerships buying their cars from him, not from Detroit. By 1928 the Noyes Buick distributorship had achieved more than twenty million dollars in turnover and expanded its facilities to include two hundred fifty employees, an immense freight yard for staging cars, a formidable five-story, 220,000-square-foot headquarters building, and a plush, theater-like showroom dedicated to comfortably introducing new models to visiting dealers and salesmen.

Harry K. Noyes, a typical 1920s entrepreneur (as a youth he had worked as a waiter for twelve dollars a month), dabbled in other ventures as well, most successful, a few not. He was for a time chairman of Boston's second largest bank, a cash cow in the prosperous pre-depression years; at the same time he owned Boston's Bay State Fishing Company, which even in those pre-regulation days hardly made a nickel. As newly moneyed Americans (like Waldo Brown) were wont to do, Noyes also found diversion in the fledgling sport of aviation, and in 1920 he boldly flew at great physical risk to Havana in an open-cockpit aircraft.

Naturally, as another privilege (or perhaps requirement) of his class, Harry K. Noyes was also a dedicated yachtsman. He built a series of motoryachts, all named *Seyon* (the mirror image of his family name), and kept several at a time around the Boston area. Among his favorites was a classic Trumpy cruiser he moored off his home in Marblehead. He used her as a refuge from shoreside disquiet, often enjoying a cruise or a family dinner in the utter plutocratic isola-

One of the Noyes family's several motoryachts named Seyon *(Noyes in reverse).*
(Mystic Seaport Museum, Inc.)

tion only a private yacht can afford. In sum, Harry Noyes was head of an exemplary upper-class New England household, with mansions, maids, autos, aircraft, yachts, and advantages at their ready disposal.

It was into this comfortable family that Harold Edward Noyes was born in 1898. After attending Andover Academy and Dartmouth College (spending his summer holidays working in his father's automobile shops), young Noyes volunteered as a naval aviator when the United States entered World War I. He was sent to MIT for three months of military schooling, then transferred to Pensacola Naval Air Station for flight training. Sometime in the period (at Andover, MIT, or during his training) Harry Noyes met and befriended Waldo Brown, and the two men's destinies became creatively and socially entwined. While Brown had managed to get assigned to a domestic coastal patrol, Harold Noyes, two years younger, fully expected to go to war in Europe, where the life expectancy of a tenderfoot pilot was measured in hours. But, as they sometimes merci-

fully do, this war ended before Noyes was shipped overseas. After the war, a veteran flyer at twenty, he returned home to Marblehead to marry his sweetheart, Ruth Pike, and accept a position as a salesman in his father's Buick empire.

In many respects Harry Noyes—he was christened Harold but changed it officially to Harry to affect a bit of salesman-like accessibility—was the model "chip off the old block." Like his father he was handsome, dapper, well groomed, and personable, with an aptitude for selling cars that furthered the company's bounty; he gained celebrity, won awards, and was promoted to treasurer and sales manager of Noyes Buick. Harry, also like his father, enjoyed yachting in the grand style and gravitated to the vanity of motoryachts run by professional crews. Harry was captivated by the bounding advances in internal combustion engines. He was enthralled by power and speed on land, on water, and in the air; he had little interest in the hands-on sport of sailing. This was, after all, the era of international flying and motoring pioneers

such as Curtiss, Sikorski, Martin, Dornier, Sopwith, Blériot, Benz, Bugatti, Oldfield, and Amelia Earhart—the world was on a fast track to mechanization through the burning of fossil fuels, and the well-to-do freely indulged their compulsion for showy, high-profile playthings. Harry Noyes was no exception.

Drawing from their common interest in motoryachts, and seeing a way to add to their fortunes while having a bit of fun outside the auto game, in the mid-1920s father and son founded Noyes Marine, a boat dealership and service company in Boston where they sold Chris Craft speedboats, ACF cruisers, and Johnson outboards—trailblazing commercial names. From his automobile service experience, Harry devised a clever way of easing service customers into the waterside shop. He built a shed over the water with a lifting garage door. This allowed yachtsmen to drive their boats in and moor alongside the mechanics' dock. It was a popular idea that brought in many customers by word of mouth. Unfortunately, no amount of inventiveness could stave off the crushing effects of the crash. Despite their mutual enthusiasm for puttering with boats, a few years into the Great Depression the two Harrys decided that some consolidation of their fortunes was necessary. They closed Noyes Marine.

But that was not the end of their involvement with the business of boating. In the early 1930s, about the same time the British introduced the CQR anchor to America, Harry and his father became unintentionally involved with a local yacht yard. The elder Noyes had built some of his yachts at George Lawley & Sons, a grand old shop in nearby Neponset that had built many fine craft including the J-Class yachts *Yankee* and *Whirlwind.* Over the years Noyes had worked closely with old George's capable son Fred. But Fred apparently had a falling-out with his father; he quit and started a new yard not far away in Germantown under his own name. As easily happens in the boating business, then and now, Fred Lawley soon ran into financial difficulties and asked some of

his clients for assistance. The senior Noyes, out of sympathy, arranged the public sale of stock for the yard. The capital infusion helped, and for a time the yard kept body and soul marginally above water. But Fred still didn't seem able to manage the business end of things; he was eventually forced to resign. The Noyes men had no choice but to take the yard over. They renamed it Quincy Adams Yacht Yard. Once again father and son were in the boating business, this time all but involuntarily.

With little time to spare from their more profitable family enterprises, they brought in a talented manager, Ralph Richmond, to run the yard's day-to-day operations. Harry, who was by then as well diversified as his father, was named president of Quincy Adams, a nominal title at best as Richmond ran the place and Harry just carried the payroll. The Quincy Adams Yacht Yard, not unexpectedly, became the younger Noyes' Bay State Fishing Company—an albatross that never made any significant return on the family investment; its books were written eternally in red. But it

was dear to the Harrys and they kept it operating for love of the game, not conscious that they were also saving it for history.

Harry and Ruth Noyes had a fine little family of three sons and one daughter, the last born in 1927. In keeping with the doctrine of proper Bostonians, Harry tended to be formal with his children—Harry, Pike, Hope, and Bradley. He didn't share his thoughts with them; he kept them at a distance to engender respect, even a bit of fear. The children sat at the table properly, with the cook and maid; they were served at a certain time; they spoke when spoken to; they went to the best private schools. They quickly grew into little adults.

Although Harry was outwardly formal and reserved (but unfortunately took to the bottle sometimes), he was a tender, loving father who set aside ample time to play with his children. In that regard, around 1930 something happened to Harry that would change his life forever. To bring a little weekend diversion to the family's Swampscott

An independent Fred Lawley and his shipyard, before the two Harrys acquired and renamed it Quincy Adams Yacht Yard.
(Mystic Seaport Museum, Inc.)

Harry Noyes' exquisitely shaped, superbly sailed, world-champion Eight-Meter, Gypsy.
(Mystic Seaport Museum, Inc./Rosenfeld Collection)

an Eight-Meter racing sloop, *Gitane,* from Henry S. Morgan. *Gitane*—48 feet 6 inches overall and designed by Frank Paine—was built in 1929 by George Lawley and was as pretty an Eight-Meter as there was. Harry renamed her *Gypsy* (which was her original name before Morgan owned her) and put her into the local racing circuit. And he began taking home silver. Big time. In 1935 he was awarded the Hutchinson Trophy for winning the most races two years running. Within a few highly compressed years, Harry the fatherly neophyte had become Mr. Noyes the resolute champion.

Like his father, Harry Noyes bought and maintained several yachts at a time (at one point he owned ten boats over fifty feet, all impeccable and handsome, which he moored in Marblehead, Quincy, or Boston. But in 1934 all the fine yachts in Harry Noyes' mini-fleet—large and small, power and sail—suddenly diminished in his eyes by the appearance of Waldo Brown's *Tioga.* She was the first boat Harry Noyes ever fell completely in love with. It is not certain that Brown had any interest in selling *Tioga;* she was just two years old and the apple of his eye. But it is clear that Harry, after seeing her only a few times, went up to Brown (a very dear friend) and cocksuredly said to him: *Waldo! I've just got to have that boat!* Brown, who had been bitten by the racing bug and was thinking of building a smaller daysailer (as well as get a cash infusion into his new dredging company) quickly acquiesced to Harry. Noyes bought *Tioga.* (Brown went back to his and Herreshoff's drawing boards for that new boat, a 30-Square Meter he named *Gem,* with which he competed actively against the hottest boats in this development class.)

While Harry continued racing his Eight-Meter, *Tioga* became the family's favorite cruiser. They sailed *Tioga* happily for only one summer season, however, before Harry realized that they needed (or, more likely, that he wanted) a larger yacht to accommodate his family and entertain his friends. He put *Tioga* up for sale. Harry had been so

summer home Harry bought a sixteen-foot, sloop-rigged, lapstrake dory. It was for the children, he posited, so one day he took his oldest boys, Harry and Pike, out for a demonstration sail. But the fatherly Noyes succeeded in demonstrating only that he didn't know much about sailing. Jogging along in a bit of fresh breeze he innocently trimmed the jib to weather, lost control of the helm, and put the dory on the rocks. The boys were not hurt; nor was Harry's pride.

The irrepressible salesman reasoned, of course, that the fault lay not with the helmsman but with the helm. He bought a larger boat, an eighteen-footer, and put her on the rocks as well.

A friendly neighbor, "Uncle" Frank Blaney, whose father was Swampscott dory champion, took Harry under his wing and taught him the finer points of sail trim and helmsmanship. In no time, Harry came to enjoy sailing so much that in 1932 he bought

TICONDEROGA

pleased with *Tioga* in every respect, from her sweet lines to her swift performance, that there was no question that his next boat would also be drawn by Francis Herreshoff. In the spring of 1935 Harry contacted the designer, whose office was not far from the Noyes estate in Marblehead. Noyes asked Herreshoff if he would design a scaled-up version of *Tioga*, with all the same charms as the original, a yacht that he also planned to name *Tioga*. Herreshoff, who was not particularly overwhelmed with work at the time, accepted the commission; with his established preference for clipper-bowed boats, Herreshoff was eager to get to work on such a design. And he was certainly flattered that Noyes would so quickly come to him after one season with *Tioga*. At the outset, therefore, planning meetings between Herreshoff and Noyes went well. The two men discussed details amiably and the meetings were productive as they teamed up to achieve the desired size, shape, rig, and interior arrangement of the new *Tioga*.

The designer/client process wasn't complex either, as *Tioga of Marblehead*, a development out of both *Joann* and *Tioga of Boston*, was designed in less than nine months, from hull lines and scantlings to decorative garnish. So casual were the meetings that Harry often brought eight-year-old Bradley who, like Waldo Brown's son John, sat quietly in a corner in awe of the striking designer with his splendiferous manner and trim goatee. There was no hint of the misunderstandings that lay ahead of Herreshoff and Noyes. Within a few months those misunderstandings would precipitate a cooling in their designer/client relationship, then estrange them to such a degree that Herreshoff (who believed that this second *Tioga* was a major plateau in his rising career) would not bother to travel the twenty-odd miles from Marblehead to Quincy to attend her launching in August 1936.

The story has been (very) often told that in ordering this *Tioga* from Herreshoff, Harry Noyes wanted only a daysailer—a pleasant,

airy boat for leisurely family outings, simply laid out, easily handled, with no decksweeping headsails to trouble the ladies or exhaust the men. He wanted a cozy elliptical cockpit with high coamings and a table on which to serve gracious picnics to adults. He wanted open deck space so his children and their chums could climb about the boat safely and comfortably, far from their elders. Such a

boat would naturally have some minimal overnight accommodations, should the family want to sleep aboard at a mooring, or enter *Tioga* in the occasional weekend club race. But Harry did not apparently intend to cruise long distances on *Tioga*, as he still owned larger yachts for that purpose. And Harry (as the story also goes) didn't intend to race *Tioga* very often or very seriously

Waldo Brown's Tioga of Boston, *the first boat Harry Noyes fell in love with.*

(Courtesy of Bradley Noyes)

either. He was actively campaigning *Gypsy*, and on August 8, 1936, at Marblehead Race week, he was soon to win the International Eight-Meter Championship, just two days before *Tioga* was launched.

When Noyes and Herreshoff concluded that the new *Tioga* would be 72 feet on deck with a modest 16-foot beam, Harry rushed home to his family and unreeled a long tape measure on the lawn to show his children her principal dimensions. But that length—72 feet—has a fortuitous significance: it was just under the 73-foot limit set by most rules governing offshore racing events, particularly the Bermuda Race. Surely Harry Noyes, whose racing exploits had earned him no small recognition and satisfaction, could not have wanted his new *Tioga* to be a totally noncompetitive daysailer. Yet he didn't want

her to be totally Spartan, either. These ambivalent ingredients unfortunately became added factors in the equation that further alienated Herreshoff and Noyes after the new *Tioga* was launched.

Herreshoff, to be sure, disdained the very idea of designing the second *Tioga*, or nearly any boat for that matter, for a client to compete in offshore. He held a distinctly negative view of ocean racing, which he deemed unwise. He later wrote a very pointed opinion on the subject to a friend:

> As for ocean cruising, I must say that I have done very little of it, but can imagine that in the right kind of boat, at the right season, in the right place it is a wonderful life. . . . But ocean racing I must say I detest in every way: it develops a type of boat that is no good for

racing and no good for cruising, and is unsafe for ocean cruising.

In the September 1935 issue of *Yachting*, Leonard M. Fowle reported that Marblehead Race Week had been the best ever, with fine weather, good breezes, and stiff competition. He also noted that Harry Noyes and *Gypsy* not only dominated the Eight-Meter class, but won the Ladies' Plate, the deForest prize, the Corinthian Series, and the Hovey Gold Bowl (the symbol of Eight-Meter prowess) with four firsts, two seconds, and a third. (After beating all comers three years in a row, including the illustrious Charles Francis Adams, Harry retired the Hovey Gold Bowl the next year, when he won the world championship.) Elsewhere in that issue of *Yachting*, a small news item made note that

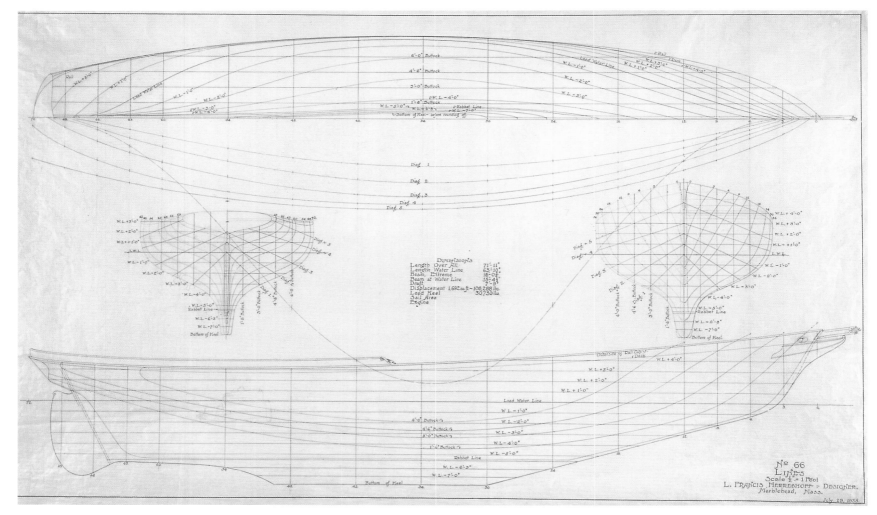

Herreshoff's lines for Tioga of Marblehead, *with a more aggressive bow and reduced wetted surface, keys to her ultimate speed.*

(Mystic Seaport Museum. Inc.)

around Massachusetts Bay yacht designers were busy drawing new boats and were optimistic about a big winter of new-boat building—the Great Depression was finally showing signs of fading. The trend, the news item concluded, was toward ketches, and it noted that L. Francis Herreshoff was also working on plans for a large ketch for Harry Noyes.

Those plans, Herreshoff's Design No. 66, were well defined by the first *Tioga.* Like her predecessor, Herreshoff drew her as a clipper-bowed, leg o' mutton ketch conceived, as Herreshoff the naval architect would often clearly state, without regard to measurement rules. She would also be, as Herreshoff the artist would also emphatically proclaim, all grace and seaworthiness, decorated with "garnish of carved decoration to delight the sailors' eyes."

But in many significant ways the hullform Herreshoff shaped for the new *Tioga* reflected a momentous evolution—not so much in his artistic expression as in his technical thinking. Herreshoff had progressively and thoughtfully refined each succeeding clipper-bowed design to improve speed, maneuverability, stability, and ease of handling. This boat was simply the next logical step. But she turned out to represent a giant step for Herreshoff. Indeed she became the pinnacle of his architectural evolution.

To begin with, rather than give the hull the deep, rounded forefoot of his prior designs, Herreshoff cut the forefoot back to reduce wetted surface. He gave the entry what amounted to a pre-modern "knuckle" below the cutwater. The gripe (connecting the stem to the keel) ran in a straight line

from the knuckle to the keel's flat bottom, with no separately angled leading edge to the keel fin. This straight line was a complete departure from the shapes of Herreshoff's earlier clipper-bowed designs, indeed from all of his designs. It was, though, common to many spoon-bowed racing yachts that were designed to rules (and it clearly harked back to his father's stunning *Gloriana* of 1891, which revolutionized yacht design with her extreme cutaway forefoot and short waterline). Francis Herreshoff was surely onto something, so much so that he was much later to describe *Tioga's* forefoot as "more like later yachts," a hint that, regardless of his avowed disdain for "the rule," he was well aware of the many speed-producing qualities engendered by that rule.

To regain the buoyancy lost by the cut-

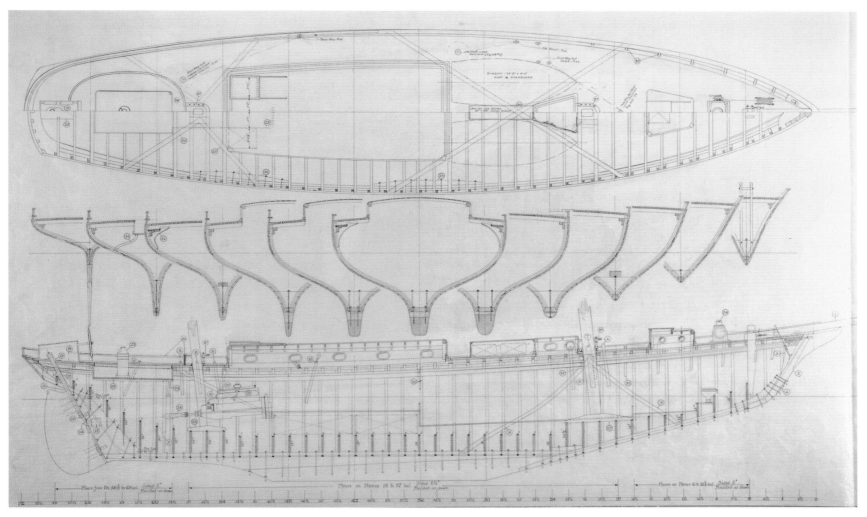

Tioga's construction drawings, which effectively sculpted a solid yacht, but later engendered great discord.

(Mystic Seaport Museum, Inc.)

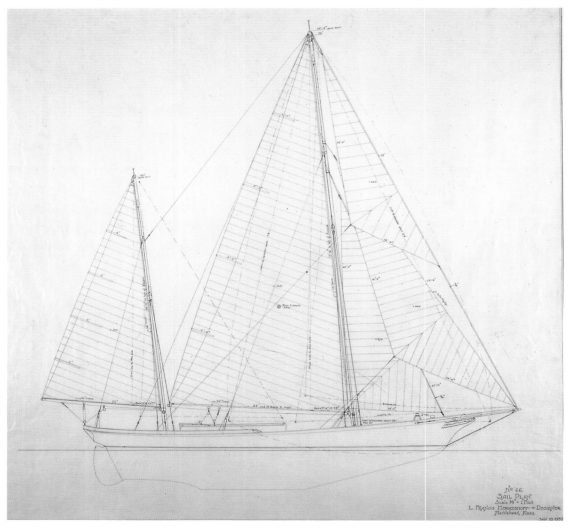

Herreshoff's balanced sailplan for Tioga of Marblehead, *which soon proved inadequate to Harry Noyes.*
(Mystic Seaport Museum, Inc.)

away forefoot Herreshoff gave the waterlines less hollow than his prior designs. He again prescribed lead ballast to assure her sail-carrying ability. At the after end of the keel, though, he cut away the deadwood into a broad arc from abaft the lead ballast to the rudder stock. This accomplished several things: it reduced wetted-surface friction to help her in light airs; it reduced the side turning force aft to make her more maneuverable; it set the rudder somewhat apart from the keel so that her fine after sections formed a sort of rudder skeg; and it exposed the rudder blade's lower area to smoother water flow to improve its hydrodynamics.

Herreshoff did not give *Tioga* a particularly tall rig. As with many of his designs, he set the mainmast truck as high above the waterline as the hull's overall length including bowsprit (which was 86 feet), proportions that perhaps satisfied his own view of a golden mean. He raked the mainmast 5½° and the mizzenmast 7° (Herreshoff was a firm believer in the added efficiency of a sail set on a raked mast). He drew a sailplan that called for an easily handled division of area into a jibtop (264 square feet), flying jib (394), forestaysail (376), main (1,271), and mizzen (500), with no Genoa jib.

Herreshoff drew up a number of deck and trunk cabin arrangements, including a flush-deck design, settling on a low superstructure with a small raised crew companion forward. As to the interior, *Tioga* had a great deal of room below as a result of her long waterline and wide after sections. Herreshoff divided the space plan as follows: In the forecastle he placed berths for four crew, with

their toilet crammed publicly between them. Immediately abaft the crew quarters he set a large galley, with the mainmast and its massive step set in its midst like a great tree. In the waist, he drew an owner's double stateroom to starboard, and a narrow cabin with upper and lower berths to port meant, as he explained, for two boys. There were two bathrooms: one to port, one to starboard. The saloon, about 14 feet square, had four large folding berths, a table on slides, a tiled cabin stove, a sideboard, and a chart table. Herreshoff prescribed teak floors, varnished overhead beams, other wood work in oak, and lots of bronze fittings, to give what he called "a seagoing effect" to this daysailer that he surmised would never go to sea.

Herreshoff specified for *Tioga's* auxiliary a Lathrop Mystic Model six-cylinder, 175-horsepower gas engine, which he expected to drive her at better than ten knots through a Hyde 24-inch by 14-inch three-bladed feathering propeller. He set the engine and shaft off-center, to port, rather than on centerline. (Herreshoff felt that a centerline shaft interferes with the keel bolts, or centerboard, and weakens the deadwood. He felt that it also allows greater speed, maneuverability, and easier steering in reverse. Finally, an offset propeller obviates a rudder aperture, which reduces the blade's effective area and generates speed-killing turbulence.)

Regardless of his mission to create a mere daysailer, Herreshoff was not casual about Design No. 66. He no doubt sensed that he had found some rare combination of shapes that would produce a very fast yacht. In a public relations broadside he wrote to describe the design for clients (and anyone else who would care to read and believe it), he concluded with this challenging remark: "It will be very interesting to see how she will go with the modern yachts of her same sail area, for she can meet them on even terms as far as outside ballast, hollow spars and modern rigging are concerned." In other words, Herreshoff knew he had a swift craft on his drawing board, and he couldn't wait for Harry Noyes to prove it for him on the water.

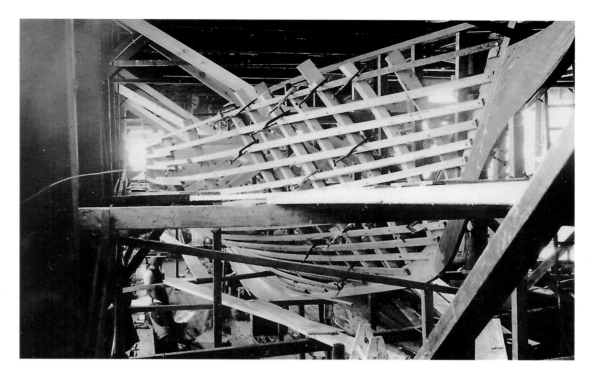

In that same publicity sheet Herreshoff wrote that *Tioga of Marblehead* was being built out of "selected material by craftsmen who have served their time in the best yacht yards and she is one of the highest grade yachts under construction at the present time." One reason for that bit of promotion was that Harry Noyes had naturally elected to build *Tioga* on his own turf, at the Quincy Adams yard; Herreshoff was probably buttering up his client for future reference. But it was true: Harry had every intention of seeing that *Tioga* was of the highest grade, and he even managed to import a handful of fine woodworkers from Italy, for comparably low wages, just to work on *Tioga*'s construction.

Herreshoff began *Tioga*'s drawings immediately and by August 1935 he had completed the scantlings, principal construction drawings, and some fitting and equipment specifications. He ordered the hull to be fabricated with a skin of bronze-fastened, double-planked, two-inch mahogany over steam-bent oak frames. The decking was to be of Port Orford cedar (which turned out to be one of his several mistakes). Then he set to work on details and machinery layouts. He obtained from Lathrop the engine's installation cut—a scaled engine "footprint" that he used to set space requirements on the drawing for a generator, plumbing, exhausts, and the other systems he had to pack into a very small engine room. He also specified to Abel Gomez, Quincy Adams' foreman, a minimum of five percent antimony (a hardening element) in the nearly 31,000 pounds of lead to be poured for the ballast keel. And he gave Gomez the detailed fabrication drawings for the hollow, extra-lightweight Sitka spruce spars.

Construction on *Tioga* advanced through the winter of 1935/36 without incident. (Parallel to *Tioga*'s construction, Quincy Adams was building two other craft: a 44-foot cutter and a 57-foot yawl, both designed by John Alden.) In January 1936, after a visit to check *Tioga*'s progress, Herreshoff reported to Gomez his great pleasure at the yard's workmanship. At the

Tioga under construction during the winter of 1935/36.
(ABOVE) She is being framed up.
(LEFT) Her lead ballast has emerged from its mold.
(BELOW) Her planking has begun.
(Courtesy of Bradley Noyes)

(ABOVE) *Bradley, his pup, Harry and Ruth Noyes survey* Tioga's *progress.*
(RIGHT) *The lead ballast is ready for its disputed keelbolts.*
(Courtesy of Bradley Noyes)

(BELOW) Tioga's *hand-carved starboard trailboard, before it was mounted and gilded.*
(Mystic Seaport Museum, Inc.)

same time he recommended that Gomez buy the bilge pumps, cleats, backstay and halyard winches from the Herreshoff Manufacturing Company (his loyalty remained to its quality, though his family no longer owned the company). Herreshoff soon specified the interior decor: the saloon and after cabin were to be of white-painted panels and bulkheads, with a teak-and-holly sole and mahogany overhead beams, the more or less standard American yacht style of the day. He also asked that Gomez be prepared to build a dining table of knotty white oak with a chiseled pattern, and he sent a handmade sample of the chiseling as a guide to Quincy's cabinetmakers (Herreshoff was himself a master woodworker).

In late January 1936 Herreshoff sent a copy of his promotional description to Quincy Adams, in hopes that Richmond or Gomez might hand out copies to curious visitors, who were showing interest in the new construction. (He admitted in a covering letter, with some irony, that he wrote the blurb with the press in mind, keeping it simple because journalists of his acquaintance couldn't handle much burdensome detail.) By mid-February he had finished twenty drawings, and reported to Harry Noyes that "so far everything seems to be very nearly perfect." About this time, Herreshoff asked the patternmakers to begin making deck, rigging, and interior fittings, and he ordered the Lathrop engine with an updraft carburetor (at Harry's request). As part of his all-inclusive service, Herreshoff sent Noyes tentative insurance quotes "for a $30,000 boat." Based on the yacht's being moored under a shed most of the time, he quoted for six months a rate of $225, and for eight months $262. (That evaluation of *Tioga* by Herreshoff of $30,000 will forever remain an enigma, as we shall later see.)

Herreshoff would visit the yard periodically. Harry Noyes would also come often from his Boston office to see the work's progress. He sometimes came alone. On occasions he would pick up Bradley at his private school and take him along to the Quincy yard. Occasionally, Harry and Herreshoff would visit the yard together to jointly inspect details and discuss the next steps. But it was becoming clear by March 1936 that their once-harmonious alliance was no longer absolutely in tune. The friction apparently started when Herreshoff went to the yard for an inspection and soon thereafter wrote a caustic letter to Noyes calling his client's attention to some baffling changes he had discovered in the hull scantlings:

> I noticed that the deck beam at the after end of the cockpit had been shifted from the position shown on the design. I thought I had better give you some notes in writing on this for I have found that, where things have been changed so that they do not work out successfully, the architect is blamed. The reasons why the cockpit should not be carried farther aft are: 1. There will be no place for a man to stand when steering; 2. The alteration makes the rubber exhaust pipe come too near the cockpit; 3. Frame 66 needs to have a crawl space associated with it so someone can reach the transom inside, and 4. The resulting uneven spacing of the deck beams is not desirable, nor is the unevenness of the deck fasteners.

The alterations stood. They were only the beginning of the problems. By April Herreshoff had become a bit testier in reaction to other liberties Harry and the yard had taken with his construction plans and specifications. (On at least one occasion he and Harry had a shouting match about these matters in front of the yardmen.) Later, in prescribing *Tioga*'s ground tackle, Herreshoff became even more acerbic. He urged the yard to buy genuine Herreshoff anchors (a 200-pound starboard bower and a 175-pound port bower with folding stock), but he concluded his specification with this well-aimed arrow: "These are very carefully figured out and rechecked by three or four systems, English and American. I did not guess at these weights and they should not be cut down."

One of the famous golden dolphins.
(Jim Brown)

On June 30, just six weeks from launch day, Herreshoff informed Richmond that he was at work on the last design details: he had sketched up the scrollwork for the trailboards and was working on the stern scrollwork and the forward end of the taffrail bulwarks, which he was decorating with two carved teak dolphins. He concluded, however, with a brusque remark about Harry's decision (or indecision) on the four-cylinder electric generator: "I don't know where it is or what it is," he wrote, "so that you people will have to work this out." Francis Herreshoff clearly felt he was losing control.

On that same day, Herreshoff revealed another source of his annoyance with Noyes that would ultimately blow up into a full-scale quarrel: he was unhappy with the payment he was receiving (or rather *not* receiving) for his work. Having completed the full set of forty-four drawings, he felt he was immediately due the final payment of $608.46 he had invoiced for completion of the job. (About the same time he wrote to the Britt Brothers, who had built the first *Tioga* and her sistership *Bounty*, complimenting them on their work and expressing his desire to build once more with them. His happy liaison with Quincy Adams and Harry Noyes was already fated to be brief, after the building of just one boat.)

In part, no doubt, Herreshoff was reacting to an unexpectedly willful, independent-minded client, one who didn't reflexively accept everything the designer prescribed. The ordering of *Tioga*'s sails was a good case

in point. As early as May 1935 Herreshoff had begun seeking a sailmaker for Noyes. For his own quite pecuniary reasons, however, Herreshoff was quite partial to the Ratsey & Lapthorn loft on City Island, the Bronx. Long before he sent out bid requests to other lofts, in fact, he mailed Ratsey a blueprint of the sailplan and a general description of *Tioga*—consciously giving them an inside track to obtain the order. Not until ten months later, however, did he seek formal bids from three sailmakers: Prescott & Wilson (New York City), the City Island Ratsey loft, and the original Ratsey loft (Cowes, Isle of Wight). He sought quotes for main, mizzen, working jib, jib topsail, and forestaysail. He asked for separate bids on some lighter sails: balloon jib, Genoa jib, mizzen staysail, and spinnaker. He asked the lofts to quote separately on each sail because he understood that Noyes wanted to add to the inventory over time, starting with the working sails only and leaving his options open later for the more race-oriented sails. Herreshoff left the panel design and cloth weight up to each sailmaker, but suggested that the forestaysail and mizzen be heavy enough to serve as storm sails, and that the mizzen be very flat, to ease helm in a breeze. He also noted that with his well-divided sailplan, "cut up into four or five sails," reefing would seldom be necessary, so he recommended that the sailmakers dispense with reef points. (But if they insisted on inserting reef points, he preferred them to be set deeper at the leech than the luff, to keep the booms from drooping.)

Despite Herreshoff's preference for the City Island loft, in May 1936 Noyes instructed him to order the working sails from the English Ratsey loft, shutting out Herreshoff's City Island friends. Herreshoff obligingly wired Cowes, asking for the best Egyptian cotton, in eighteen-inch panels, suggesting that the light sails might be ordered later for economy's sake, because "we are having pretty hard times in this country at present." Herreshoff also sent the bad news to his friends on City Island, revealing his sometimes bitterly parsimonious side: "This decision was made against my wishes for at the time getting sails through the customs is very bothersome and I get about fifty percent less commission." (The cost of *Tioga*'s sails, in 1936 pounds sterling, were: main, 135.14; mizzen, 51.15; working jib, 41.80; forestaysail, 40.50; and jibtop, 22.10. The total of 290 pounds would be about $450 today.)

No doubt Herreshoff was not pleased to be trifled with by a willful client, and he was extremely sensitive to setbacks, particularly if they involved money. As it turns out, there were extenuating circumstances to his troubled mood. In the spring of 1936 he was having financial difficulties, owing to the depression-driven paucity of design work. And he was also suffering periodic bouts of ill health. Further, while Quincy Adams was building *Tioga* Herreshoff was busy moving his residence and office to a small house he had bought at 25 Front Street, Marblehead, where he hoped for some stability after years of renting offices and living in boarding houses. As a result, Herreshoff was distract-

ed by the time, effort, and expense of the move, which he had long sought but which exacerbated his financial predicament. The house, for which he paid the not inconsiderable sum of three thousand depression dollars, and the higher renovation cost, put him in the embarrassing position, at the age of forty-eight, of having to consider accepting an interest-free loan offered by his father, with whom he maintained a rather distant, correct relationship (old Nat often signed his letters: "Your affectionate father, Nathanael G. Herreshoff").

Yet, once Herreshoff completed the move and was comfortably settled, the financial squabble with Noyes worsened, as they argued over his fee. As was the custom, a designer's fee was set from the total building cost of a yacht, usually ranging between ten and fifteen percent. Herreshoff, however, came to suspect that, as owner of the Quincy Adams yard, Noyes was charging himself significantly less than the normal rate he would charge an outside client for a yacht of *Tioga*'s size, quality, and detail. The truth of the matter is elusive—there are no extant

records from the yard. While it seems likely that *Tioga* cost as little as $42,000 to build, by his own public estimate Herreshoff believed that the boat should have cost between $65,000 and $70,000 if it had been built for an outside client. (To further confuse the issue, some time after *Tioga*'s launch another client came to Herreshoff for a set of *Tioga* drawings to build a duplicate; Herreshoff wrote that he should expect to pay Quincy Adams $90,000 to build it.) In short, Herreshoff all but accused Harry Noyes of being a crook, of unethically cutting his design fee by the unscrupulous ruse of manipulating *Tioga*'s building costs downward (though his insurance quote, noted earlier, had been for a yacht of only $30,000 value).

(Years later, Harry's son Bradley tried to clear up this aspect of his father's rift with Herreshoff. To put the actual price of *Tioga*'s construction onto a logical scale, he noted that 1936 was still a depression year and that Herreshoff was paying sixty cents per hour, "and half a bottle of wine for lunch," to Aage Nielsen for his assistance with *Tioga*'s drawings. And he recalled that within a year of *Tioga*'s completion, Quincy Adams built a pair of 72-foot Sparkman & Stephens (S&S) yachts—*Windigo* and *Ptarmigan*—for clients who paid around $40,000 each, give or take a couple of thousand dollars. Bradley Noyes felt that, by his own recall, the yard wasn't playing games with a special price for his father, as Herreshoff so fervently believed.)

There was still more to the story. It would seem from Herreshoff's frequent correspondence that complaints about the designer/client relationship (legitimate or otherwise) came only from his side. But that was hardly the case. In fact, before the Quincy Adams yard finished *Tioga* they executed more scantling changes owing to differences between the yard's practices and Herreshoff's drawings. For one thing, the Quincy Adams managers refused to attach the lead ballast to the keel using lag screws, as Herreshoff prescribed. They always did it

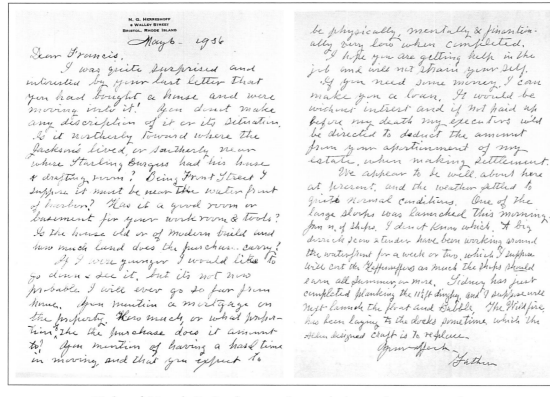

Nathanael Herreshoff offers his son architectural advice and a no-interest loan.

(Mystic Seaport Museum, Inc.)

The invitation Harry and Ruth Noyes sent to 300 Massachusetts Bay yachtsmen.
(Courtesy of Bradley Noyes)

by screwing heavy keelbolts into large nuts set in pockets deep in the ballast keel. (When they poured and finished the keel, their way, Herreshoff came to inspect the work. A couple of the yardmen hastily covered the bolts with empty screw boxes, and when they ran out of boxes one of them tossed his hat on the last exposed bolt. Herreshoff didn't notice.)

Perhaps the most notorious change, and one that should never have been necessary, was the eleventh-hour rebuilding of the saloon floor. When *Tioga's* hull was complete in the early summer of 1936 the finished trunk cabin, built in a separate shop, was brought to the main shed to be joined to the deck. Once they set it in place, to their astonishment, the yardmen found far less than six feet of headroom in the saloon. Noyes immediately ordered his carpenters to lower the saloon sole, which in a finished hull is more easily said than done: they had to trim floor timbers, cut down and rebuild tanks, and reroute plumbing.

The event accelerated the breakdown of the accord between Noyes and Herreshoff. It

was never forgotten by the designer. Many years later, responding to a question about the trunk cabin incident, Herreshoff said: *"It didn't have full headroom because it's not a goddam dance hall!"* Still later, when he was a guest aboard the yacht for the 1962 America's Cup races, Herreshoff sputtered in response to a similar query: *"I was asked for a goddam daysailer!"* (Never reluctant to employ an appropriately salty expletive, Herreshoff seems to have reserved his most saline for Harry Noyes.)

Though he was never able to articulate it without agitation, Herreshoff probably did have a justifiable complaint: Noyes truly wanted much more than a daysailer. That is easily seen in the almost ludicrous panoply of weighty creature comforts he requested for *Tioga's* interior. Yes, he wanted speed; but he seemed unwilling to sacrifice a single human comfort in attaining that speed. So, at his order (and surely to Herreshoff's chagrin) Quincy Adams installed: an oversize galley stove; a hotel-size electric refrigerator and deep freeze; a large generator; two ship-to-shore telephones with their own heavy

batteries; the best available navigating equipment; over-large fresh water and fuel tanks; a hot-and-cold pressurized water system; two showers; a central heating system with cast-bronze radiators warmed by hot water pumped from a large galley boiler; and a cast-iron bathtub in the owners' suite. It could not have made Herreshoff very happy to see the added weight, which resulted in *Tioga's* floating considerably below her design waterline for nearly thirty years after her launching.

Regardless of the tension, Herreshoff completed his obligations, right down to designing *Tioga's* garnish and ordering it from R.H. Peterson, of Revere, Massachusetts. It consisted of two trailboards with raised oak leaf scrolls ($90 each); two carved teak dolphins for the forward end of the topgallant rails ($50 each); a carved eagle nameboard, cast bronze border rope, and other detailing ($175 for the set). Peterson completed the carving; the yard did the painting and gilding. By the end of July 1936 *Tioga* (with lowered saloon sole and trunk cabin securely in place) was painted and varnished inside and out, and made ready for launching.

In 1934, when she was nine years old, Hope Ellen Noyes—Harry and Ruth's only daughter—received from her younger brother Bradley a sort of hand-me-up gift. It was an eleven-foot, cruel-sounding, Brutal Beast one-design dinghy, drawn by Starling Burgess. Harry had given the dinghy to Bradley for his birthday. But this Beast wasn't just an off-the-shelf stock boat; it was a custom-built brightwork boat built lovingly by the men of the Quincy Adams Yacht Yard (only a father with deep devotion to his children and a shipyard at his disposal could manage that). But, after racing the Beast a bit, Bradley (destined to become a world-class ocean racer on his own) wasn't pleased with the boat and the sail that came with it; he suggested that his father give the boat to his big sister.

Hope's reaction, however, was no better

Hope Ellen Noyes, Brutal Beast champion.
(Courtesy of Hope Smith)

than lukewarm: she had a wish for a very different sort of beast. Being Harry's only daughter, and filled with girlish charm and guile, when Harry offered her the boat she jumped on his lap and entered into a delicate negotiation: "Daddy, dear, I don't want a sailboat," Hope said. "I want a horse." Harry countered with a bargain: "All right. If you learn how to sail the boat," he said, "I'll buy you a horse." Harry thought with fatherly confidence that once Hope jumped aboard the Brutal Beast and sensed the exhilaration of single-handing among her young peers, she would never again hear the call of the equestrian life. Harry miscalculated; his daughter didn't. She accepted the dinghy, named it *Bounding Clam,* and proceeded to master its vagaries. Plump little Hope polished the *Clam's* bottom, trimmed its sails, and mastered its tiller; in two summers she became Brutal Beast champion in Marblehead's first junior division, which included

George O'Day, Bobby Coulsen, Barbara Connelly and other stellar youth. Harry bought her a horse.

To further reward his daughter, Harry asked Hope to do the honors at *Tioga's* christening. As August 10, 1936, neared Ruth and Harry sent out more than three hundred invitations for that very special Monday event. Yardmen hurriedly completed the final tasks of getting *Tioga* ready and cleaned up the premises. When the guests arrived that afternoon, they found the main building shed decorated with flags and bunting. *Tioga,* on her launching cradle, already carried her yachting ensign set astern, and she was dressed with code flags draped over mast stumps set temporarily in her partners. Folding chairs were set about the shed, as were tables for refreshments. A band played.

Harry had arranged for his motoryacht *Kyrrah* (named for his father, Harry K., in reverse) to bring down from Marblehead more than thirty kids of the Brutal Beast Class and other junior yachtsmen, along with his sons Harry, Pike, and Bradley. At the same time, their parents—a who's-who of Massachusetts Bay yachting—gathered in the shed to admire *Tioga's* gleaming white hull with its pale-blue taffrail bulwarks, blue

boottop, and gilded garnish. Just before the scheduled launch time of 1800, the shed was crammed with society guests, photographers, local journalists, reporters from two Boston newspapers (the *Globe* and *Herald*), and anxious yardmen. Everyone bubbled with great excitement over the traditional moment to come. It was hardly noticed by the crowd that the designer of this handsome craft was nowhere to be seen.

Hope, a bit shy and shaky before the crowd, had up to the last moment begged her father to relieve her of the launch responsibility. She believed it would have been wiser, and less taxing to her youthful psyche, if her mother christened the boat. But Harry insisted. As Hope recalled many years later: "It was a beautiful boat, with gold leaf and twirls and swirls. I remember the dolphins carved out of teak. There was a band. It was like a tea; all these older people, in their twenties and early thirties . . . champagne . . . sandwiches. The most impressive thing was that I had this huge bottle of champagne, this enormous bottle of champagne, and I had to swing it. It was hanging from the bowsprit, all wrapped in red, white, and blue ribbons to keep it from shattering, with long streamers coming off it.

Harry's motoryacht Kyrrah, *which brought local kids to the launching.*
(Courtesy of Bradley Noyes)

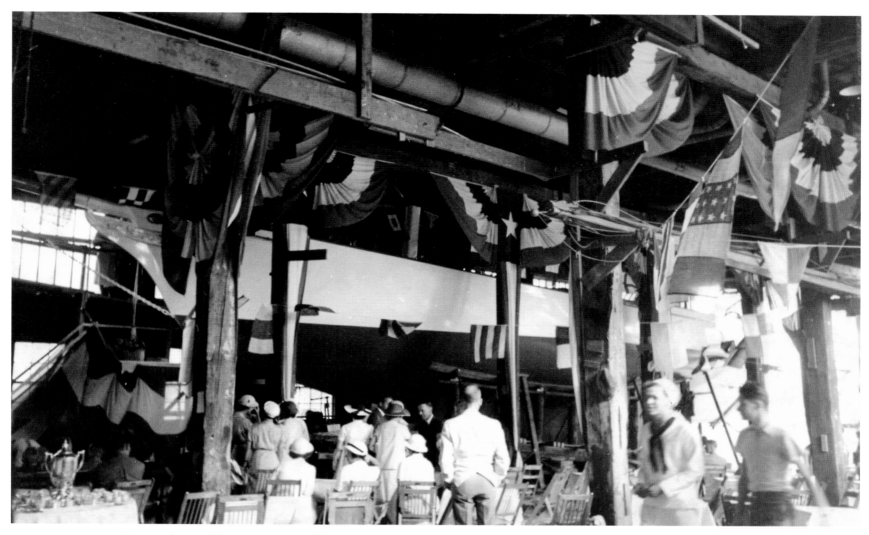

Guests gather amid bunting, music, and champagne in Quincy Adams' main shed, just before Tioga's *launch into history. . . .*

(Courtesy of Bradley Noyes)

"All I said was: 'I christen you *Tioga,*' and —*pow!*— I hit it right on the bow, but it didn't break. Then my father leaned down and whispered: 'Take it in both hands.' And I did: I took it in two hands and gave it a mighty swing. I remember when it smashed you could smell champagne all over—*What a waste!*—but at the age of eleven you don't worry about things like that. . . . It was quite a day."

It *was* quite a day. Because, just as Hope rared back for her second swing of the bottle (which one press report likened to Jimmy Foxx smacking a home run), yardmen drove the wedges out from under *Tioga's* keel—as they had done countless times without incident—to free the cradle so it might slide gently down the rails at the proper moment. The flying bottle struck the bobstay, and this

time it smashed, merrily spewing its bubbly contents. As though it had been pushed by Hope's "mighty swing," *Tioga's* 54-ton hull began to slide stern-first quickly down the ways. After the hull had moved just a few yards down the rails, however, the starboard-side cradle poppets, which apparently lacked the usual diagonal supports, suddenly gave way. The cradle collapsed, accompanied by the hideous noise of splintering wood. *Tioga* careened sharply to starboard, her forward caprail grating horribly along the shed's door frame as she emerged into the daylight. As she flew, her bowsprit barely missed jamming against the shed wall, which would surely have snapped it off like a matchstick. The cheers and applause of the guests were instantly drowned out by shrieks of panic as *Tioga* fell over to that sharp angle, then, as

she hit deep water, plunged back just as precipitously to port. In a split second, three men standing on *Tioga's* foredeck—Charlie Rudolph (Quincy's rigger), Duncan Bernard (a yardman), and Johnny Rhyn (Harry's Eight-Meter sailing master)—were given the ride of their lives: all three were spilled heels-over-head in the air like acrobats, much to the horror of the crowd (and their fellow yardmen, who saw disaster and blame suddenly flashing before their eyes). As gravity returned the three men to the deck, Bernard instinctively grabbed the port rail below him with one hand in an effort to break his fall until the hull returned to level, at which time he could no longer hold on and he splashed over the side into the water, barely missing the jagged wood wreckage that lay everywhere around. Inside the shed, the guests

frantically pressed forward to see the great fall, while yardmen scrambled about to make sense of it all. But Arthur Hansen—a writer, photographer, and local character who was covering the event for the *Herald* and working as a stringer for the Associated Press—coolly waited until he thought the hull could fall no more and tripped his camera shutter. Hansen captured the topsy-turvy moment on one precious prize-winning frame.

As *Tioga* became fully immersed, her momentum unbridled, she hurtled full-bore in reverse about a hundred yards until the yard crew managed to fetch her up with her mooring lines before she could collide broadside with *Kyrrah,* standing well off the slipway to allow guests a good overview of the proceedings. They got their overview (and someone aboard captured the action with an 8-millimeter movie camera). Yardmen quickly reined *Tioga* in and brought her alongside the work dock; the swimmer was picked up by a tender, stunned, sopping, and abashed, but happily unhurt. The shaken guests returned to the party. It was all over.

Or rather, it was just beginning. Immediately, with the help of local salts and saltier journalists, a mythology began enveloping this yacht named *Tioga*—an aura, a mystique, a distinction that has ever since stuck to her like barnacles to a poorly painted hull. Everyone saw significance in this near-wreck of a launching. All realized that if the cradle had collapsed a split-second earlier, the flying *Tioga* would have hit the building with the full force of her weight and done major damage to herself, her occupants, and the shed. The more cheerless observers therefore called up the old bluewater superstition that a mishap at the start of a vessel's life must be taken as a forewarning of calamity to come. Optimists, on the other hand, saw that her friskily independent reach for her element represented "the luck of the sea and starboard tack in the pinches," and that *Tioga* was unquestionably destined for a brilliant future.

The launch to end all launches. . . .
(Mystic Seaport Museum, Inc./Arthur Hansen)

Harry Noyes, who naturally fell in with the optimists, was unperturbed. He later said, nonchalantly, that he entertained no fears for the future. Fear would not have been the right emotion for this exceptional occasion; elation was. And *Tioga* would live up to the expectations of all the wiser salts who saw in her cocky, crazy, hair-raising launch a bright future: a very bright future indeed.

Following a brief recovery period, the guests were served much-needed drinks and a buffet supper, while the yard crew stepped *Tioga's* masts. Then guests were ushered aboard for a quick tour of the boat. After the party, *Tioga* was hauled overnight for inspection. She was indeed damaged, but not seriously—she sustained a long scrape on her starboard caprail, where she slid along the shed's door frame, and her keel timber was gouged for some length just above the ballast, where she had no doubt caught part of the cradle. Repairs were made and she was touched up, relaunched, and delivered the next day to her Marblehead mooring. On that day, August 11, 1936, the feast of words celebrating *Tioga's* birth began. The *Globe* said she was one of the most graceful craft launched for a Boston yachtsman in many a year; the *Herald* said that if she is as fast in proportion as the first *Tioga*, she should win prizes in many an event. Both newspapers breathlessly described *Tioga's* break-neck self-launch in fable-making prose, carrying their metaphors well beyond the limit; it was truly a field day for the press.

Coincidentally, just two days after *Tioga's* much-publicized launch, Francis Herreshoff wrote to his father in Florida, reporting rather indifferently that nothing of great interest had happened lately in Marblehead "excepting possibly Race Week." His only mention of *Tioga's* launch was a speculation, late in the letter, based on newspaper reports and hearsay, that "inexperienced yardmen" had not built her cradle properly. There was no mention of pride, no note of joy, no sharing of triumph. How sad it must have been for the designer to be so restrained when he had created such a superb yacht. A few days

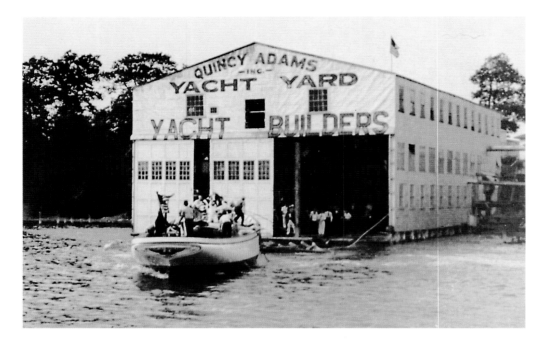

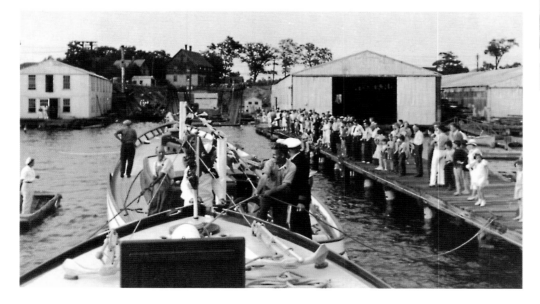

(LEFT) Tioga *flies out of the shed and is captured.*
(TOP) *In the aftermath yardmen calmly stepped her masts.*
(ABOVE) *The gouging of her keel was minimal.*
(Courtesy of Bradley Noyes)

Tioga, with her original single-spreader rig, fuels up in New London.
(Mystic Seaport Museum, Inc.)

later, he reported with slightly more energy to his father that *Tioga* had arrived in Marblehead and was "making a very good impression." Three weeks later, Nat Herreshoff answered the letter by chiding his son for designing a double-ender for Bill Strawbridge, which he felt was "not at all good looking, and the opposite to the *Tiogas* and *Bounty* that you designed." The well-established coolness toward his father, coupled with the rift with Harry Noyes, seemed to doubly militate against Francis Herreshoff's expressing his true sentiments about *Tioga.* Here was an artist who had sired a boat of exceptional grace and worthiness, but who already felt her slipping away, like a child who has left home . . . never to return.

*T*ioga's crew of four, including her skipper Nelson Porter, lived aboard that first summer, crammed into the forepeak. Crewmen worked for ten or fifteen dollars a week in those days, the captain earned three hundred dollars a month. (Harry also had one permanent crew, Johnny Rhyn, for his Eight-Meter, along with four paid hands on the family's big powerboat, so he was supporting a fair proportion of Marblehead's best professional seamen.) The family daysailed *Tioga* for the

rest of the summer of 1936, and Harry did some day racing with his sons and friends. (Nearly every time they went out sailing, however, Hope would develop a mysterious case of "asthma," and have to stay at home, although her affliction was never quite debilitating enough to prevent her from riding her horse in the family's absence.)

Guests aboard *Tioga* were mostly the Noyes' friends and their children—Waldo Brown came occasionally. Harry was not much inclined toward using the boat for business entertaining: *Tioga* was pure family delight. But in that idyllic summer of 1936, something was bubbling in the grotto of Harry Noyes' mind. It is true that he had asked Herreshoff for a family daysailer. Yet Harry began to feel, even at this early stage, that this *Tioga* had a potential beyond his elementary expectations; this feeling emerged during an occasional family outing or local club race when she showed sudden, wholly unexpected, bursts of speed, particularly on a reach in a fresh breeze. Then Harry entered *Tioga* in her first distance-racing event, the 138-mile Jeffrey's Ledge Race, which her predecessor had dominated under Waldo Brown. Both *Bounty* and the old *Tioga* (now named *Reejak*) were entered as well.

After several days of hard easterlies, the wind at the start of the race turned fresh out of the southwest, kicking up a terribly rough sea. Time allowance was given at the start: the smallest boats crossed the line at 2100, September 5; the 72-foot *Tioga,* scratch boat, started at 0300 September 6. After less than a month in the water her rig was not well tuned and her sails hardly had the sailmaker's folding creases worked out of them. She had no spinnaker, and the friends and kids Harry enlisted as crew were green and not familiar with her. Yet, on the first close reach and the 40-mile running leg *Tioga* passed every one of the 23 competing boats except John Alden's *Grenadier,* which was sailed hard by a top-notch crew. When *Tioga* hauled on the wind to head for the finish, however, some of the kids got seasick and Harry noticed that the mast was flexing a good deal, too much for comfort. He lowered sail and powered into Gloucester for two or three hours of rest. When the breeze abated he set sail again and proceeded to be first to finish (in no small part because the only other boat in *Tioga's* class withdrew in the rough conditions, along with half the rest of the fleet). Though she was first over the line, *Tioga* was set back to third from last overall among the dozen or so surviving boats, a reality that would plague this beauty nearly all her life.

A few days later Francis Herreshoff, eager for *Tioga* to make her mark, wrote to his father of the event. He reported (finally with some pride) that for the first time in years the fleet was not dominated by John Alden's designs: five were by Alden and five by himself, a sign of his arrival. But Francis was not kind to Harry Noyes' fatherly action. Though he noted that *Tioga* nearly led the fleet, he concluded that the reason she dropped out for a time was that "the owner and crew evidently got panicky" when she hauled on the wind. Another unkind cut.

Harry Noyes' sense of *Tioga's* speed, in this event and others, raised his appetite for distance racing, and further added to the strain between him and Herreshoff. Late in the summer of 1936 he apparently asked

The Noyes children — Harry, Hope, Pike, and Bradley — enjoy a day's dress-up outing.
(Courtesy of Bradley Noyes)

blocks and doubled the Yankee and mainsail halyards to carry greater loads, and they designed a larger Yankee jib and an overlapping Genoa jib, as Harry wanted. *Tioga* the alongshore daysailer was fast being outfitted for muscular offshore work.

And as though these shakedown troubles weren't enough, Harry had discovered that Herreshoff's cutaway in the keel, meant to make *Tioga* easy to turn, apparently made her *too* easy to turn: she had so little lateral resistance aft that she was quite squirrelly to steer. At the end of the summer of 1936, Harry hauled *Tioga* and had the cutaway filled in to improve her tracking. He also had the decorative top of the rudder cut off—he had noticed that the eye-catching scrollwork, elegant as it was, induced a good deal of turbulence and drag, and slowed *Tioga* down. Can there be any question that Harry was trying to convert *Tioga* into a less-than-casual machine? (As further proof of that, in 1936 Harry added a new cruising queen to his fleet, the 96-foot steel schooner, *Wildfire*. Built in 1923, *Wildfire* became the family cruiser while Harry tuned up *Tioga* for more combative sailing purposes.)

Herreshoff to order the optional Genoa jib, which had been excluded from the original sail order. Herreshoff seems to have rebuffed Harry, as he stubbornly kept to his view that *Tioga* didn't need a Genoa jib to go fast. Also, as Harry had noted in the Jeffrey's Ledge Race, *Tioga*'s mainmast was rather, well, resilient (the Noyes kids dubbed it the "rubber" mast). Apparently, the hollow box sections Herreshoff had specified for lightness were *too* light; the single-spreader rig didn't support the spar well enough, and the mast flexed undesirably. Consulting Herreshoff again for a solution, Harry received something on the order of this blunt, nontechnical reply: *You asked for a large, comfortable daysailer, so—damn it!—shorten down your sails and be comfortable!*

Noyes bypassed Herreshoff and contacted the John G. Alden office in Boston to have them redesign the rig. Alden did some calculations on the mainmast section (which was 13 inches by 9½ inches). They found the section inadequate and recommended that Harry lift the mast out, remove all fittings, strip it to bare wood and glue on a reinforcing shell to stiffen it. They designed

a much needed two-spreader shroud arrangement to improve the athwartships support of the mast, and they added a jumper above the top spreader and a removable baby stay to control the mast fore and aft. They added

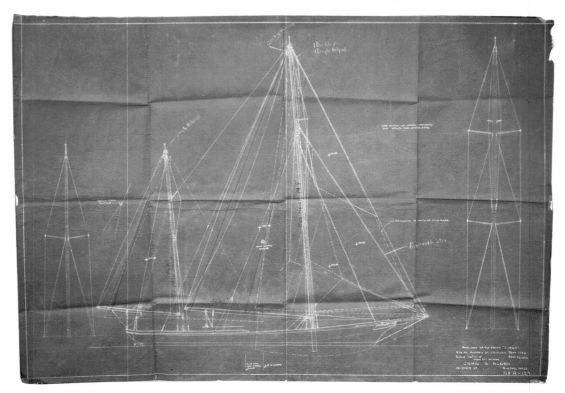

Alden revised Tioga's rig (ABOVE) to include double spreaders (OPPOSITE).
(Courtesy of Bradley Noyes)

There are those, with usually flawless hindsight, who recognize that the combination of Herreshoff's superb hullform, Alden's rig and sailplan, and all of Harry's alterations, were the fundamental sources of *Tioga*'s ultimate power and stability in a breeze. The combination of a hefty ballast, the well-distributed beam, and a stiffer mast, with the wider choice of sails, made it possible for Harry and his crew to maintain her balance and keep her on her feet in heavy weather while other less-stable yachts were forced to reef early to reduce heeling and helm. History was to prove them right.

Tioga was relaunched and sent down to Florida for a winter of family cruising. The younger children lived aboard with Ruth Noyes, and took school lessons ashore with other boat kids. Between daysails and short cruises, Harry did some racing. Early in 1937, he entered *Tioga* in her first big blue-water Florida event: the Biscayne Bay Yacht Club's Lipton Cup Race. *Tioga*'s performance was nothing less than embarrassing. The wind was light at the start of the 30-mile triangular race and, as is always their privilege, the race committee shortened the course during the starting sequence by flying new signals. *Tioga,* whose entire crew missed the signals, sailed the original long course. There is no record of her finish, but someone in the crew scrawled a hasty entry in her log that said it all: "They changed the course on us after the start and nobody told us anything about it." Despite her potential, *Tioga of Marblehead* was a long way from being alertly, professionally raced.

In the Miami to Nassau Race, however, probably with the same bunch of now slightly more seasoned sailors, she did quite a bit better against some really tough competitors, including Spencer Berger's 71-foot Alden yawl, *Mandoo Too,* and *Stormy Weather,* a Sparkman & Stephens creation sailed by the redoubtable Rod Stephens. In a strong southeasterly, which gave her brisk reaching conditions on the first leg, she kept up with the fleet all the way, and finished third in just under 32 hours (more than 3 hours behind

Wildfire *(TOP) replaced* Tioga *as the Noyes family's favorite sailing cruiser.*

(Mystic Seaport Museum, Inc./Rosenfeld Collection)

36

In her early days Tioga *raced against well-sailed competitors such as* Stormy Weather.
(Mystic Seaport Museum, Inc./Rosenfeld Collection)

Chowder Race (not exactly the sporting equivalent of the Fastnet, but to Massachusetts Bay yachtsmen an endearing, central event). It turned out to be an unusual heavy-weather bash into stiff seas, in which 37 boats started. Seven Class "A" boats did not finish; two were dismasted and two badly damaged. *Tioga,* whose new rig held up superbly, finished 34 minutes ahead of the second boat and saved her time to take the event overall. At least around the Boston area, the derision about this "largest daysailer afloat" began slowly to abate.

After another winter in Florida, in early June 1938 (the summer of the great hurricane), *Tioga* was first to finish in a rainy, foggy, light-air Boston Yacht Club 90-mile tune-up. But she needed 20 hours 30 minutes to accomplish it (for a sluggish average speed of 4.4 knots over the bottom). No one who sailed that drizzly passage, however, could have been prepared for her next racing adventure: the New London to Marblehead Race. Starting on June 24th, this 171-miler took the fleet in a broad anti-clockwise semicircle from Sarah Ledge, across Block Island, Vineyard and Nantucket Sounds, around Cape Cod to the finish at Marblehead Rock north of Boston. After a half-hour postponement owing to a lack of wind, *Tioga* started at 1000 in a light southwesterly. Though it was slow going at Fishers Island, and she was becalmed for a brief time, by early afternoon the breeze veered more to the west, and freshened by evening to a gusty 30 knots. *Tioga* passed the early leaders, *Huntress* and *Reejak,* and took the lead. Then, as she came well off the wind, her crew set a ballooner (Harry had obviously further expanded her sail inventory) and she lifted her skirts and flew. Averaging well over ten knots, she rounded Pollock Rip Lightship at 2030 and ran for the northern tip of the Cape. She rounded Peaked Hill Bar at 0030 the next day, having covered 130 miles in 14 hours, then trimmed up for an inspiring close reach of 40 miles in a piping southwesterly, during which she averaged nearly 11 knots over the bottom. She finished at 0437, with

Mandoo Too and less than 2 hours behind *Stormy Weather). Tioga* was second overall on corrected time (one of the rare moments in her racing life that she moved up in the fleet after being given her time allowance against a larger, scratch boat).

In the spring of 1937, about the time Amelia Earhart was lost in the Pacific, the Noyes family did some cruising in Florida and the Bahamas. *Tioga* was then brought north again to Marblehead. She did no major races in the early summer, just some club stuff. (By the casual use Harry was making of his long and lovely creature, and his own

characterization of her, she had already been dubbed by local yachtsmen, sometimes derisively, as "the largest daysailer afloat.") *Tioga* did join the leisurely midsummer cruises of the Eastern and New York Yacht Clubs. About then Harry bought a hundred-foot motoryacht, *Marjelou,* and sold his Eight-Meter *Gypsy. Tioga* was now his racing boat of choice.

Aside from the club cruises, *Tioga* did compete in one memorable race in the summer of 1937. In a last-minute decision, Harry entered her in the Boston Corinthian Club's annual 15-mile Grand Handicap

In company with her forebear Reejak *(ex-*Bounty*)* Tioga *sails in the 1938 Eastern YC cruise.*
(Mystic Seaport Museum, Inc./Rosenfeld Collection)

an elapsed time of 18 hours 37 minutes; she had to wait more than 2 hours for the next yacht, *Lion's Whelp*, followed by *Reejak*. *Tioga's* average speed for the race was 9.2 knots, and she broke the record of 20:17:42 set in 1911 by the 136-foot steel schooner *Elena* with well over three times her sail area. (In 1912 *Elena* had made the same passage in just under 16 hours, but that was in an easterly gale and a different race, for the Clark Gold Cup.) Of the twenty-four starters, six were either disabled or withdrew in the heavy conditions. Though *Tioga* could not save her time to win the Lambert Trophy (her passage was corrected to 18:25:48), the smirk was wiped off the faces of many a local sailor as she entered the books with her first elapsed-time record. It was certainly not her last.

Leonard M. Fowle, the master sailing writer of the *Globe*, sailed on *Tioga* often as a visiting crewman. He was first among journalists to sense her extraordinary qualities, and he became a notorious enthusiast for *Tioga's* many exploits. He wrote of her thrilling Marblehead triumph:

[K]nowing her hull form, the crew at times must have had some of the sensation of an aquaplane ride. . . . The skipper reported that she performed beautifully in the hard weather and the crew never had a qualm about hull, rig or sails during the passage . . . a tribute to *Tioga* and Francis Herreshoff, her creator, as many of the other racers, craft of more typically modern cruising lines, frequently had to shorten canvas.

In a later column Fowle raved about *Tioga's* ability to "race like a fool and outdistance anything," even with a blown-out Genoa, a baggy forestaysail, and a rather full-cut main (which she carried in more than one race). Fowle also gave rave reviews to *Tioga's* caliber as a sea boat: with her "amazing smoothness of motion," he found it "impossible to tell her speed just by sound or motion, as she parts and closes the water so easily."

A more youthful, spontaneous reaction to *Tioga's* first record-breaking sail came from Bradley Noyes, who enjoyed the wild

ride of his eleven-year life: "We were just crashing though the water, around the Cape. The navigation was by guess, by golly, by radio-direction, and by how-close-can-you-come when you're going around the buoys in the fog with lots of current. *Tioga* had a wonderful motion. It was a thrill to go out, especially when we had any wind. I steered her a lot, but you didn't have to steer her. She was a real sailing boat, and she could sail for an hour or two by herself; she'd just get in the groove and go. She had that long run in the keel. But she didn't have the feel of modern boats: she had an Edson steerer, the geared type; it had no feeling. You couldn't feather the boat to weather—of course, she wouldn't go to weather anyway. My father talked about putting a centerboard in, which probably would have helped a lot." (What a baptism for an eleven-year-old.)

Perhaps the last word on this early triumph of *Tioga's* was had by Francis Herreshoff, in a calmer moment. Years later, in his *Common Sense of Yacht Design*, he wrote enthusiastically about *Tioga's* record-breaking run from New London to Marblehead, claiming that larger yachts, such as the 87-foot *Istalena*, "could never have done that in her palmiest days. . . . [O]ver a short waterline, pot-bellied racers are a joke, and our rules radically wrong when they develop a racing yacht slower for the sail area than a useful cruiser." (Herreshoff the writer at his militant best.)

After smashing her first record, *Tioga* was permitted to take a more leisurely turn on the Eastern Yacht Club cruise; she won her class in one long (136-mile) and one short (40-mile) race. But this event allowed her to participate in another historic happening. Leonard Fowle pulled off the first real-time reporting of a sailboat race by radio-telephone from aboard a yacht. The unprecedented report, called in from *Tioga* as the race progressed, warranted an eight-column spread across the front page of the *Globe's* sports section, and made Fowle even more of a celebrity than he ever dreamed of ashore.

Following the cruise, *Tioga* handily won

the Boston Lightship Race, breaking that record in a come-from-behind bout with B. Devereaux Barker's 64-foot *Good Hope*. And she finished third in the New York Yacht Club cruise behind two tough competitors: W. A. Stewart's *Queen Mab* and De Coursey Fales' magnificent 59-foot schooner, *Niña*. Then she went on to take line honors in the Monhegan Race, in moderate airs, missing the record by just one minute, six seconds, taking second on handicap to *Spookie*, a 45-foot S&S cutter. To climax her first fully proficient racing season, *Tioga* took line honors and first overall in the Jeffrey's Ledge Race (where she had made her wholly forgettable racing debut two years earlier).

In the winter of 1938/39, as was his pleasure, Harry had captain Nelson Porter bring the boat once more to Florida for family fun. He had planned to send one or two of the younger children off to school in Switzerland in the spring, but rejected the notion when the potential for a European war grew daily. (Instead, he built a sweet little sloop for his oldest son Harry, to an Aage Nielsen design, and named her, appropriately, *Tioga Too*). In the spring, in Marblehead, Harry did some around-the-buoys racing on the big *Tioga* in his home waters, then brought the boat down again for the New London to Marblehead Race, in high hopes of surpassing his record. With a light, variable breeze and fog, however, it was a small-boat race, and *Tioga* had little chance of coming near to her previous pace; she had to settle for third place among the big boats after *Baruna* and *Avanti*, two S&S yawls. A 36-foot sloop, *Lucky Star*, won it overall on corrected time.

Waldo Brown and Harry Noyes became close friends the moment they met as young lions during World War I. They sometimes hunted together, and they remained sailing mates throughout the postwar period. When Brown wasn't off racing his 30-Square Meter *Gem*, he would happily come along at Harry's standing invitation to race on *Tioga*. In fact, such was the candor and depth of their

friendship that when Harry went off on one of his intermittent benders, it was Waldo Brown who acted as the instrument of his salvation, taking him to a Boston drying-out clinic and helping him sort things out afterward.

In the spring of 1939, Harry Noyes (forty-one) and Waldo Brown (forty-three) were in the prime of their lives, continuing on similar paths. (Brown also had a falling-out with Francis Herreshoff, over the creation of the Yankee One-Design class. Herreshoff subsequently addressed him as Mr. Brown in a letter on that subject.) Brown was immensely popular, accomplished, and confident. In the summer of 1938 he had come within a fraction of a point of winning the 30-Square-Meter international series in Marion, after a fierce boat-for-boat competition with John Lawrence on his *Moose* (designed by Knud Reimers). He had recently completed several intense years of study at

a Boston fine art school, where he developed and refined a skill at copper-plate etching, both as an expression of his artistic soul and as a means of making a bit of pocket money. He maintained a small studio apartment in Boston to do his artwork, and he was preparing several dozen etchings, many of them portraying sailing yachts and ships, for his first one-man exhibition.

Like so many of his contemporaries, including Harry Noyes and his father, Waldo Brown remained committed to aviation. (Out of his experience at Colonial Airways, Brown was being considered for an executive position with Pan American Airways.) He had also remained in the U.S. Navy Reserve, attaining the rank of Lieutenant Commander. In the latter connection, Brown flew regularly with his reserve unit to maintain his skills and rank.

On April 4, 1939, he and five other reserve pilots from the Naval Air Station at

The yawl Baruna, *one of* Tioga's *veteran competitors in the 1940 Miami-Nassau Race.*

(Mystic Seaport Museum, Inc./Rosenfeld Collection)

Asquontum, Massachusetts, were participating in the launching ceremony of the aircraft carrier USS *Wasp* at the Fore River Shipyard. As their flight of SB2U Vindicators gathered at 3,000 feet and made a turn over East Braintree to take up a V-formation for the official fly-by, the left wings and struts of Brown's biplane tangled with the right wings of the adjacent plane, flown by another experienced pilot, Ellsworth Benson, twenty-six. The two men struggled to break free, but both aircraft were damaged in the effort. Benson's crippled plane lost much of its lift and he tried to glide to a safe landing clear of the residential area below. But his plane's wheels clipped the roof of a house and it crashed into another; he and his crewman were killed immediately amid awful flames. Waldo Brown's aircraft plunged straight to earth out of control. He quickly bailed out. His crewman didn't have a chance to jump; he died in the crash. His having bailed out at such low altitude, however, Brown's parachute had no time to fully deploy.

Waldo Brown—engineer, handsome charmer, creative force behind *Joann*, *Tioga*, and ultimately *Tioga of Marblehead*—died instantly. His youthful vow not to conclude his life in an airplane crash had run its course. Days later, Frances Brown received a letter from Pan American Airways that her husband had been elected to the board.

In midsummer 1939 *Tioga* was quietly brought back to the Quincy Adams yard for a major refit. During several winters in the south, the high, searing Florida sun had caused her Port Orford cedar deck planks to spring; the deck was leaking badly. Over a month Quincy joiners removed the bulwarks and the forward house, stripped everything except the main trunk, then replaced the deck with conventional two-inch teak planks over marine plywood. One of the men who did the work was Frank Mayo; within a few years Mayo, a carpenter, was to become a forced, if not entirely unwilling, member of *Tioga's* crew. But we are ahead of the story.

In September 1939, as German troops invaded Poland to precipitate all-out war in

Waldo H. Brown, shortly before his death.
(Courtesy of John Noble Brown)

Europe, *Tioga* engaged in a somewhat more tepid battle of her own in the annual Vineyard Lightship Race. Along the way, four boats led the fleet—*Tioga*, *Baruna*, the 73-foot yawl *Escapade* (designed by Phil Rhodes), and Rudy Schaefer's 68-foot *Edlu II* (drawn by S&S). But *Tioga's* hapless tactician (very likely Harry himself), like many misguided tacticians since, elected to sail into Fishers Island Sound to get out of a foul current; *Tioga* did find less current, but also less wind. When the fog cleared at the finish in Stamford, *Tioga* was third over the line and fourth overall: just another of her so-so performances. She went south for the winter to lick her wounds.

There, between lazy daysails with the family, *Tioga* squeezed in one of the most inspiring victories of her young life, in the 1940 Miami to Nassau Race. The elapsed-time record for the 184-mile race—20 hours, 19 minutes, 40 seconds—had been set in 1936 by Vadim Makaroff's 72-foot ketch *Vamarie*. In those heady years the Miami-Nassau Race, part of the Southern Circuit of winter racing, always drew the cream of racing boats; this year, 1940, was

no exception. The race began on February 9 in a southerly of less than ten knots. *Tioga's* start didn't promise much in the way of an impressive passage; she missed her timing badly and was nearly last in her class across the line. Still, as the breeze slowly filled in, she passed everyone along the generally northeast heading and led the fleet rounding Great Isaac.

During the moonless but clear overnight fetch to Great Stirrup Cay, the breeze freshened more and *Tioga* rounded 20 minutes ahead of her nearest competitor, the 70-foot S&S yawl *Wakiva*. Then, as though planned by some unseen force, as the course turned south-southeast the breeze veered more westerly, strengthening to a puffy 30-35 knots, making it a perfect reach to the finish. It also generated a rough, gear-busting sea. Several boats, including *Wakiva*, blew out Genoas. *Borealis*, a 47-foot Alden yawl, lost her mainmast, and *Java Head*, a 44-foot Mower cutter, went to assist her. On *Tioga*, damage was minimal: a wire headsail sheet parted under the enormous dynamic pressure, but a preventer kept the sail in trim until the crew replaced the sheet. Harry had learned the ropes of ocean racing well.

By dawn of February 10, *Tioga* was reaching ferociously for the finish, alone, and when she crossed the line at a few minutes past 0730 she had traversed the course in 19 hours, 36 minutes, 30 seconds, cutting a fat 43 minutes off *Vamarie's* four-year-old record. *Wakiva* came in 43 minutes later, *Good News* 18 minutes after her, and 19 minutes later *Elizabeth McCaw* followed. *Tioga* was set back to second place overall on corrected time. This extraordinary circumstance of blazing speed combined with a handicap rating that all but prevented her from taking home top silver, was an unintended outgrowth of Harry Noyes' original plan for *Tioga*. Because of her high rating, she was often scratch boat in races. But it was generally agreed that she rated high not just because of her long waterline, but because Harry wanted a comfortable boat, which meant a heavy one—the radiators, deep-

Ruth Noyes and her men enjoy a midsummer motoryacht cruise, while Hope dreams of equestrian glories.
(Courtesy of Bradley Noyes)

freeze, and bathtub took their collective toll. Harry, in a word, brought it on himself. If, as sailors then and now have speculated, *Tioga* had been stripped down, or if the weight had at least been better distributed to lower her center of gravity, her rating would have been lower and some of her weak showings on handicap might have turned into victories. In any case, so far as *Tioga* was concerned, even without a shelf full of First-Overall silver, Harry Noyes was a very happy man.

Though Harry would sail *Tioga* as often as he could, he naturally continued to run Noyes Buick, and to play the role of entrepreneur and family provider. When *Tioga* was in Florida for the winter, he would commute by airplane back to his business in Boston, then return to join the family for weekend sailing. On one such occasion, April 16, 1940, Harry was set to fly from Boston to

Palm Beach to join the family, after completing his normal week of business. He chartered a Stinson Reliant with an FAA-licensed commercial pilot, John Hartwell. They planned to reach Florida after making a brief stopover in New York City.

Despite his qualifications, Hartwell, it seems, had very little instrument flying time under his belt. As luck would have it, over Connecticut the aircraft became enveloped by a dense fog. After failing to get a weather report, because of static over his radio, Hartwell elected to drop his altitude from 2,000 to 1,500 feet, hoping to get under the ceiling and take visual bearings on landmarks. But, his effort went awry. As he came out of the fog he was already too low. The Reliant skimmed a row of trees and tumbled into a wooded area near Middletown. Hartwell and one passenger survived with minor injuries. Another passenger, Robert Rideout, died. At forty-two, Harry Noyes (like his dear friend Waldo Brown just a year earlier) was killed instantly.

At their request, the only people who attended Harry's burial were Ruth, the four children, and *Tioga's* crew in full dress uniform. The burial was the last in the little town cemetery in Marblehead. Harry Noyes loved *Tioga* deeply. A portrait of her, under full working canvas, is engraved handsomely on his headstone.

A SLOPPY COAT OF GRAY

1940–1946

AFTER HARRY NOYES' DEATH the family had *Tioga* brought north again to Marblehead. The regular crew of four remained living aboard for the summer of 1940, still crammed into the forepeak, to tend to her needs as she lay at her mooring. They continued to honor correct yachting protocol: setting her ensign and burgee in the morning; striking the colors, and firing her cannon at sunset. But Ruth Noyes could not summon much enthusiasm for sport, so she and the younger children sailed *Tioga* only rarely that summer. Nor did they derive much pleasure from the boat without Harry, who was as much a part of *Tioga* as were her masts, keel, sails, and bathtub. Ruth Noyes proudly put on a good show of dignity, strength, and courage in her bereavement; it was the right thing to do for her public image in Marblehead society and, more important, for her children.

At the end of the summer of 1940 the crew unbent *Tioga*'s sails, stripped her of the family's personal possessions, covered her

tightly, and laid her up in wet storage at Quincy Adams, where she had been built so lovingly and launched so tumultuously little more than four years earlier. With no clear plan for the future, Ruth Noyes simply postponed any decision about disposing of the yacht. Fifteen months later, Japan's surprise attack on Pearl Harbor made that decision for her: *Tioga* went to war.

The saga of *Tioga*'s wartime life actually began in the summer of 1939, as a futuristic (and optimistic) World's Fair opened in New York's Flushing Meadows, even as Europe was on the brink. Foreseeing the possibility that America would be drawn into action in Europe, on June 23, 1939, Congress passed the Coast Guard Reserve Act establishing a voluntary, non-paid organization to relieve regular guardsmen for more urgent, possibly defensive military duty. Yachtsmen and commercial boat owners along the East Coast were asked to lend their small craft to assist the Coast Guard in its peacetime missions of search and rescue, law enforcement, and civilian training. But when Germany invaded Poland on September 1, 1939, Congress repealed the act and by February 1941 con-

verted the Coast Guard Reserve into a military wing (like the regular reserves of the other military branches). The former Civilian Reserve was renamed the Coast Guard Auxiliary and given the ancillary training role (it still functions to promote boating safety and education.)

As matters in Europe worsened, on May 27, 1941, President Franklin Delano Roosevelt declared an Unlimited National Emergency. His Executive Order 8767 of June 3, 1941, transferred Coast Guard Reserve crews into the Navy. Coincidentally, in the summer of 1941, Alfred Stanford, Commodore of the Cruising Club of America (CCA), began a vigorous campaign to convince the Navy to directly enlist private yachts and their owners to meet the need for coastal patrol craft. Though the Navy sorely needed such craft, it stiffly refused Stanford's offer. The Coast Guard, however, continued to draw in yachts and yachtsmen for nonmilitary work. Owners insisted on accompanying those boats, and although many had poor vision, were hard of hearing, or had football knees, they were accepted for limited tours of duty if they

The enemy: one of Admiral Dönitz's Type IX submarines.
(U.S. Naval Historical Center)

met the Guard's lower physical requirements. (Contrary to many of their earnest expectations, this did not give the healthy men among them a deferment from the regular draft.) In an effort to better organize coastal patrols, on November 1, 1941, Congress transferred the entire Coast Guard to the Navy's jurisdiction. Five weeks later, on December 7, 1941, the Japanese attacked Pearl Harbor.

The declaration of war against the Axis powers by President Roosevelt and Congress the next day mobilized the nation as never before. There was an immediate increase in the number of owners offering their yachts to the government, and among the first to respond were Mr. and Mrs. Joseph E. Davies. He was the former ambassador to Russia; she was Marjorie Merriweather Post, heiress to the great cereal fortune. They had no sons to offer to the war effort, so they volunteered their most prized possession: the 3,000-ton, 360-foot three-masted barque *Sea Cloud*. (Launched in 1931 in Germany, as *Hussar*, she was the pride of Marjorie Post's first husband, Edward F. Hutton, the great investment mogul.) Oddly, Mr. and Mrs. Davies were turned down by a thoughtful but authoritative spokesman for the government and very close friend of theirs, President Roosevelt. He interceded to convince them not to turn *Sea Cloud* over for service. An avid yachtsman, Roosevelt felt she was too valued to risk being sacrificed in time of war. But *Sea Cloud*'s time would come, soon enough.

The American declaration of war also changed the face of the battle for supremacy on the Atlantic by giving a green light to Germany's Admiral Karl Dönitz to expand his naval war to America's vulnerable shores. In January 1942, Dönitz, whose fleet of U-boats was already doing grave damage to Allied shipping around Europe and Africa and along North Atlantic sea routes, initiated Operation *Paukenschlag* (Drumbeat) to attack Allied merchant shipping at its source: the United States East Coast. He shifted a handful of his deadliest, most sophisticated

long-range type VII and type IX submarines (all well over 200 feet long) to the western Atlantic, stationing them singly or in small packs from the mouth of the St. Lawrence River to Cape Hatteras, giving them *carte blanche* to attack ships carrying war materiel to Europe. On January 12, 1942, one of the type IX submarines, *U-123*, made *Paukenschlag*'s first kill, the 9,000-ton British merchantman *Cyclops*, less than 300 miles southeast of New York City.

Within a few weeks, between Newfoundland and Bermuda, German U-boats sank 35 ships totaling 200,000 tons; further out on the Atlantic they sank more. Dönitz's submarines were having a turkey shoot, destroying unprotected ships at will, preventing urgently needed fuel oil, supplies, and munitions from reaching the Allied effort in Europe. Thousands of survivors were being brought into Atlantic coast ports, further testimony to the need for an expanded fleet of civilian patrol craft under Navy jurisdiction. (The Navy and Coast Guard had designed and ordered a fleet of proper patrol and picket boats, but these were not expected in service for some time.) Yet, despite the enormous losses, Admiral Ernest J. King, Chief of Naval Operations and Commander in Chief of the U.S. Fleet (described by his daughter as even-tempered: "always in a rage"), continued refusing to conscript private yachts into the Navy. Being a bit of an Anglophobe, he sent most of his spare destroyer escorts to the Pacific Theater.

As a result, in the first quarter of 1942, U-boats on the North Atlantic, in what one naval historian called a "merry massacre," sank 216 ships totaling 1.25 million tons, including many tankers. Even when the ships were sent along supposedly safer near-shore routes, U-boats struck with impunity, often sinking them within sight of the beach. The United States found itself in a two-ocean war with barely a one-ocean navy. The CCA's patriots again offered the Navy's Eastern Sea Frontier Command the loan of 30 auxiliary sailing yachts between 50 and 90 feet, with skippers (their owners) and skeleton crews;

by April 1942 the offer was increased to 70 yachts and 100 smaller craft. When the Navy again refused, a spirited outpouring of newspaper editorials and letters to Navy commanders from prominent yachtsmen and politicians ensued. Many of these letters made the strongest possible reference to the essential role that civilian craft had played at the heroic evacuation of 250,000 retreating British personnel from Dunkirk in 1940.

In May 1942, Admiral King, feeling the pressure and facing months before the delivery of his new cutters, finally relented. Navy commanders were ordered to select as many auxiliary sailing yachts, motoryachts, fishing boats, or other privately owned craft as were "capable of going to sea in good weather at least 48 hours at cruising speeds." The yachts were assigned to the Reserve and recommissioned with gray paint and CGR identity numbers. On the East Coast they were divided into six task groups: Northern, Narragansett, New York, Delaware, Chesapeake, and Southern. In the New England area, the crews of the vessels were assigned to watch for and report all enemy activity, in particular U-boats attacking ships or laying mines; aircraft heading to bomb New York or Boston; or surface craft delivering scouts, spies, saboteurs, or ground forces. And they were instructed to pick up survivors.

At the same time Admiral King changed his mind, President Roosevelt relented too, with respect to *Sea Cloud*—the exigencies of war overcame his senses of beauty and friendship. Mr. and Mrs. Davies turned their gorgeous yacht over to the Coast Guard, in return for which they were paid the princely sum of $1 per year. *Sea Cloud* was taken to Baltimore and stripped of her massive rig, 32,000 square feet of sail, fine furnishings, and gilt figurehead; only the perfume of wealth remained below as a reminder of her recent past. Her steel hull was armor plated and she was equipped with eight 40-mm and sixteen 20-mm anti-aircraft guns, two 3.5-inch guns, depth charges, and new anti-submarine weapons. Her palatial suites for 16 guests and quarters for 60 crew were con-

The 360-foot barque Sea Cloud, *launched in 1931 by Edward F. Hutton and his wife Marjorie Merriweather Post.*
(Mystic Seaport Museum, Inc./Rosenfeld Collection)

verted to accommodate 175 military men in a less palatial habitat. She was also equipped with a full weather station, an early radar, submarine-tracking sonar, and advanced radio communications. She was painted flat gray and renamed *IX-99*. Thus, this largest, most luxurious and private of all yachts was converted into a Navy weather station, to assist supply and troop convoys in reaching the European Theater in the most efficient manner. As *IX-99*, *Sea Cloud* was stationed for most of the war in the North Atlantic between the Azores and Greenland. Her trained specialists radioed weather parameters back to the U.S. Navy operations headquarters six times daily, operating in calm and storm, in the heat of summer and the pack ice of winter. She set a fine example for owners of lesser yachts to come to the aid of their nation.

Most of the lesser yachts that entered Coast Guard Reserve fleet, officially called the Coastal Picket Patrol, were fitted out to carry 300-pound depth charges, sidearms, and one or two machine guns. Yacht owners usually remained onboard (often with the rating of Chief Boatswain's Mate). At first, their crews were largely made up of young men, still covered in the sweat of farms and factories, who had never been to sea; according to Coast Guard documents, they also included "college boys, adventurous lads of shore villages, Boy Scouts, beachcombers, ex-bootleggers, and rum-runners. Almost everyone who declared he could reef and steer, and many who couldn't, were accepted." With

such a ragtag group, totally lacking military discipline and deemed to have "too much yachting spirit," the Coastal Picket Patrol, which was unofficially nicknamed the Corsair Fleet, became popularly known as the Hooligan Navy. It wasn't long, however, before these unkempt Hooligans became trim, sea-wise defenders of America's shores.

Eventually, some 50,000 Temporary Reservists served the Coast Guard during the war, many of them assigned to beach patrols, lifeboat stations, and securing more than 21,000 miles of port waterfront and 8,000 waterfront facilities. Many among the 5,000 or so who joined the Picket Patrol were ordinary citizens; many were seasoned yachtsmen such as Vic Romagna and Rudy Schaefer (who was instrumental in arranging for the

donation of several yachts to New York's Third District, including his own *Edlu*). Other celebrities joined the Hooligans as well, notably Arthur Godfrey (the radio entertainer), Arthur Fiedler (the founding conductor of the Boston "Pops"), and Ernest Hemingway (who volunteered himself, his yacht, and his private cache of weaponry: hunting rifle, machine gun, pistol, and a gaggle of hand grenades).

It was in this chaotic milieu of military improvisation and civilian uncertainty that, in the spring of 1942, Ruth Noyes and dozens of other aristocratic New Englanders loaned their precious, often gold-plated, yachts to the Coast Guard. Before *Tioga* left, however, captain Nelson Porter (knowing his beloved yacht might be shot at and abused,

The same Sea Cloud —*with her three masts, bowsprit, and gold-plated luxuries in storage* —*goes to war.*
(U.S. Naval Historical Center)

and certainly slathered with artlessly applied military paint), laid four thick coats of varnish over her exterior surfaces, stem to stern, to deter the military gray from seeping into the wood grain and ruining her for all time. (*Tioga* would end the war with her machinery, equipment, rig, and sails in generally appalling condition, but Porter's trick worked wonders in mitigating the degeneration of her structural and cosmetic woodwork.)

On July 7, 1942, Tioga was officially accepted into service "for the duration," commissioned *CGR 2509*, and assigned to District I, Boston. A band of green reservists boarded her at Quincy Adams on July 8, and under the guidance of Chief Boatswain's Mate R. Nelson Porter (yes, he signed up to be her military skipper as well) towed her to a working dock and took her covers off. Over a week they cleaned her; connected her plumbing, electrics, and engine; stepped and rigged her masts. On July 15 they delivered her to the Coast Guard base at Chelsea, Massachusetts, where, as expected, they painted her hull, deck, house, and spars General Issue battleship gray. Then she was taken under power via the Cape Cod Canal to the Steamboat Pier on Nantucket, where she was equipped with a pair of .30-caliber machine guns and small arms. On August 4, 1942, she was given a three-hour shakedown under sail. *Tioga* was in the Navy now . . . albeit the Hooligan Navy.

Boats chosen for picket work, like *Tioga*, were nearly all made of wood, as they were less susceptible than metal boats to magnetically triggered mines and were more difficult to detect by enemy sound equipment. The majority were sailboats, which could serve silently for long periods under sail alone, without using their auxiliary engines, to further avoid detection. And sailboats had greater cruising range and better motion in heavy seas than motorboats; they could remain offshore in heavy weather to listen and observe, while motorboats, with their

A rugged Corsair sails under rough conditions.
(National Archives/U.S. Coast Guard)

The logo designed for the Corsair Fleet by The Walt Disney Company.
(The Disney Publishing Group)

tendency to roll in a seaway, usually had to be recalled when the wind and sea worked up. Thus, sailboats were deemed to be far superior to motorboats for picket duty (which added a pointed new argument in the eternal "ragman" versus "stinkpotter" squabble).

Normal Picket patrols ran along the Atlantic and Gulf Coast continental shelves. Smaller boats did brief patrols within the 50-fathom curve; larger yachts such as *Tioga* could poke their bows as far as 150 miles offshore for a day or two. They patrolled in a prescribed pattern, looking for U-boats in assigned squares of about 15 nautical miles on a side. Life in the Picket Patrol was generally tedious and uneventful. Sorties could be pleasant enough for the sailors in summer, but winter's storms and ice posed serious

problems for vessels and men, many of whom had never been to sea in winter or summer. The yachts had to be rerigged and equipped with storm sails and other winter equipment, and only the most worthy were kept at sea during winter gales.

The Pickets contacted submarines by detecting their sound (or visually when they surfaced) and tracked them as long as contact could be maintained. They checked oil slicks, and took samples of oil for shoreside analysis. They investigated gunfire, and radioed convoys of U-boat activity in time for the ships to alter their courses. Most pickets were very lightly armed, so having sighted a German submarine they would normally radio a report to Navy vessels stationed in the vicinity or to aircraft based in the district.

CGR-1004 (in civilian life, the schooner Mendham*) searches for U-boats on the stormy North Atlantic.*
(National Archives/U.S. Coast Guard)

Some had opportunity to set depth charges when they detected submerged U-boats. Relatively few of them observed U-boats on the surface; if they did the boats usually dived upon being sighted. (Contact with submarines was usually anonymous, but one German skipper, who surfaced beside a reserve boat off the end of Long Island, reportedly stepped on deck and shouted, in too-impeccable American slang: "Get the hell out of here, you guys! Do you want to get hurt? Now, scram!")

Tioga's—that is *CGR 2509's*—first patrol took place on August 5, 1942, when she sailed out of her home port with a crew of seven, in a typically thick Nantucket fog, and made her first "contact" by nearly running down some friendly fishing boats. On August 8, according to a cryptic entry in her log, she was "challenged by [a] bomber." Otherwise, her commander, Nelson Porter, wrote in the log that there was "nothing to report." More revealing, log entries show that no matter where the wind was coming from *Tioga* was nearly always tacked rather than jibed during patrols, even while sailing off the wind, mute testimony to her crew's limited (perhaps fear-driven?) sailing aptitude.

The area *CGR 2509's* group was assigned to included the periphery of Cape Cod, from Quincy to Nantucket, and offshore along the continental shelf. On patrol she would be motored out to deep water and her sails set. Her assigned grid lay generally within a square between latitude 41° and 42° N and longitude 69° and 70° W, within which she would sail in a pattern for three or four days until returning to port. During her 48-hour breaks her crew would spend time doing mundane chores such as drying clothes, bedding, and sails; taking on gasoline and lube oil for her engine; loading in gas for her Shipmate galley range; and bringing aboard often remarkably large quantities of coal and kindling wood for her heating stove (which seems to have been used more regularly than any other major piece of gear, certainly including her weapons).

Some time after her commissioning,

CGR 2509's seven-man crew received three .38-caliber pistols, ninety rounds of ammunition, belts and holsters, seven sheepskin coats, one box of flares and rockets. But they seem never to have fired the guns except in practice (though the sheepskin coats were well used). It was not, however, until she had been in service over a year that, on August 17, 1943, *CGR 2509* had her submarine-detecting sounding gear installed. Soon after Navy experts checked it out and approved it for operation, it failed on patrol; it took weeks to be made operative again. *Tioga's* most heroic accomplishments in the ensuing

The Hooligan Navy sharpens up.
(National Archives/U.S. Coast Guard)

In heavy weather Corsair Fleet sailing yachts just hunkered down under shortened sail.
(National Archives/U.S. Coast Guard)

months were her reporting a disabled fishing boat, *Santa Maria*, and challenging a big ship 30 miles east of Nantucket, which turned out to be an unappreciative American destroyer (she was to repeat this odd feat in her postwar civilian life as well).

Let us face the truth. The war was not an ennobling experience for *Tioga;* rather, it reduced this marvelous white stallion to a gray dray. Although her log is filled with endless reports of damage and engine break-downs (shattered pistons, bent connecting rods, burned-out bearings, broken spreaders, crunched stanchions, and a smashed wheel box), none were combat-related. The rest of the entries are so excruciatingly uneventful one would hardly think *Tioga* was at war, sailing in submarine-infested waters: "general washdown," "painting mast," "general survey," "inspection," "studied phonetics," "splicing," "drying sails," "studying codes," "blinker and semaphore drill," "gun drill." Drills, drills, and more drills.

One man who recalls the tedium quite well was Frank Mayo, who served on *CGR 2509* for about eight months. Before the war Mayo had worked briefly at the Quincy Adams Yacht Yard, where he helped rebuild *Tioga's* deck. A friend had advised him that if he was going to stay in the boatbuilding business after the war, which he planned to do, he had better go to sea to gain experience in order to better understand how his boats behaved. The friend suggested that Mayo join the Navy. But Mayo, who had been deferred from the draft twice by the time of

By mid-1943 the Coast Guard and Navy began taking delivery of their own picket patrol boats.
(Mystic Seaport Museum, Inc.)

"We worked patrols out of Nantucket until we got caught in a nor'easter and got pretty well blown apart out there. We were trying to beat up and get up around Provincetown, get in back of the Cape. We were working our way up there, and the staysail traveler literally tore right out of the deck. Of course, the minute the staysail traveler went, the staysail went; it was blowing so hard we couldn't hold her off the wind. And of course the mizzen, that was gone to shreds in a matter of a minute or so. So, we turned around and we ran—we were doing five and a half knots under bare poles for fifty-six hours. We ended up way the hell and gone, down off Long Island."

But Mayo also got a remarkable taste of *Tioga's* very special ability to perform in a blow: "There is nothing like sailing on that boat . . . you can't imagine it. . . . Speed. Just sheer unadulterated speed. That sucker will go like the wind. Fifteen, sixteen knots under sail. Effortless. Absolutely effortless."

Later, on two occasions, *Tioga* was sent south for temporary duty. On December 15, 1942, she was assigned to Task Force 90.5, of the Fifth Naval District, Norfolk, and returned to Nantucket on January 8, 1943. On January 29, 1943, she again was assigned to Norfolk, and returned April 1, 1943, this time to Newport, Rhode Island. It is in connection with her two southern sojourns that one of the great fables about *Tioga* was born. In February 1947, a civilian again, she was dismasted in the Miami-Nassau Race. Immediately, a story began circulating in the yachting press that during one of her trips to Norfolk she passed through a waterway lift bridge that the operator started to close too quickly; her Coast Guard crew was unable to stop her in time and she hit the bridge, splitting her mainmast between the spreaders. In Norfolk, the story continued, the Navy did a crude jury repair by hastily glueing and screwing the pieces together, without bothering to unstep the mast. The clumsy repair, the story concludes, was the direct cause of her dismasting.

Pearl Harbor, decided to join the Coast Guard. In a rare exhibition of military logic, he was assigned to *CGR 2509*. According to Mayo, he signed up on a Thursday afternoon in Boston; the next morning he went to Chelsea Coast Guard Station and picked up his sea bag and uniform; on Saturday he was aboard the boat; on Monday he was sailing offshore looking for German submarines. "I never went to boot camp," Mayo recalls. "Nothing. I mean . . . boom, you're gone."

As Mayo also recalls: "[I]f you saw a U-boat, or any suspicious activity, you could radio back to somebody on land, and hope they could get out there. But that's about all it really amounted to. It was pretty much boredom, really . . . it was four on, four off. And . . . you'd just go out, put in your time, and come back. You practically never saw anything out there. . . . The only excitement was trying to find your way back into Nantucket in the fog."

Perhaps the most genuinely exciting episode Mayo experienced was a storm at sea.

As we shall see, neither the U.S. Coast

Guard nor the U.S. Navy had anything to do with the damage to *Tioga*'s mast, or with her subsequent dismasting. Not a thing.

During 1943, as American mobilization peaked, the Atlantic coast U-boat threat abated through the successful Allied destruction of a good portion of Admiral Dönitz's undersea fleet. At the same time the Coast Guard began taking delivery of its new 38-foot picket boats and 83-foot cutters. After an earlier reduction in the Hooligan Navy by 35 percent, in October 1943 the Navy Command decided to disband the Coastal Picket Patrol completely. This was made official on November 13, 1943, though a few of the largest yachts, including *Sea Cloud*, were retained as needed. The letter of commendation that went to yacht owners from the Patrol Force Commander, Captain R.L. Jack, remarked on the splendid work done by all the pickets.

CGR 2509 was decommissioned on September 27, 1943, and officially returned to civilian life on May 31, 1944, though she was not yet delivered to Marblehead. The Decommissioning Board, apparently with at least one member who knew his sailing yachts, cited her as "one of the best known yachts on the East Coast, with her clipper bow, trail boards, monkey rail, elaborately carved transom . . . an extremely handsome and picturesque craft. She has proved very able and very fast." The Coast Guard letter to Ruth Noyes, dated July 19, 1944, states:

> The Coast Guard appreciates your public spiritedness in making this craft available to the service and to your country. In the great war in which we are now engaged, every citizen and every resource plays a part in the goal of victory. When the call came for motorboats and yachts to meet the extraordinary emergency and duty responsibilities of the Coast Guard in providing for anti-submarine, coastal, harbor and security patrols on an unprecedented scale and beyond our regular resources, you patriotically responded in the proffer of your vessel. In returning

Tioga's award for time served.
(Courtesy of Bradley Noyes)

the vessel to you, please be assured of our grateful acknowledgment of the contribution this made to the war effort. [Signed] *R.R. Waesche, Vice Admiral, USCG, Commandant.*

Later, *CGR 2509* was brought back to Marblehead, towed helplessly into the harbor by a tug. The tugmen dropped her off at her old mooring, which had waited empty during the war, and there she lay for the summer, sad, dreary, and broken. She was still painted a dismal battleship gray and was in dreadful condition. She had a number of broken frames and was leaking badly. Her bilges were full and rancid. Her engine didn't work. Her sails, the few that remained aboard, were generally tattered, useless rags. She had been stripped of every yachting amenity, and most of her original brass fittings were gone. Her bronze-runged boarding ladder was gone. Her fog bell was gone. Though she had served proudly in the military, her signal code flags were gone: she couldn't even be dressed

properly for the occasion of her return to civilian life . . . her return home.

It is perhaps a curious accident of history that just as the dishevelled and abused *Tioga* was returning home, all gray and grimy, with a look of fallen grace, Francis Herreshoff was lamenting what he perceived to be America's loss of innocence and grandeur. In October 1943 he wrote:

> There must be some reason for the present American foolishness. . . . The general trend seems to be away from the truth. Maybe it is all some democratic influence where the people have been taught that everybody is just as good as the other fellow. . . . But if there is any logic in such a thing there would be nothing to live for: no reason to strive for greater perfection or higher culture.

As compensation for *Tioga*'s service the Coast Guard gave Ruth Noyes a plaque, a citation, and a modest check for $11,000 to cover damage to the boat. While *Tioga* sat on her mooring, Mrs. Noyes investigated the cost of recommissioning her, which were exorbitant. With her spirit broken, she began to think of selling *Tioga*, though her children all wanted her to keep the boat. But they were grownups now. One by one they had left the nest. Bradley, the youngest, had entered the Navy in 1945, when he was eighteen, and barely escaped the planned invasion of Japan when atomic bombs dropped on Hiroshima and Nagasaki forced the Japanese to surrender unconditionally. (Waldo Brown's son John, a Navy pilot stationed in Hawaii at the same time, awaited the same invasion. Both returned home from the war unscathed, to sail again.)

While Bradley Noyes was still in the service, late in 1946, his mother wrote him that *Tioga* had been sold. Young Bradley did not see the finest yacht of his childhood again for twenty years. The rest of the world, however, saw her often in sports-page headlines and enthusiastic reports that, over the next two decades, would celebrate her as an invin-

Dull gray paint still camouflaging her beauty, Tioga *returns to her birthplace, Quincy Adams Yacht Yard.*
(Courtesy of Al Grenier)

cible racing machine, and a yacht of surpassing grace. With that in mind, perhaps it is fitting to end this story of war and monotony with another of Frank Mayo's vivid recollections, recorded nearly half a century after he served on *CGR 2509:*

You figure that when she set the Trans-Pac record [in 1965] from California to Honolulu, her Kenyon [speedometer] went to twenty-four knots. She pegged it for fifty-six hours. . . . And she had a big Genoa, that went from the front of her bowsprit, and went into a snatch block practically at her stern. And it was masthead, up ninety-six feet. Took six men to carry it. You got that thing out—no reef points—they'd carry it until it blew out.

And the jibs, the skipper told me that they would take the windward sheet and bring it around leeward, and put both jib sheets to try to hold the jib. And they would take those big Merriman snap shackles and literally pull them right apart, two of them at once. That's how hard they used to drive her. But, you know, sixteen, eighteen, twenty knots. Nothing to it. And dry. Absolutely bone dry. And the easiest vessel in the seaway. . . . No resistance whatsoever. Beautiful. . . .

In 1965, the year of the Honolulu race Mayo refers to, and for all her life, *Tioga's* speedo, which wasn't a Kenyon but a Triton in those days, read no higher than 20 knots; she pinned it only rarely, and only briefly;

never even remotely for 56 hours at a time. Her mainmast was only 86 feet tall. Her Genoa sheeted well forward on the rail, not at the quarter; two or three men could carry it; it wasn't blown out, just ripped occasionally. True, the crew sailed with a preventer on the Genoa sheet, she broke a lot of those Merriman shackles (and lots of other gear), she was dry and, of course, she sailed like a dream. And yes, she was, and is, beautiful. *Oh,* so beautiful.

But Mayo can be excused for his tendency to aggrandize this magnificent boat. He was suffering from the same contagious affliction that nearly every virtuoso commentator on *Tioga* would subsequently suffer, and whose effects would haunt this graceful craft all her life: Mayo had a severe case of Highly Infectious Hyperbole.

UNDER MERCURIAL COMMAND

1946–1951

ALLAN PINKERTON CARLISLE came into the world in the upper-class town of Islip, Long Island, in 1910—the year of Stravinsky's *Firebird*, George V's coronation, and Mark Twain's death. It was also the year of Halley's Comet, and if one follows the stars faithfully one might conclude that a comet would have been an omen for this newborn child, all for the good. And to a great extent, it was. Allan Carlisle was born into two prominent families, and thus into great wealth, privilege and, in the case of his mother's lineage, security. She was the daughter of Allan Pinkerton, a transplanted Scotsman who founded the Pinkerton Detective Agency (which became famous for solving a series of train robberies in the 1850s and foiling an assassination attempt on Abraham Lincoln in 1861). Pinkerton men later supplied armored vehicles for much of the world's cash and negotiable holdings on the highways and byways of America. Allan Carlisle's father, Jay F. Carlisle, was a renowned Brooklyn socialite,

Karin Booth Carlisle.   (Edmund 'Skip' Eveleth)

horseman, sugar-trading specialist, and member of the New York Stock Exchange. Oral spoons are rarely as silvery as Allan Pinkerton Carlisle's.

But, comets notwithstanding, the omens were destined to have their down side for Allan Carlisle as well. Because, at his birth Carlisle was guaranteed a lifetime of comfort through a Pinkerton trust fund from which he would derive the annual interest. But, as often obtains, generous gifts may harbor a forbidding penalty, and Carlisle—pleasant-looking, personable, educated in private schools, and extremely bright—paid that penalty throughout his seventy-five years, struggling to find balance with his own birthright. As a child of ordained privilege Carlisle could be decidedly self-indulgent; but as a man of restless energy and intellect, he could indulge honestly in culture (he was fluent in German and French, a collector and dealer in antiques, a musician and composer of published songs). From his fine upbringing Carlisle came naturally to believe in style, poise, and tradition; but these values ran sadly counter to trends he witnessed in his

later life. Carlisle was also very spiritual, in a philosophical rather than theological way: he had a somewhat lofty, orthodox view that mankind should have high ideals and be unyielding in pursuit of those ideals (a difficult burden to carry in a century that had concluded the "War To End All Wars" by the time he was eight years old, but a century that had many more wars yet to fight).

Though at times he lived the socially entwined life of a Gatsby, attending Saturday night parties in his family's Long Island mansion (where George Gershwin might be playing one piano and Allan the other), in his heart Carlisle didn't derive much joy from society and its trappings. Given his choice he might have been born to some wealth, yes, but on a lesser island and in an earlier age. And, as was not unusual in his day (as Harry Noyes did for other reasons), Allan Carlisle suffered most of his life from that common disease of the noble misfit: alcoholism.

Surely all of these are rationales, affluence aside, for Carlisle's becoming a hands-on yachtsman and meticulous navigator. In his youth he sailed actively in the confines of Long Island Sound, and later he found solace and absolution on the open sea. He came to love classic wooden boats, whose bilges were redolent with yesterday, over anything that remotely smelled of today. In the same sense that Carlisle understood the historic importance of an old boat, he had great respect for the sea. Early in his sailing years he learned the art of celestial navigation and, unlike many sailors who go through the motions but easily revert to electromechanical backup, he used it freely and frequently, rejecting electronic navigation as it came into vogue. Carlisle was certainly too bright and accomplished to be seen as a Luddite, but he did selectively disdain much of the progressive world around him.

When he was still in his twenties, Carlisle moved to the south of France, where presumably he found life more ingenuous. While he could have afforded a larger yacht, he preferred to keep a modest wooden sailboat there, cruising the Mediterranean with friends whenever he could. But when the Nazis invaded France in 1940, legitimized the Vichy government, and split the country asunder, Carlisle fled to the United States. He left his boat, most of his possessions, and his idyllic life behind; but he brought home a wife—a temperamental, be-furred German woman named Daisy.

On their return, the Carlisles moved to Long Island. When the United States became involved in the war, Allan volunteered as an officer's trainee to fight in Europe. But he was rejected because of Daisy's German origins. He enlisted in the Navy instead, and was assigned as a boatswain on a Pacific supply ship. Carlisle served under Executive Officer Sonny Tufts (the Hollywood star) and Captain Huntington Hartford (the A&P supermarket heir, and a kindred spirit whose dissonant life later paralleled his own). Aboard ship Carlisle further perfected his celestial navigation and he became a fine, confident seaman. As a gunner, he also perfected his eye in one magic night by heroically shooting down three Japanese Zeros.

During the war Carlisle was also in an airplane that lost its landing gear and was forced into a fiery belly landing. Unlike Waldo Brown and Harry Noyes, who tragically fell from the sky and died, Carlisle survived the crash. But for the rest of his life he resisted flying with a devotion bordering on the religious, drinking premeditatedly before and during any flight he could not otherwise avoid. Indeed, whenever he chose to travel to Europe, which he did often after the war, Carlisle would look urgently for a yacht going over and offer to deliver her; or he would just take an ocean liner. The sea was Allan Carlisle's first love; flying was his last resort.

Right after the war Carlisle virtuously bought a sorely neglected wooden schooner, *Blue Waters,* which he had found up the Miami River. She was a sort of dry-rotted "handyman special" and he planned to rebuild her. In the summer of 1946 he managed to her sail up to Long Island Sound, to A.E. "Bill" Luders' shipyard, in Stamford, Connecticut, for some work. (Luders and Carlisle were old buddies, having attended prep school together in Pennsylvania.) But when Luders' crew hauled *Blue Waters* to

estimate the work required, she began to fall apart on the ways. Facing prohibitive reconstruction costs (and the denial of hull insurance) Carlisle saw that *Blue Waters* was beyond redemption; he had the yard cut her into scrap timber with a chainsaw. He salvaged her fittings. He sold her tanks, wheel, rig, and sails to a friend. And he sold the ballast lead to Bill Luders for use in the boats he was building. So much for good intentions.

At the same time, however, Carlisle's good sailing companion, Gordon Raymond, a husky professional skipper and Manhattan-based yacht broker, told Carlisle of another classic wooden yacht that might be more to his liking. She was a ten-year-old Francis Herreshoff ketch lying in Marblehead—well-found but needing work, much devoted work. Raymond, an old friend of the Noyes family as well, had the exclusive rights to sell *Tioga.* He had been running an advertisement for her in *Yachting,* but he hadn't sold her (perhaps because he was forced to use a prewar sailing photo of her in the ad, which may have put potential buyers off when they saw her true postwar condition). But it didn't put Allan Carlisle off; hearing her name he was ready to buy *Tioga,* sight

The bitter end for Allan Carlisle's Blue Waters: *she's cut down scrap wood by Bill Luders' chainsaw team.*
(Courtesy of Al Grenier)

(TOP) Tioga *in 1936 and* (ABOVE) *as Allan Carlisle bought her, still in 'uniform,' in 1946.*
(Top: Billy Letts/Above: Courtesy of Al Grenier)

unseen; he put in a bid through Raymond. It seems that before the war he had seen *Tioga* sailing in New England; he believed her to be the most beautiful boat ever built. Carlisle had always wanted to own a boat that was eminently graceful and particularly fast; he didn't care for a boat designed to a rule. According to everything he knew about her, *Tioga* fit his ideal perfectly.

Carlisle went to see *Tioga* at the Quincy Adams yard where she was in the wet storage shed, still painted a dismal navy gray. Her masts were unstepped; she was caked in bird droppings. Considering her lowly condition and the deep scars of her abuse, the Noyes estate attorneys probably listed her value at well below her replacement cost, perhaps as little as $10,000 or $12,000. Carlisle, however, reportedly paid the estate $18,000 (or possibly as much as $27,000); she was worth every penny to him.

A week after he scrapped *Blue Waters* Allan Carlisle owned *Tioga* (and he logically hired Nelson Porter as her skipper). Carlisle expected to haul her immediately at Quincy Adams to have their experienced hands strip off her military dress (and Captain Porter's buffering varnish) and carefully restore her to unsullied condition. But Quincy Adams had lost many of its best shipwrights, and the yard had been temporarily converted to fabricating wooden doors for the postwar housing boom. Quincy couldn't accept the job.

With the help of Charlie Rudolph, Quincy's chief rigger, and other locals including Al Grenier (who lived next door and had worked as a teenager on *Tioga*'s construction), the crew stepped her gray masts. Carlisle then brought her to Bill Luders' yard where he spent at least $50,000 to refurbish her. That initial expense, and the enormous financial burden of her later upkeep and racing program, would form a pattern that bedeviled Carlisle's ownership of the boat for the next dozen years or so. It would force him to charter her to more competitive, deep-pocketed men to cover his expenses, and it would propel him to sell her (and buy her back) more than once when the burden

became too great, until he was compelled to give *Ticonderoga* up for the last time in 1959.

Yes, *Ticonderoga*, not *Tioga*. One of the strict terms of the sale by the Noyes estate was that the boat would have to be renamed: for bittersweet reasons Ruth Noyes and her children wanted to keep the name *Tioga* in the family. Out of respect, Carlisle gave serious thought to a new name. He sat aboard quietly one day with a notepad, sketching ideas with a long yellow pencil. (He rejected naming the boat *Daisy*, as his wife had insisted, as their marriage was about to end in an unpleasant divorce.) After pondering for a while, Carlisle had an inspiration: by the simple expedient of inserting CONDER between the TI and OGA on J.H. Peterson's golden nameboard, he could give *Tioga* another imposing Indian name, *Ticonderoga*. (The name is marked in history by the fort between Lake George and Lake Champlain, built by the French as Fort Carillon in 1755, and abandoned by American Revolutionary forces to the English in 1777.) Carlisle's thought process, however, was surely enhanced by his discovery of that very name embossed on the long yellow pencil he was using to scribble his ideas.

Allan Carlisle sailed *Ticonderoga* out of Northport, Long Island, or the Luders yard, for the remainder of 1946, and quickly got to know his new responsibility. And responsibility she was. It wasn't too long before he realized that this yacht, by any other name, would cost as much. The upkeep, supply, and professional crewing of a 72-foot ketch (unlike the several smaller boats he had owned) absorbed no small part of Carlisle's annual Pinkerton allowance. To make matters more expensive, Daisy Carlisle (who sailed with her husband on rare occasions, usually with two big Labrador retrievers, when she wasn't tooling about ashore in a red Lincoln

Continental) insisted that the crew be kitted out in starched professional uniforms, complete with jacket, officer-style cap and necktie. The crew found these attractive on land but useless under way—hats blew off, jackets cramped their movement, and neckties got caught winches. But Carlisle was saved from the burden of these expenses, in part, by the collective memory of his boat's reputation and her astonishing beauty. There were, he discovered, a good number of sailormen willing to charter her, particularly among the bankers, publishers and financiers in his social sphere. This helped him defray expenses and allowed him to enjoy *Ticonderoga* the rest of the time. (To enhance that enjoyment, and keep a steady eye on *Ticonderoga*'s condition, Carlisle went along as sailing master or navigator on most of *Ticonderoga*'s racing charters.)

For the winter of 1946/47 Carlisle brought *Ticonderoga* to Palm Island, in Miami. He and a couple of drinking buddies (and a couple of willing female companions) cruised the Bahamas before he brought *Ticonderoga* to Palm Beach for some varnish, then back to Miami in February 1947 for her first postwar competition, the Miami-Nassau Race. For that race Carlisle chartered *Ticonderoga* to Dr. Matthew T. Mellon of Palm Beach and Bar Harbor, Maine. Carlisle, who navigated, invited a crew of seasoned racing yachtsmen from around New York, including the great Cornelius "Corny" Shields. Gordon Raymond served as sailing master; paid hands Al Grenier and Billy Letts, and another yacht broker of Carlisle's acquaintance, Frank Duffy, provided knowledge of the boat that the rest of the crew of fourteen lacked.

The 1947 Miami-Nassau race, with *Ticonderoga* scratch boat in a fleet of fourteen boats, started in a howling nor'easter, which in its opposition to the Gulf Stream produced unusually rough seas. The New York crew had only a brief shakedown to familiarize themselves with the boat; they didn't know how she maneuvered, and they underestimated the drawing power of her

With fresh paint, new sails, and under her new name, Ticonderoga *is steered to weather by a proud Allan Carlisle.*

(Mystic Seaport Museum, Inc.)

Ticonderoga (second from right) has a middling start in the 1947 Miami-Nassau Race. The worst is yet to come.

(Mystic Seaport Museum, Inc./Rosenfeld Collection)

sails. After the gun they struggled too slowly to get her in trim, and she was seventh across the line. But that crack New York crew settled down and quickly worked her out into the lead, taking the stiff seas in stride and pushing her along at 10 to 11 knots.

They were carrying *Ti*'s working-sail complement of the big Yankee jib, staysail, full main, and mizzen. Although she was overpowered and occasionally on her ear, scooping water over her leeward rail ("drowning the dolphins," as the expression was born), the New Yorkers refused to shorten sail. They also believed that the rigging was slack, so on several tacks someone took up on the leeward cap-shroud turnbuckle,

which steadily increased the compression load on the mast. About nine miles beyond the Miami sea buoy, hardly an hour after the start, Gordon Raymond gave the wheel to Corny Shields. Shields was taking a moment to adjust to the feel of the helm when *Ticonderoga* hit a wave and the shock caused the headstay's lower turnbuckle rod to snap at the barrel. With a sharp crack that sounded like the report of a cannon, the mainmast shattered about 20 feet off the deck. As the broken section fell over the starboard side, the main boom fell on the house, barely missing Billy Letts' head but crushing the little clinker-built dinghy lashed there. The triatic stay, still attached to the fallen mast sec-

tion, simultaneously ripped off the top of the mizzenmast. It was hell to pay on deck.

With no sails set and drawing, *Ticonderoga* was dead in the water, at the mercy of very rough seas. Without the stabilizing effect of the spars and sails, the boat rolled miserably; there was no way the crew could bring the rig safely back aboard without great personal risk. Besides, crewman Bill Lundgren, Carlisle's insurance agent, wanted to prevent the underwriters from forcing Carlisle to re-use any gear in their settlement, so he insisted that the crew dump the spars, rigging, and sails overboard. They began knocking out the rigging pins and, in the absence of cable cutters (which Carlisle had thought

Gordon Raymond stands calmly amid the wreckage as a Coast Guard PBY comes to Ticonderoga's assistance.
(Billy Letts)

unnecessary), they broke up the wire rigging and wooden spars with any tools they could find: bolt cutters, a sledge hammer, and an axe. It was a frightful mess. And it got worse. The floating mast sections and loose wire were gnashing so violently against the boat, they began chewing away at the counter planking, endangering the hull's integrity. Without thinking, someone started the engine to back *Ticonderoga* away from the drifting wreckage. Of course, the shaft and propeller immediately became fouled with 1x19 rigging wire and the engine froze. Finally, within an hour a Coast Guard PBY patrol aircraft arrived and dropped oil bags to weather of *Ticonderoga* to smooth the seas

so the crew could finish the job. When the rig was clear, the escort cutter *Pandora* hove alongside. In *Ticonderoga's* first postwar reunion with her former service, *Pandora* took her in tow to the Merrill-Stevens yard in Miami. Once the situation was under control Carlisle calmly, and characteristically, announced: *"Rum for all hands!"*

The rest of the fleet sustained a battering by 50-knot winds and very rough seas. Eight boats were disabled. In an unrepeatable freak accident, a huge sea broke over a 36-foot Cuban boat, Angel Naya's cutter *Windy,* parting her mainsheet and carrying away her doghouse and two crewmen. Once they could reave a new sheet and regain some con-

trol, *Windy's* crew recovered one of the men; the other was lost. Only a handful of the starting boats finished this most brutal of Miami-Nassau Races, which was won by Harvey Conover's 45-foot Sparkman & Stephens yawl, *Revonoc.*

Along the waterfront the word went out that *Ticonderoga* lost her mast because Raymond, Shields, and the New Yorkers had pushed her too hard, failing to reef when prudence demanded they do so. That was probably so, and their over-tuning of her rig may have been the proximate cause of her dismasting. But it wasn't the entire truth. The mast gave way in the same area the Coast Guard most assuredly had *not* damaged it during the war, but Allan Carlisle most assuredly *had.* The real story of *Ticonderoga's* dismasting goes this way:

During the winter Carlisle had taken a bunch of his sailing cronies along to deliver *Ticonderoga* to Florida. He planned some cruising before turning the boat over to Dr. Mellon for the Nassau race. It was on the way south that the great myth of her broken mast took form. Carlisle was at the helm, motoring *Ticonderoga* through the Intracoastal Waterway near St. Augustine, Florida, (not Norfolk, Virginia). As they approached a lift bridge, the crew signalled the operator to open the span, which he did. Carlisle began speeding down the channel in forthright fashion. But, for some unfathomable reason, the bridge attendant began to lower the bridge too soon. Carlisle was horrified as

he saw it coming down, but the boat was moving too fast; it was too late and there was nothing he and his pals could do but watch as the mainmast fouled the bridge and snapped. Quietly, Carlisle had a hasty repair done in Florida, then gave the boat over to Mellon for the race.

"It was a miracle that no one was killed," Carlisle later told friends. It seems quite likely as well that he told other friends (who were not aboard for the delivery) that the mast had been broken during the war by an irresponsible Coast Guard, and badly repaired by the Navy at Norfolk. Every recounting of her history henceforth blamed the Guard for *Ticonderoga's* first dismasting (there were a few more to come). While America's military services may be blamable for much that is sinister in this storm-tossed

life, they were truly blameless in this case.

Ticonderoga, needless to say, didn't race the rest of the winter season, nor could she be chartered. As a result, Carlisle lost what would surely have been a most inspiring (and surely profitable) charter party: the Duke and Duchess of Windsor. England's ex-King Edward VIII and his American-born wife Wallis Simpson wanted to sail to Mexico's Yucatan Peninsula to study rare birds. Instead of birdwatching with royalty, however, Carlisle brought *Ticonderoga* back to Long Island Sound, once more to Bill Luders' yard. Luders' expert carpenters repaired the hull, built new spars, fitted heavier rigging, reinforced the chainplates, and generally put *Ticonderoga* in shape. When she was rerigged and tuned, Carlisle entered her in the Newport to Annapolis Race in June 1947; it hardly tested her new rig. The race, in very light wind, was an exceptionally slow one, particularly for the big boats. It was won overall by the 45-foot S&S sloop *Alar;* *Ticonderoga,* in a good boat-for-boat tussle with *Baruna,* finished third, but was near the bottom of the fleet on corrected time. Not one of her sterling performances. Her next performance, however, made up the difference, and more.

Not sailed since 1939, when many races were canceled owing to the war, the Marblehead to Halifax Race was revived in the summer of 1947. Carlisle chartered *Ticonderoga* to a few members of the Miami Yacht Club. He went along as navigator and provided a core crew, including some hardy Marblehead schoolboys, to do the deckwork. Before the race, Francis Herreshoff drifted by in his handmade kayak to see *Ticonderoga,* but didn't come aboard or meet Carlisle. (Those who did greet him were astonished to see dried blood on his face: he had just gotten his beard caught in his lathe.)

The heading out of Marblehead, once the fleet attained deep water, was generally ENE to Cape Sable, then NE to Halifax, a total of 360 nautical miles. The wind at the start, on July 19, was fresh out of the southwest, a perfect situation for *Ticonderoga* to

Bill Luders' experts step Ticonderoga's *new masts.*
(Courtesy of Bill Luders)

Dick Bertram: one of the gallant giants of offshore racing.
(Courtesy of Dick Bertram)

carry her full wardrobe of reaching sail. But the entire coast, from the Gulf of Maine to Nova Scotia, was socked in by thick fog, making it a navigator's race (many boats finished without ever seeing land or other boats, and Carlisle depended fully on his dead-reckoning ability and his one concession to electronics: a Bloodworth radio-direction finder).

To make matters even more stimulating, the Canadian Lighthouse Service chose that week to remove for servicing the last turning mark of the course, Sambro Lightship, without placing a relief vessel on its station. The absence of the light (and radio beacon) caused no small amount of consternation among the fleet's navigators. A U.S. Coast Guard cutter, *General Green*, accompanying the fleet, did manage to hastily improvise a light at Sambro's station, but in the absence of visibility, and without a duplicate radio signal, she helped only marginally.

Ticonderoga had a brilliant sail all the way.

She reached the Sambro Light position long before the cutter did, however, and rounded the buoy the Canadians had left behind at 1400 on Monday, nearly striking Three Sisters Shoals as she headed for the finish. In doing so, of course, Carlisle got a perfect fix on her position in the fog, while the rest of the fleet was still searching for the Sambro turning mark. *Ticonderoga* finished at the Royal Nova Scotia Yacht Squadron jetty in 50 hours, 32 minutes, 5 seconds, breaking the course record. She was more than 6 hours ahead of the second boat. One of her toughest competitors, Rod Stephens' 45-foot *Mustang*, was more than ten hours behind. (Stephens later claimed that *Ticonderoga* had cut the Sambro buoy, but he didn't protest officially.) *Ticonderoga* kept her time and swept the race, winning trophies for First to Finish, First Overall, and First in Class "A." *Ticonderoga* was back in her old form, even if, in that pea-soup fog, no one but her crew had witnessed that magnificent form.

This was the golden era of offshore racing. And one of the men who added the greatest luster to that gold, and who had his hand on *Ticonderoga*'s wheel for many a watch during this period, was tall, slender, handsome Dick Bertram. Bertram, one of the great names in offshore racing (sail and power), started crewing on *Ticonderoga* with Allan Carlisle early in 1948 (one of the several years he also won the International Championship in the Lightning Class). Bertram and Carlisle had met on the racing circuit, bumping into each other in harbors everywhere. Being worldly and cultured men, they discovered shared interests and became close friends. Bertram always found Carlisle to be extremely bright, but he also recognized Carlisle's troubled side, and tried to become his mentor in some ways. One way in which that mentorship manifested itself was that Bertram, who lived in south Florida, helped Carlisle find crew for *Ticonderoga*'s southern racing ventures, and he often came along as watch captain on the distance races. In those days the CCA Rule favored comfortable boats (rather than some of the skinned-out machines that were later to dominate ocean racing). The Southern Circuit (later the Southern Ocean Racing Conference or SORC) was an important and far more satisfying series of competitions under the CCA Rule than it later became under the International Offshore Rule and other more ambiguous handicapping systems. The fleet consisted of a solid group of hardy regulars. Northeastern, Southern, and Great Lakes sailors would bring their boats long distances to race. Everybody knew everybody else, and the camaraderie ashore was as spirited as the rivalry at sea.

During the many races Bertram sailed, and sailed hard, *Ticonderoga* would break gear. For one thing, she had more sail area compared to other boats her length, and her gear was generally overloaded. More to the point, the higher drawing power of her postwar sails overwhelmed the original fittings chosen or designed by L. Francis Herreshoff for her more pliable Egyptian cotton sails. The crew would often carry a great spread of modern canvas, far beyond the prudent range of wind strength and into a Gulf Stream chop; the shock loads and stresses on the gear were enormous, and blocks, fittings, and shackles would fly apart with great regularity. *Ticonderoga*'s prime winches were also woefully undersize, so racing her in a breeze, although fun at the core, was utterly brutal physical work for all hands.

In January 1948, Dick Bertram's first winter aboard, *Ticonderoga* sailed the Fort Lauderdale to Cat Cay Race. Nobody found the work very hard in this case: *Ticonderoga* never finished. The light southerly at the start built into a long night of 40-knot squalls, then faded again in the morning, leaving the fleet to face a beat from Bimini to the finish in a zephyr and against an eminently foul Gulf Stream current. *Ti*'s crew elected to drop out, motor home, and hit the bars. For the rest of the 1948 Circuit *Ticonderoga* was chartered to a big-time, hard-drinking Texan from Fort Worth, Dr. Hub Isaacks, who

would become a regular, if sometimes troublesome, client of Allan Carlisle's.

For their first race, Isaacks and a few friends reported to *Ticonderoga* wearing hand-tooled leather cowboy boots and ten-gallon hats. Needless to say, *Ti*'s regulars, who were there to do the sailwork (and were more appropriately attired), persuaded them to remove the boots before they came aboard. On February 10, 1948, with the Texans tucked safely out of the way, *Ticonderoga* and ten other yachts started the annual Miami-Nassau Race; Carlisle came along as sailing master. This time her crew worked hard and her mast stayed up. After a modest start in a ten-knot norther, *Ticonderoga* passed the initial leader, *Revonoc*, and worked well ahead of the fleet. But with the breeze filling in from the north, the opposing north-flowing Gulf Stream wasn't moving up to its usual velocity; all the navigators overestimated the set. The fleet got caught well short of the mark, having to beat up to the turn at Great Isaac. Despite the windward work, *Ticonderoga* held the lead, rounding 36 minutes ahead of *Revonoc*, followed closely by two S&S boats, *Ciclon* and *Stormy Weather*. As the wind veered more to the east, *Ticonderoga* kept nibbling out a longer lead, and after rounding Great Stirrup she had her favorite meal, a close reach in a fresh breeze to the finish. *Stormy Weather* followed her across the line by an hour and a half; *Ciclon* came in 15 minutes later. *Ciclon* won the event on corrected time; *Ticonderoga* fell to fifth. But she took home line honors, which by now she was getting accustomed to, and which Hub Isaacks was rather enjoying. So, to be sure, was Allan Carlisle.

Ticonderoga wasn't entered in any significant races up north during the summer of 1948, and with good reason: Allan Carlisle was rather distracted. Having divorced Daisy (and foiled her attempt to take possession of *Ticonderoga*), he had set up residence in California. He was spending much of his spare time in Hollywood, the prime reason being Karin Booth. Booth was a voluptuous young MGM actress whom Carlisle dated

Ticonderoga sports new baggywrinkle in 1947.
(Mystic Seaport Museum, Inc./Rosenfeld Collection)

Ciclon beat Ti in the 1948 Miami-Nassau Race.
(Mystic Seaport Museum, Inc./Rosenfeld Collection)

when he was in town and, after a while, found himself in love with beyond measure. He was between races, deliveries, and other diversions. He sent Booth a wire at the studio that read: "Will you marry me, or not?" Booth was performing in her first movie, *Unfinished*

Dance (a ballet melodrama starring Cyd Charisse and America's favorite crying machine, Margaret O'Brien). Booth said "Yes." When the picture was finished they were married in Palm Beach, aboard a friend's yacht. There were no boats for Carlisle to deliver, so to get to Florida he had to be poured onto an airplane by some of his best pals. The Carlisles spent their secluded honeymoon aboard *Ticonderoga*, cruising the Bahamas with two crewmen, Billy Letts and Louis Hickman, and a very fine cook.

The Carlisles settled in California so that Karin could be near the studio. Several years later, in Beverly Hills, Carlisle started the one business that seemed to absorb and stimulate him almost as much as sailing: he opened Carlisle Galleries. It was a delightfully cluttered, utterly charming nautical antique shop, a great attraction among the non-nautical crowd, and the sole California source of rare museum-quality marine instruments, paintings, and curios. But even in this endeavor, Carlisle remained restless and detached. He was never comfortable with Southern California culture, and he complained to intimates that selling fine antiques to residents of Beverly Hills was like casting pearls before swine (an odd attitude for a man who, in different circumstances, could have been on the other side of the sales counter). But he had many good clients and he kept the shop open more as a hobby than a business.

Karin Booth had no particular love of sailing at first. It could not have fit into a creamy-skinned beauty's career to spend long days under the ocean sun, her hair wet with salt spray, her skin beaten by wind, her hands calloused by rope. But she soon began daysailing with Carlisle, cruising on holidays, meeting her man and serving martinis when *Ticonderoga* returned from a race. Eventually, she fell sweetly under *Ticonderoga*'s irresistible spell, and went along on warm-weather races. Out of the joy of sharing, Carlisle would often put his beautiful wife at the wheel for a "photo op" as *Ti* headed across the finish line.

But Carlisle couldn't share *Ticonderoga* or

Barefoot and blissful, the Carlisles share Ticonderoga's *delights.* (BELOW) *Allan and his firstborn, Allan III.*
(Courtesy of Allan Carlisle III)

himself all the time. Though he was a loving man, even after Karin bore him two sons there remained a part of him that his family couldn't reach. He would disappear from home for weeks at a time to go sailing. It wasn't a matter of his not caring; it was that he loved *Ticonderoga* so much he felt compelled to remain aboard to protect her from abuse by the men he was forced to charter her to (particularly those with hand-tooled leather boots).

As was usual, Carlisle chartered *Ti* for the 1949 Circuit. In the first event, the Fort Lauderdale to Cat Cay Race on January 28, *Ticonderoga* had a close bout with Walter Gubelmann's 72-foot S&S yawl *Windigo* and Gilbert Verney's brand new 52-foot Alberg yawl *Katuna*. *Ticonderoga* was scratch boat in a 15-boat fleet (as she often was) and she led all the way despite light and shifty airs, lots of close-tacking against the Gulf Stream along the Bahama Bank, and a parted mainsail headboard. She finished first; *Katuna*

made up her time, winning overall and knocking *Ticonderoga* down to second.

The second Circuit event, the Miami-Nassau Race on February 15, turned out to be an unusual beat nearly all the way, as storm-warning flags fluttered vigorously in

Nassau Race, a 23-boat fleet started on Valentine's Day in a 25-knot southeasterly, under shortened sail, with *Ticonderoga* scratch boat. The conditions, however, changed radically over the course, with winds dropping to near-calm for hours, then freshening again. Two of the dominant racers of the day, *Blitzen* and *Escapade,* took all the honors and *Ticonderoga* was somewhere in the middle of the fleet. She was more impressive in the Governor's Cup, and had an exciting boat-for-boat race with *Windigo.* In a sailing

breeze of 15 knots, after the start the two 72-footers sailed in close quarters, with *Ticonderoga* rounding the first mark a minute and a half ahead of *Windigo.* But *Windigo,* despite a shorter waterline, set an enormous spinnaker and made up the distance on the run and caught *Ticonderoga* about 200 yards from the finish. As she tried to pass to weather, *Ticonderoga* threw her a big luff and *Windigo* responded. Then, just before they both piled up all-standing on a sandbar, they bore away to jibe for the finish. As she came

(*LEFT*) Escapade *and* (*ABOVE*) Blitzen *competed against* Ticonderoga *in the 1950 Circuit.*
(Mystic Seaport Museum, Inc./Rosenfeld Collection)

across the wind *Windigo*'s beautiful 'chute, which had gained her all that distance, split into pieces of confetti. *Ti* finished ahead by seconds, but they reversed positions on corrected time.

Under Hub Isaacks again, *Ticonderoga* was scratch boat in her first entry into the St. Petersburg to Havana Race, on March 18, 1950. The race runs just 284 nautical miles, but it is a splendid challenge to navigator and crew, passing through three potentially turbulent bodies of water—Tampa Bay, the Gulf of Mexico, and the Straits of Florida—plus fickle winds and gyring currents (which were not well understood in those pre-satellite days). The largest fleet ever to sail the race, 26 yachts, started in fairly light winds. Once more *Ticonderoga* and *Windigo* sailed a boat-for-boat race for line honors. After a slow start, with *Windigo* in the lead, the fleet exited Tampa Bay and the wind died for a time. Then it picked up fresh out of the east. The fleet enjoyed a swift smooth-water reach in Florida's lee, conditions that *Ticonderoga* relished so well she passed *Windigo* and set a new record for the leg to Rebecca Shoals. When the big boats

The race from the St. Petersburg YC (above) to Havana presented an appealing transition for American sailors.
(Mystic Seaport Museum, Inc./Rosenfeld Collection)

hit the Straits the breeze went flat again, and *Windigo* closed on *Ticonderoga*. But her crew fought back, and in the freshening Tradewinds worked farther ahead over the last 50 miles, holding their lead to the finish, crossing the line more than 24 minutes ahead of *Windigo*. *Ticonderoga* couldn't hold her time and was second overall by a scant 5 minutes. When Isaacks and his Texans came ashore in Havana, they disappeared into the delights of Cuban night life, leaving the regulars to sail *Ticonderoga* back to Florida.

In that all-male domain of ocean racing, in that *machismo* era of Hemingway, Errol Flynn, and hordes of oversexed men sailing the blue sea without their wives to observe or constrain them, all American sail-racing roadsteads led to that most magical, maddening, musical of towns, Havana. With smoky casinos, noisy night clubs, cheap thrills, cheaper rum, and easy women, the allure of Havana was a powerful one for American sailors with simmering hormones and pockets stuffed with almighty Yankee

dollars. If a man were to sail just one race each year, St. Pete to Havana was the race he would sail. There was no second choice. Allan Carlisle also believed that Havana was the greatest sailortown of all; there was no harbor on earth he would rather sail to. He found in Havana an unmatched hospitality, a refuge filled with ineluctable sounds, heady fragrances, wanton rhythms, and a grand spirit of license. But, unlike many of his freewheeling brethren, who left their women behind, Carlisle shared his love of Cuba's

One of Havana's great attractions: gambling at the Hotel Nacional.
(Center for Cuban Studies/Constantino Arias)

Caribbee, Alden's *Malabar XIII* and Conover's *Revonoc;* she was eighth overall. In the 30-mile windward/leeward Nassau Trophy race, sailed in 20- to 30-knot winds, *Ticonderoga* was again first to finish but fell to fourth behind *Caribbee, Revonoc,* and *Belle of the West,* a 47-foot Kettenburg cruising sloop.

Then Hub Isaacks and his band of defiant, leather-booted Texans returned to charter *Ticonderoga* for a fee of around $6,000, for the big thrash from St. Petersburg to the big bash in Havana. Baxter Still was helping Carlisle with his charters by then—sailing on *Ticonderoga* when he could and providing the nucleus of the crew—so he shared in the fee. Carlisle went along happily as navigator. This time *Ticonderoga* had unexpected competition from a new source, Garner Tullis' 77-foot Rhodes ketch, *Windjammer.* After working out to an early lead in light airs, with small boats near her, *Ticonderoga* was first among the big boats to pick up a fresh norther to open her lead. But once the breeze filled in, *Windjammer's* fatter sailplan filled in as well and she began closing the gap. Pouring it on, Isaacks, Carlisle and the crew drove *Ticonderoga* to finish two hours ahead of the bigger boat. But after all the light air, the smaller boats dominated the handicapped standings and the fleet prize was won by a 39-foot Rhodes ketch, *Lady Patty.*

With four firsts-to-finish and a new

dives, cantinas, and music with Karin. She would fly down to meet him when he raced there, and at least once she sailed the race at his side.

As was Carlisle's routine, he brought the boat north for the summer of 1950 for cruising charters, then south again in early 1951 for the Circuit. About then *Ticonderoga's* original six-cylinder Lathrop gasoline engine, undermined by its abuse during the war, finally went to pieces. Carlisle bought a used Chrysler in-line, eight-cylinder engine to replace it. When his crew dismantled the Lathrop to remove it and install the Chrysler,

they discovered that the Coast Guard, owing to a shortage of wartime spares, had replaced half the pistons with non-Lathrop ones. (It is a marvel that the Lathrop had run that long.)

Under charter to Charles Granville of Chicago, *Ticonderoga* had a splendid 1951 Circuit series. She set an elapsed-time record in the Lipton Cup of 3 hours, 16 minutes, 34 seconds, only to be beaten on handicap by a 32-foot Hinckley sloop with the odd name of *Larry.* In the Miami-Nassau Race, *Ticonderoga* was again first to finish in just over 29 hours, beating Carleton Mitchell's

Dr. Hub Isaacks accepts Ticonderoga's *trophy.*
(Center for Cuban Studies/Barcino)

Despite some troubled times, Allan and Karin Carlisle always shared Ticonderoga *with their dearest friends.*
(Edmund 'Skip' Eveleth)

record in the Lipton Cup, the 1951 Southern Circuit was a triumphal moment in *Ticonderoga's* racing life. It was an ominous one, however, for Allan Carlisle. Owning *Ticonderoga* had been a struggle for him; the high cost of keeping her afloat and the high cost of living ashore competed fiercely for his resources. *Ti's* support was wearing him down. By the time he had her brought to Long Island Sound for a summer of cruising, his charter income was only intermittent and he was exhausted. He felt he had no choice but to put *Ticonderoga* up for sale.

But, as though the financial burden weren't enough, in August 1951 *Ticonderoga* became the focus of a perplexing medical mystery. Three people—Lie-Nielsen's wife, Maggie, a relative of hers, and one crewman—contracted poliomyelitis. After determining that the common thread in the three victims' lives was time spent aboard *Ti-*

conderoga, medical investigators checked the boat thoroughly. They postulated that a leak in the galley sink drain pipe had allowed fresh water and food residue to settle in the bilge, where it was missed by the pumps. It festered, undetected long enough for the polio viruses to multiply in the confined heat of summer. Two of the cases resulted in some paralysis; Maggie Lie-Nielsen's infection left no after-effects. *Ticonderoga* was thoroughly disinfected before she resumed her role as a source of health and joy—at least for most of the folks who sailed her.

Allan Carlisle had been hanging on to *Ticonderoga* in hopes that his financial situation would improve. It didn't. He sold *Ticonderoga* at the end of 1951 to John Hertz. It was a painful moment after five difficult years. Dick Bertram was there; he arranged the sale. Bertram knew well that Carlisle

could no longer afford to own the boat and live ashore in the grand manner. But Bertram also felt, with sadness, that Carlisle could have kept *Ticonderoga* if, instead of lavishing her with the highest-price upkeep, which he did with loving abandon, he had found more modest ways of maintaining her. Allan Carlisle sold *Ticonderoga* to John Hertz because of his financial problems, and for no other reason.

In a curious turn of events, however, his finances did improve some years later. After Hertz had returned her to Bristol condition, Allan Carlisle bought *Ticonderoga* back. Yes, because *Ticonderoga* was his bank account's albatross, Allan Carlisle couldn't keep her; but because she was his heart's delight, he couldn't let her go. When he bought her later, however, to paraphrase the sentimental song, Allan Carlisle's equity wasn't better the second time around.

UNDER RESTIVE COMMAND

1951–1960

IN THE LATE 1940s John Hertz had a house in Miami Beach, and it was there that Dick Bertram (who had established a south Florida yacht brokerage) sold him that beamy, sluggish old gaff ketch, *Tonga*. She was a boat perfectly suited to velvety cruising, not hard-edged racing—like many other ponderous cruisers of her type, she'd sometimes need a quick boost from her engine just to come about. But Hertz raced her on rare occasions anyway (presumably jibing his way up some of those difficult weather legs). In making the deal, Hertz and Bertram discovered that they had both attended Cornell University, which created a door to a friendship that remained open for more than twenty years.

Bertram had raced on *Ticonderoga* with Allan Carlisle for two years before leaving to join Carleton Mitchell's *Caribbee*, and later his *Finisterre*. Though he no longer sailed her, Bertram still loved *Ticonderoga* very much. He wanted her to have a financially sound owner after Carlisle, someone who, like Carlisle, genuinely responded to the needs of

older wooden boats. He talked to Hertz about *Ti's* potential, and reminded him that she was a supremely comfortable boat to cruise as well as a fast one to race. Bertram suggested that a transition from *Tonga* to *Ticonderoga* (names that share the same letters in the same order) would be a natural sort of progression.

In September 1951 Carlisle had *Ticonderoga* moored at City Island, the Bronx, seriously for sale. When he heard from Bertram that Hertz was interested, Carlisle telephoned the skipper, Lee, and asked him to take Hertz for as long a test sail cruise as he wanted. Hertz was also on City Island, where he moored *Tonga*, and the day of the demo a blustery fall nor'easter was blowing. Lee and three crewmen, including a local teenage deckhand, Peter Gerquest, picked Hertz up at the dock, along with *Tonga's* skipper.

With the wind blowing hard, they set out into the gale under "jib and jigger," and once out on Long Island Sound they turned to the east and began tacking to show Hertz her good windward speed and easy motion under shortened sail. Hertz stayed on deck just long enough for them to reach Execution

Rocks, a distance less than five miles, then he went below and poured himself a whisky, the first in a series. *Ti's* crew sailed Hertz to Oyster Bay for an overnight stay, then across the Sound the next day where he debarked. Hertz took possession of *Ticonderoga* later in the autumn of 1951 when she was lying in Oxford, Maryland. He paid Allan Carlisle around $100,000 for her. He was clearly in better financial kilter than Carlisle was, in large part because of his access to substantial family funds through his father, John Daniel Hertz.

A dirt-poor immigrant from a small town near Budapest, John Daniel Hertz and his parents had settled in Chicago in 1884 during the great wave of Eastern European Jewish immigration. John Daniel dropped out of school after the fifth grade and ran away from home for a while, paying his way in a waif's home by selling newspapers. His father found him, but that didn't keep young John Daniel down. First he found work driving a livery wagon. Then at sixteen, after quickly learning English, he became a sports reporter for the Chicago *Record*, then a sometime prize fighter and fight manager. In

Hertz's beamy ketch Tonga *was a most unlikely predecessor for* Ticonderoga.
(Mystic Seaport Museum, Inc./Rosenfeld Collection)

John Daniel Hertz.
(Courtesy of the Hertz Corporation)

1900, in order to raise himself out of this poverty-stricken rut, John Daniel Hertz took a job as an automobile salesman. Like the senior Harry Noyes (but unlike the unlucky Waldo Brown) Hertz made such a triumph of it he soon bought a partnership in the agency. By 1903 he was making a comfortable enough living to marry.

Never satisfied with the status quo, Hertz soon initiated a "ride-for-hire" division of his agency: he provided chauffeurs for the better cars he took as trade-ins, and rented them out as luxury-class livery. In 1915 he captured the low-end livery market by organizing a modest Chicago taxicab company. But he shrewdly painted the vehicles bright orange-yellow, a color he learned to be scientifically proven distinctive and highly visible. The Yellow Cab Company spread to a thousand American cities (yellow is still a standard taxi color in many of them). Born in 1879, Hertz was a millionaire by the turn of the 1920s. In 1923, when auto registration exceeded 13 million vehicles (a far cry from the 100,000 of Harry Noyes' day) Hertz bought out another rental agency and renamed it the Hertz Drive-Ur-Self System. He eventually sold the company to General Motors, under the name Hertz Rent-A-Car. Hertz then began to manufacture taxis and buses and operate urban transportation fleets, including the Chicago and Fifth Avenue Coach Companies, which he later merged into the giant multi-city Omnibus Corporation.

At the 1929 crash, while most Americans struggled to stay solvent and healthy, John D. Hertz retired at the age of fifty with an enormous fortune—the American Dream on a wide screen. But he by no means slowed down. In 1934 he became a partner in the banking firm of Lehman Brothers. He served the Roosevelt Administration during the war, and was awarded the Department of Defense Medal For Distinguished Public Service. In his spare time he raised thoroughbred horses and his distinctive yellow silks adorned the likes of Count Turf, Reigh Count, and Count Fleet. In a compelling and profoundly challenging sense, any son of this self-made colossus of a father would surely have an oversized pair of shoes to fill. That barefoot son, John Hertz, Jr., was born in 1908.

The junior Hertz attended the Culver

Military Academy as a youth and entered the advertising business in 1932 after graduating from Cornell University. Before the war he was an executive in several New York advertising agencies. In the early war years, under his father's aegis, he was active in public fund-raising programs, notably for Greek War Relief, and he was publicity director for several War Loan drives before he went into military service. In 1942 he married a radiant movie star, Myrna Loy, who was at the peak of her beauty and popularity. After the war, in the early 1950s, John Hertz, Jr., became president, then chairman, of the advertising agency Buchanan & Company. Hertz's life seemed, in the common parlance, golden.

But despite his affluence, John Hertz, Jr., was in truth a black sheep. At an early age he developed a similar syndrome to the one that haunted Allan Carlisle: the inability to fully cope with endowed wealth. He too had a family trust fund, which enabled him to squander much of his time riding horses or playing polo. To Hertz, though, the onus of wealth was to become more unsettling than to Carlisle. Although he was intelligent, well educated, and could be a perfectly charming man when sober, he got caught in a web of alcohol, and possibly opiate, abuse to the extent that he sometimes lost control of his life. His childless marriage and his friendships with Dick Bertram and other sailing companions suffered under the strain. Though he knew countless people from the sporting and business worlds, he didn't have many close friends. John Hertz was a true loner.

Hertz would stay up late at night, sometimes drinking alone, then call someone, often Bertram, to talk endlessly (Bertram had to muffle his telephone bell at night to prevent Hertz from waking him). And though John Daniel Hertz loved his son, he felt unsure of him. He tried to wean him away from polo ponies and chemicals by setting him up at Buchanan (which was part of his empire). But Hertz's relationship with the agency at times bordered on the bizarre. As with his friends, he would call clients in the middle of the night to discuss accounts, often under the influence of something other than his professional desire. This put the agency's staff under some pressure to keep him out of the picture.

When Hertz bought *Ticonderoga* she became, in a sense, *their* relief valve as well has *his*. He loved *Ticonderoga* so much she turned his lifestyle suddenly onto a new, fresh tack: he quickly lost interest in other, more profligate matters. He surrounded himself with marine experts who compensated for his own modest nautical skills, and began to spend as much time as possible sailing. Even so, to assure that he would remain away from the office, Buchanan executives began discreetly paying one or two of his sailing professionals outlandish sums (as much as $200 per day) to keep him engaged with the boat: racing, cruising, even doing mundane deliveries between venues (which owners *never* do). In short, his family and business associates

Hertz spent his every spare moment aboard Ticonderoga, *and continually refurbished her.*
(Mystic Seaport Museum, Inc./Rosenfeld Collection)

That little rule-beater Hoot Mon *leads the pack as usual.*
(Mystic Seaport Museum, Inc./Rosenfeld Collection)

treated John Hertz, Jr., as a child, because he often behaved as one.

But when it came to caring for *Ticonderoga*, John Hertz behaved as a thoroughly responsible adult. After several years of Carlisle's scrimping, *Ti* was not in the best condition. Hertz brought her promptly to the great Minneford yard on City Island for a no-expense-spared refit, investing nearly $90,000 in the work. The yard overhauled her mechanically and redid the interior and varnish. This was the first of several substantial refits that Hertz would give *Ticonderoga* in the years he owned her, resulting in a steady upgrading of her condition and value.

As Baxter Still would later say: "You have to give credit to John Hertz. If it weren't for him, there would be no *Ticonderoga*."

When *Ticonderoga* was ready, Hertz had her taken to Miami, where he would moor her in the winter and enter some of the events in the Southern Circuit. (He chose to do relatively little racing up north in the summer, preferring to cruise in New England, with Bar Harbor, Maine, as his homeport.) On January 10, 1952, *Ticonderoga* was remeasured by the New York Yacht Club's top professional, Robert Blumenstock, and given a new handicap rating. Her first race under Hertz was for the Lipton Trophy, on

February 9. Unfortunately, the fleet confronted light, fluky winds; it was no fun for the Class "A" boats. *Ticonderoga*, *Caribbee*, *Escapade*, and *Doris III* fought it out for line honors. *Ti* was second to finish, 30 minutes after *Escapade*, but all the big boats moved well down in the standings on handicap. *Hoot Mon*, a light-displacement 40-footer designed by Worth Brown, won overall. Modeled after the Star boat (but with a yawl rig, enormous forward overhang, and round bilges), *Hoot Mon* angered most traditionalists, who claimed she was a rule-beater, unseaworthy, and, worst of all, ugly. She remained a source of controversy for several years because she continued to win (and, of course, to be ugly).

If the 1952 Lipton Trophy Race was slow, the Miami-Nassau Race was slower; it was in fact the slowest in the event's long history. With hardly a breath of wind at the gun, the fleet of 19 boats was forced to anchor behind the line for fear of drifting over early in the current; it took more than a half hour for all of them to finally pass the committee boat after the gun. *Escapade* averaged only 5.7 knots over the bottom for the 184-mile course, yet she finished first. *Caribbee* finished second, winning overall. *Doris III* finished third and *Ticonderoga*

fourth. She moved down to seventh overall. Hertz's team had not yet gotten the knack of sailing *Ti* in light airs.

But they quickly found the knack when it breezed up. In the Nassau Cup Race, sailed in steady 15-18 knot easterlies and a flat sea, *Ticonderoga* led the fleet all the way; after 30 miles of sailing she finished well over three miles ahead of the second boat, *Doris III*. In doing so she established a new course record: 3 hours, 37 minutes, 41 seconds. As was not unexpected, a smaller boat, the 50-foot *Water Witch,* took the race from *Ti* on corrected time, but by only 2 minutes.

Ticonderoga and Hertz next sailed the St.

Petersburg to Havana Race. The fleet of 29 top racing boats started from St. Pete on March 8th, under a new rule penalizing premature starters an hour, so the maneuvering was over-cautious until the fleet got well clear of the line. *Ticonderoga, Caribbee,* and *Doris III* (now under charter to Hub Isaacks) led through the first leg in Tampa Bay, *Caribbee* clearing the bay first. On the 190-mile leg to Rebecca Shoal, a northeasterly filled in at 15 knots, veering to easterly and freshening at night to 25 knots. *Ti* had fallen well back but, she passed the leaders in perfect reaching conditions. In the midst of the leg, as the breeze strengthened, *Doris III*'s headstay

Baxter Still's Doris III *(here with Allan Carlisle on the foredeck) often raced against* Ticonderoga.

(Mystic Seaport Museum, Inc./Rosenfeld Collection)

79

(TOP) *Bellatrix, whose St. Pete-Havana record was invulnerble until* Ti (ABOVE) *sailed into Havana.*
(Top: Mystic Seaport Museum, Inc./Rosenfeld Collection/Above: Center for Cuban Studies)

parted and she retired. She was not alone. In the near-gale that ensued many other boats broke down. By the next morning, *Ticonderoga* was roaring along under full sail having broken her 1950 record passage to Rebecca Shoal; at the Dry Tortugas she was about two hours ahead of *Caribbee.* The wind increased to 30 knots, with puffs to 45; *Nemesis,* the Coast Guard's escort vessel, clocked *Ticonderoga* at 13 knots as she headed for the Straits of Florida. There the wind opposed the current causing a rough, steep sea. *Ti* turned for Havana and the wind, veering more to the south, headed her, converting her last 80 miles into a choppy and wet tight reach, then an even wetter beat to the finish.

Despite the windward going, which *Ticonderoga* never liked, she swept across the finish line off Havana's Morro Castle in 31 hours, 36 minutes, 15 seconds. She broke the record, set in 1949 by the 58-foot Cuban schooner *Bellatrix,* by more than 3½ hours, averaging 9 knots. There was, however, not a single spectator boat at the finish line to applaud her: no one in all of Cuba was expecting a boat to arrive so soon. *Ti* even caught the *Club Nautico Internacional de la Habana* race committee with their proverbial pants down: from the shore they saw her sails heave into view in the half-light of evening. They jumped into the committee boat and sped out to the finish line to give her the traditional cannon salute. Alas, in their haste they forgot the cannon; they spontaneously shouted *Hooray!* in their best Cuban accents. *Caribbee* finished nearly three hours later, followed by *Malabar XIII. Caribbee* won overall; *Ticonderoga* was set back to third on corrected time. It hardly mattered after that performance.

Though *Ticonderoga* never got the gun on this occasion, the race committee recovered the cannon and there were guns, rockets, and Roman candles going off all night as more yachts finished. But most of the firing and pyrotechnics didn't come from the committee: the race finished on the very day that Colonel Fulgencio Batista y Zaldivar had overthrown the government of President

Cubans celebrate the Batista revolution in front of the Presidential Palace, while a soldier (arrow) brandishes a machine gun.
(UPI/Corbis-Bettmann)

Prio in a swift but bloodless *coup d'etat.* Thousands were celebrating the event, some wildly firing weapons in the air (and some in more horizontal directions). As the fleet finished the sailors could see the flare of guns ashore. *Benbow,* a 57-foot schooner from the Great Lakes, finished under a hail of bullets, one of which lodged without harm in her mainmast. As the American yachts finished, though the Cubans kept the immense yacht club bar open for their crews, most were urged by American consular authorities to return immediately to the safety of the sea. The escort cutter *Nemesis* took wives, sweethearts, and children, who had flown down for a holiday with their sailing men, back to the

sanctuary of Florida. Needless to say, although a few of the more gutsy Americans remained ashore at the yacht club for a few days (including a carefree Dick Bertram, who rarely refused an opportunity to belly up to a bar), the spirited fiesta that the *Club Nautico* had zealously planned was canceled.

Ticonderoga's record remains in the books today by virtue of its merits, of course. But not entirely so: within seven years Fidel Castro would overthrow Fulgencio Batista and take his decades-long turn at the Cuban helm. After a brief attempt by the St. Petersburg Yacht Club to extend the race's life in 1958, Cuban waters became generally off-limits to American sailors. Races to the

vibrant, musical, boisterous Havana were suspended until further notice. But with that victory, *Ticonderoga* became the first and only yacht ever to hold the elapsed-time record in each of the SORC events.

Under John Hertz *Ticonderoga* had a first-class Bahamian crew. Hertz was generous in paying his professionals — a change from the Corinthian days when sailors raced for the challenge of it. Yet despite his generosity, by virtue of his somewhat edgy, often cheerless persona, Hertz had a terrible time keeping skippers. (One of them, Jay Wolter, who had sailed from his native Estonia with his family to escape Communism, had once been castigated by Hertz for instinctively fending off as Hertz was about to hit a bridge with *Ti*'s bowsprit.) Hertz was so tough on his skippers that, according to Mike Anderson, he had nearly thirty of them in one year. Anderson should know: he was one of the few skippers to last much longer than a handful of days in Hertz's employ.

Anderson got the job in the winter of 1952/53 when Hertz was living aboard a houseboat in Miami Beach. *Ticonderoga* was hauled at the Miami Shipyard where Hertz was having her hull strengthened with a bronze ring frame for the mast step and chainplates, bronze angles for some frames, and a stronger backup for the baby stay. As usual, Hertz was looking for a skipper. Baxter Still, who knew everybody and anybody on the waterfront, introduced Anderson to Hertz. The interview, as Anderson vividly recalls it, consisted of Hertz asking him one question: "What would you do if I was bringing the boat in, and was about to smash the bowsprit into the dock and do some serious damage." Knowing of Jay Wolter's unhappy experience, Anderson quickly replied: "I would just say to myself 'It's a good thing I wasn't at the helm,' and leave it at that." "You're hired," Hertz replied. "Other captains would have told me what I did wrong. I like your honesty."

Anderson, a gentle, quiet, humorous man—the sort you want running your yacht—learned honesty on his native Losinj, a tiny island in the Adriatic about 70 nautical miles from Trieste, now part of Slovenia. A mariner since his youth, he came to the United States in 1937, moved to Florida in 1939, and became skipper of a big motor-yacht. When she was sold, he met the owner of a Nat Herreshoff yawl, *Scarab*, and became her skipper. In 1940 *Scarab* broke the Miami-Nassau race record, and Anderson became more enamored of sailing.

After Hertz hired him, Anderson's first duty in the spring of 1952 was to bring *Ticonderoga* north to City Island to have work done at the Minneford yard. While she was there, a young salesman from a midwestern

The 1952 Bermuda Race aboard Ticonderoga *went from a snooze to a thrash in just a day.*
(Three photos: LIFE Magazine/TIME Inc./Peter Stackpole)

coatings company convinced Hertz to use a newly developed vinyl paint to renew *Ti*'s topsides. Based on the salesman's convincing pitch, Hertz authorized the shipyard to use the paint, which they applied without an undercoat. After some tune-ups and weekend sailing, Mike Anderson's first major event on *Ticonderoga* was the 1952 Bermuda Race, starting from Newport on June 21.

This was also *Ticonderoga*'s first Bermuda Race. It turned out to be a confused jostle at best, and an uninspiring prelude to what has since been a nonstop series of undistinguished runs for *Ti* to the gracious Bermuda

Isles. The wind was moderate from the SSW as the record 58-boat fleet sailed across the starting line; most boats were barely able to lay the rhumbline on starboard tack for the first day or so, with no allowance for the Gulf Stream set. *Doris III* and the Naval Academy's 62-foot cutter *Highland Light* led the fleet, followed by three Sparkman & Stephens maxi yawls, *Baruna*, *Bolero*, and *Kittyhawk*. After a time the wind filled in from the southeast and everybody flopped to port tack. Then the breeze went to the ESE at 25 knots, making the Gulf Stream crossing a bit rough for the small boats; the Class

"A" yachts, however, including *Ticonderoga,* had a romp and opened the gap. *Doris III,* navigated by none other than Allan Carlisle, advanced to the lead. But she was carrying a set of new sails made of an experimental material from Union Carbide that unexpectedly stretched under pressure: the stronger the breeze, the more the sails bagged out, the farther back she fell. In the long run it hardly mattered, because the bottom fell out on all the big boats when the wind died in midcourse. Some of them lost steerage, drifted backwards, or just furled sails to prevent them from slatting to shreds in the swell. *Ticonderoga* spent about fourteen hours becalmed. At this irritating moment, some wiseacre on the escort boat set up a large arrow pointing to Bermuda; the joke was not fully savored by the overheated crews.

As sometimes happens on the wide

ocean, however, the wind was still blowing fresh to the north and most of the Class "B" and "C" boats caught up with the big boys south of the Stream; it was a race again. The wind continued to periodically fill, shift, and fade until a mild sou'wester came off the continent and held for the rest of the race. The Naval Academy's 71-foot Alden yawl *Royono* was first to finish, but she fell to 16th on handicap. Dick Nye's 46-foot Rhodes yawl, *Carina,* took the Bermuda Trophy, the first Class "C" yacht ever to do so. *Ticonderoga,* whose elapsed time was nearly four and a half days, and average speed just six knots, was 24th to finish; as scratch boat she was set back to 16th out of 19 boats in Class "A" and 52d of 58 in the fleet. With only six boats placing lower, her Bermuda debut could not have been much more deficient.

But there was an interesting postscript to *Ticonderoga's* poor showing. As she sailed into Bermuda, Hertz and his crew noticed something quite eerie: several long white ribbon-like objects flowing in her quarter wave, which seemed to be streaming off the hull. On further inspection Hertz realized to his astonishment that the ribbons were strips of the new paint, which had peeled off some of the planks and were trailing behind the boat. Hertz discreetly brought *Ti* to a quiet cove to clean up and avoid the embarrassment that would certainly have obtained from the critical Bermuda Race crowd.

Soon after the finish, on July 1, a scheduled 750-mile race from Bermuda to Halifax, Nova Scotia, was run. Owing to the short notice and poor advance publicity, only four boats started: *Wanderer IX*, a 64-foot Mower schooner from Canada; *Gulf Stream*, a 71-foot S&S yawl; *Teragram*, the Coast Guard's 59-foot Alden schooner, and *Ticonderoga* (minus ribbons). Conditions for the return course north, after the semi-drifter to Bermuda, were marginally better. Light northeasterlies at the start turned dusty south of the Gulf Stream, then turned to fresh southwesterlies in the Stream. Halfway up the course *Ticonderoga* led her nearest competitor by 30 miles. She was first to finish by a wide margin, with an elapsed time of just over six days. *Ti's* average speed, a shade over five knots, was slower than her Bermuda debut, but as this was the first running of the event, she set the record. Only *Wanderer* could make up her time, and won the race.

In August 1952 *Ticonderoga* competed in the 128-mile Monhegan Island Race, to climax her summer season. It was a gear-buster to end all gear-busters. Twenty-two mostly local boats started; only 11 finished. In winds that at times roared up to 50 knots or more they experienced blown-out sails, broken rudders, and fractured gear. Bobby Coulson's 40-foot George Owen cutter, *Finn MacCumhaill*, besides blowing out her jib,

Ticonderoga in 1952 sailing under Mike Anderson.
(Mystic Seaport Museum, Inc./Rosenfeld Collection)

took a large wave over the bow that stove in a portlight and filled her bilges with water. But she held on to win Class "B." Despite *Ti's* gear failure—she parted her topsail halyard and had to race without the sail—she finished first, in 16 hours, 24 minutes, and broke the course record by an astonishing 1 hour, 16 minutes. *Merry Maiden*, Irving Pratt's 52-foot Rhodes yawl, won overall. For his first racing season under the northern summer sun, despite the Bermuda fiasco and the preposterous paint job, John Hertz had nothing to be ashamed of.

Mike Anderson left his homeland on the eve of Hitler's devastation of Europe but retained his European sensitivity in America; he understood Hertz perhaps better than anyone who sailed with him, except perhaps Dick Bertram. Though they were boss and employee, the two were also friends, as close in that regard as Hertz's manifold persona could allow. Hertz respected Anderson, and Anderson honored Hertz's intelligence and sensitivity (even as he knew how alcohol was destroying him). Anderson also had the European sensitivity to recognize (and dare to quietly articulate to others) that John Hertz suffered from one other form of personal execration brought on by his religion. It cannot be denied, in retrospect, that in the 1950s and beyond, the tight little culture of yachting, yachtsmen, and yacht clubs (and other public and private cultures as well) did not look kindly upon the entry into their midst of Jews, blacks, Catholics, and other minorities. As a result of these insidious exclusions John Hertz felt, as a Jew, alienated from both sides of the issue. While he struggled for acceptance by the elite yachting community, he joined yacht clubs only where he knew he was welcome: Miami Beach, Bar Harbor, and the Knickerbocker, in Port Washington. (On more than one occasion, his several captains and crews witnessed him breaking down into tears when the turbulent conflict brought on by his religion and his exclusion rose to strike him.)

Mike Anderson recalls that many in the

yachting world often snubbed Hertz (though it was sometimes because Hertz could be an irksome man). On one occasion, a minor race in Maine, the snubbing became unbearable even to Anderson. Hertz was steering toward the finish in Blue Hill Bay. *Ticonderoga* was leading the fleet, but she was overcanvassed. The crew wanted to drop the mizzen staysail; to accommodate them Hertz bore away to ease the pressure on the sail. He inadvertently crossed beyond the channel markers and *Ticonderoga* grounded hard on a ledge. She hit with so little forgiveness—the ledge was about three feet shallower than her keel—some crew were knocked off their feet. Hertz flew over the binnacle into the cockpit. Luckily, his nurse of twenty years was aboard (Hertz was also a bit of a hypochondriac, and often brought her along for hands-on curative attention). Though bruised, Hertz quickly shrugged the somersault off. When it became apparent that *Ticonderoga* wasn't taking water (proof of her superb construction by Quincy Adams) Hertz got a tow off the ledge from a small fishing boat and set sail to resume the race. The fleet had all passed *Ticonderoga*, but in a few miles she re-passed all but one boat, *Good News*.

The issues that Anderson recalls most bitterly were that no one in the race came to their assistance, and later, when Hertz hoisted the cocktail flag in the harbor, no one came to commiserate. Finally, a few people did reluctantly drift over, but when they left Anderson discovered that some minor household items were missing. Hertz asked the crew to leave quickly and they set sail for the Hinckley yard, in nearby Southwest Harbor, for repairs. Hertz used the opportunity to replace some of the loose ballast pigs in *Ticonderoga's* bilge with a single lead block molded to fit a cutout in the keel deadwood. And he added lead-sheet sound insulation to his cabin (in addition to his other tensions, he was extremely sensitive to noise). *Ticonderoga* cruised New England the rest of the summer, then Anderson brought her south again for the 1953 SORC.

Upon finishing first in the 1953 St. Pete-Havana Race on Caribbee *(ABOVE), Carleton Mitchell (BELOW) is congratulated .*

(Above: Mystic Seaport Museum, Inc./Rosenfeld Collection/Below: Center for Cuban Studies/Barcino)

This was the year of *Caribbee*, Carleton Mitchell's 58-foot Rhodes yawl, which won the Circuit hands down. She took the race to Cat Cay. In the Miami-Nassau Race she showed her stuff again in a very rough beat into 25-knot easterlies. Among the 23 starters there were broken spreaders, blown-out sails, and parted gear; *Ticonderoga*, scratch boat, finished fifth and was ninth overall. *Caribbee* took all the marbles in the St. Pete to Havana race as well, in fluky airs that produced no possibility of a new record for *Ti*.

She finished third, and was ninth overall. (After this unimpressive performance in the 1953 Circuit, Lee Lie-Nielsen, who had returned to sail *Ti* for the Miami-Nassau and St. Pete-Havana races, wrote to his old employer, Francis Herreshoff, that "it was a great pity to me to see her so grossly mishandled, although she is being kept up in very fine shape.") Another man in the Circuit who might have felt the same way about *Ti's* handling was skippering a yacht named *Galway Blazer*. It was Allan Carlisle. He no doubt kept his eye fixed on the prize of *Ticonderoga* as much as he did his sextant, chronometer, and nautical charts.

Allan Carlisle missed *Ticonderoga* very much, as though she were a lover who abandoned him. To make his heartache worse, he had to endure some good-natured ribbing from friends, particularly Frank Duffy, who chided the mild-mannered Carlisle for being in the limelight *only* when he was with *Ti,* and for being "nothing" without her. So, although it isn't certain when, somewhere in this period, Carlisle bought *Ticonderoga* back from Hertz. He held her, however, for only a short interval, and sold her back to Hertz. One cannot know what motivated these two similarly haunted men as they alternately fed upon and satisfied the other's needs in an odd, somewhat sad round-robin of ownership. (It surely was not for money, because neither man was so ignoble as to ever see profit as an objective in these dealings.) Karin Carlisle sometimes quipped that her husband bought *Ticonderoga* back every time Hertz made substantial improvements in her, so he wouldn't have to invest heavily in the boat's refit and upkeep (a jest that is no doubt somewhat exaggerated, but no doubt inherently true).

In this same period, Geoffrey G. Smith, a veteran yachting writer, completed a laudatory manuscript for a book on *Ticonderoga's* racing record from her launch in 1936 through the racing season of 1952. Smith summed up those first sixteen years with the unadorned statistic that she had entered thirty-seven races and had taken line honors in twenty-four of them. Though the races were both major and minor, it was nonetheless an eye-opening statement of simple fact, made more dramatic by the notion that Smith had no way of knowing that the best first-to-finish, record-smashing years were still ahead of this remarkable 72-foot ketch.

In 1953 Hertz had Mike Anderson bring *Ti* to Minneford's again for a major refit with new rigging. (According to Anderson, Hertz checked himself into a hospital room with a good view of the East River for no more medically pressing reason than his urge to admire the boat heading upriver to the Bronx.) Minneford's did all the work and made some changes to her sailplan designed by Rod Stephens of S&S, including the addition of a mule—a roller-reefed staysail set between the mainmast truck and a point about fifteen feet up on the mizzenmast, sheeted to the mizzenmast truck. The mule could be used alone or in conjunction with the mizzen staysail. Apparently it added something to her performance, as her only significant Long Island Sound start that summer was in the Cornfield Lightship race out of City Island, in early September. She covered 140 nautical miles in 17 hours, 18 minutes, 45 seconds, finishing first and setting the course record.

Back in Florida for the 1954 Circuit, *Caribbee* and *Hoot Mon* remained in the limelight while *Ticonderoga* sailed mostly in their lengthening shadows. *Caribbee* took the race to Great Isaac; *Ti* was tenth overall. *Hoot Mon* captured the Lipton Cup. Then, to everybody's continued chagrin, she won the

The versatile mule John Hertz added to the sailplan gave Ticonderoga *an added kick.*

(Mystic Seaport Museum, Inc./Rosenfeld Collection)

Ticonderoga *sails out of Tampa Bay on her way to Havana in 1954.*
(Mystic Seaport Museum, Inc./Rosenfeld Collection)

Miami-Nassau race in light northwesterlies —the first time in living memory that an offshore breeze prevailed over the entire course and the fleet started and finished under spinnakers. *Ti* was ninth in Class "A." She finally redeemed herself somewhat in the 1954 St. Pete to Havana Race. This was her fifth entry into that event and she had already been first to finish three out of four times; she had an honored reputation to uphold. She did not disappoint. Though the pace was not particularly fast, and no records fell, *Ti*

finished first by nearly three hours, but was ninth in class.

In the spring of 1954, as *Ti* neared her eighteenth birthday, Hertz became more delighted with his possession and curious about her history. He wrote to Herreshoff, who was now established in a stone house in Marblehead he called "The Castle," inquiring about the origins of *Ticonderoga's* design. In his formula answer to such queries, Herreshoff wrote to Hertz of Waldo Brown's oil painting, Harry Noyes' commission, and

Tioga's anti-rule conception. He concluded with a notable turn of phrase that still rings remarkably poetic and true: "And if beauty is a joy forever I think these several [clipper-bowed] boats will give pleasure as long as they last."

Ticonderoga's performance in the 1954 Bermuda Race, lamentably, was neither a beauty, a joy, or a pleasure. As scratch boat she made another dismal showing, taking nearly five days, six hours to reach the finish line at St. David's Head, averaging just five knots. True, her excuse was that the wind was, as in 1952, somewhat spotty and often calm, though occasionally fresh just to keep things lively. But she went too far to the wrong side of the rhumbline (a common mistake in this classic, sometimes pot-luck event) and she placed 72d in a fleet of 76 boats. *Bolero* took Class "A" honors; the winner was a Class "D" boat, Dan Strohmeier's Concordia yawl *Malay.* This race, though it will not be recalled as a triumph for *Ticonderoga,* will be remembered for the introduction of a new dimension in Bermuda Race navigation: it marked a new plateau in the solution to negotiating the Gulf Stream, as the embryonic science of oceanography was beginning to develop a clearer picture of that great ocean river's gyrations and meanders. Most yachts now carried a thermometer to take the measure of the Gulf Stream's form, to find the fair currents and avoid the foul.

By the time she sailed in the 1955 Circuit, there were signs that, just possibly, *Ticonderoga* was being outclassed by a new generation of postwar yachts. Many on the line had new shapes drawn by designers who better understood how to circumvent the rule to lower a yacht's rating and make her competitive on handicap, if not always boat-for-boat. There was no question that the new Sparkman & Stephens yachts were capable of winning on handicap. The fat little 39-foot centerboard yawl the firm designed for Carleton Mitchell, *Finisterre* (which competitors derided as slow, then accused of being a rule-beater when she proved a winner), decisively won the cold and wet season-opening race to Bimini; *Ti* finished a respectable second. That little 40-foot freak *Hoot Mon* took her third Lipton Cup in four years and won the light-air Miami-Nassau race as well, with *Finisterre* second and *Ticonderoga* 14th. And in all these races a brand-new, trim 50-foot yawl drawn by K. Aage Nielsen (who had worked for Francis Herreshoff in the 1930s) made her debut; she not only placed high in fleet standings but beat *Ticonderoga* on handicap in each event. That boat brought back to the race course a distinguished name: *Tioga.* She was the pride and joy of Bradley Noyes, Harry Noyes' youngest son. He had indeed kept the name in the family after his father's death (and he certainly must have had mixed emotions as he made *Ticonderoga* look ever more vulnerable for her age).

It is unclear why *Ticonderoga* did not make an appearance in the 1955 St. Pete to Havana Race. (It might have been that Hertz was hesitant because it was the first year for which a new Ticonderoga Trophy was offered at the finish of the race to the yacht club with the best Circuit score.) The race was won for the second time by *Hoot Mon,* with *Finisterre* second. It is clear, however, that *Ticonderoga* was in Havana *after* the St. Pete race because Hertz entered her in the Transatlantic Race from Havana to San Sebastian, Spain, on the treacherous Bay of Biscay. A dozen boats were expected, but only four made it to the line (many northern-based owners were attracted to a competing race from Newport to Marstrand, Sweden, held at the same time). The rest of the San Sebastian fleet consisted of the 72-foot *Mare*

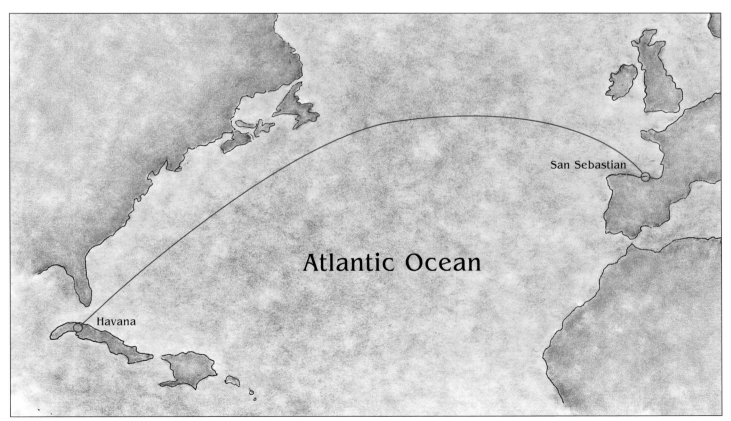

In her first Atlantic crossing Ticonderoga *raced from Havana to San Sebastian, Spain.*

(Map: Randi Jinkins)

Nostrum (ex-*Ptarmigan*, a *Windigo* sistership) sailed by Enrique Urrutia of Spain under a Mexican flag; *Siboney* (ex-*East Wind*), an 85-foot yawl chartered by a Havana Yacht Club group under a Cuban flag; and *Gaucho*, a 50-foot ketch, winner of the 1947 CCA Blue Water Medal, sailed by Ernesto and Mario Uriburu under an Argentine flag. Hertz and *Ticonderoga* had their pride and their country to defend.

For the 4,200-mile challenge Hertz brought along a fine crew including Dick Bertram and Alex Pfotenhauer (a German-born sailing master who years later became the skipper of several of Malcolm Forbes' luxury motoryachts named *Highlander*). Both *Ticonderoga* and *Siboney* defied superstition and raced with crews of thirteen men; both paid the penalty for their folly. The race started in light air. *Ti* and *Mare Nostrum* frequently exchanged the lead, remaining in sight of one another for more than a week. Then it got worse: 12 days out *Ti* was becalmed, slatting dead in the water close aboard the Spanish escort corvette *Descubierta*. Hertz tried to break the monotonous routine by radioing an invitation to *Descubierta*'s Captain and his off-duty officers to a cocktail party aboard *Ti*. Although they spoke no English and no one on *Ti* spoke Spanish, Hertz managed to convey the idea with great clarity. The Spaniards came

over, but were disciplined and drank little. In an hour the awkward mid-ocean gabfest broke up with everyone parting great friends. (The other race participants, who knew nothing of this, filed no protests.)

When the wind finally filled, the tiny fleet made its way steadily across the Atlantic, under a constant haze; Hertz described it as "no sunshine or sunburn from Biscayne Bay to the Bay of Biscay." The curse

(*LEFT*) *Enrique Urrutia, in white watch cap, skippered* Mare Nostrum (*ABOVE*) *in the 1955 Transatlantic Race.*
(Left: Center for Cuban Studies/Barcino)
(Above: Mystic Seaport Museum. Inc./Rosenfeld Collection)

of the thirteen-man crew struck *Siboney* midway up the East Coast when her mainmast began to come unglued; she was forced to withdraw and get a tow to Norfolk, Virginia. Aboard *Ti* the curse was of a somewhat different sort: Hertz on his worst behavior. Somewhere off the Grand Banks, presumably deluded by some "medicine," Hertz accused Mike Anderson and his watch of conspiring to steer a course other than the one he had prescribed. Anderson honestly denied it; Hertz didn't believe him. He fired Anderson on the spot, in mid-ocean. Hertz then summoned the boat's resident sailmaker to his cabin and appointed him sailing master, de-

Allan Carlisle bought the sloop Erivale *after he sold* Ticonderoga *to John Hertz.*
(Mystic Seaport Museum, Inc./Rosenfeld Collection)

manding that he take a solemn oath of allegiance to Hertz's authority. In the absence of a bible, Hertz told the man to swear on something "sacred"; the sailmaker put his hand ceremoniously to his crotch. Hertz went back on deck and *un*-fired Anderson, but asked Anderson to remind him, when they docked in Spain, to *re*-fire him. On another occasion a crewman shouted *Let's get a spinnaker on this goddam bucket!* Hertz, in his bunk, heard the invocation, came on deck and demanded an apology, not to him, but to his beloved boat. To cap it all off, *Ti's* No. I

Genoa split down its miter as she was heading to the finish in the Bay of Biscay.

Mare Nostrum won the race with an elapsed time of just under 23 days; *Ti* finished in 26 and a half days with an average speed of 6.8 knots. Both yachts broke the record of just under 29 days in this, the second running of the race. In San Sebastian, as in Havana, the pungently flavored hospitality of Spanish culture raised everyone's temperature. The local yacht club and San Sebastian's residents threw a grand fiesta that lasted more that two weeks (imagine if the

fleet had consisted of more than three boats). Hertz, of course, didn't fire Anderson; their bond was too strong. And he stayed sober ashore, confiding to Anderson that, having read about the Inquisition (which had begun in the year 1233 and had long-since concluded) he didn't want to make a bad impression on his Spanish hosts. John Hertz was indeed an odd man. (At about the time Hertz was indulging the fleshpots of Spain and avoiding torture by the Church, Allan Carlisle was buying a substitute for *Ticonderoga*, an innovative 55-foot Robert Clark sloop named *Erivale*, with a unique gimballed saloon table. He would sail her actively until he bought *Ticonderoga* back from Hertz one last time.)

From San Sebastian Hertz and his crew sailed around Spain to Majorca, where they were again treated royally, this time by the *Club Nautico* in Palma, and equally so by Hertz's Hollywood buddy, Errol Flynn. Hertz moored *Ti* alongside Flynn's big ketch *Zaca*, and over drinks they talked about organizing a race around the Balearics (it never came about). *Ti* then sailed on to Antibes so Hertz might have a reunion with Walter Gubelmann, who had just sailed from Sweden on *Windigo* after winning the Gotland race.

One murky black night on the 325-mile Mediterranean passage someone noticed a white flare abeam. Then another. All they could see where the flares originated was a faint light emanating from a single porthole. In the spirit of the law of the sea, they turned toward the apparently distressed vessel and with their decklight flashed the International Code: "EH" ("Can I assist you?"). Suddenly, a blinding light from above responded with code signals that were flashed so fast no one could read them. Still curious, they came closer; in the dark they saw the shadowy but unmistakable figure of a very seaworthy French battle cruiser, engaged, it turned out, in maneuvers with a pack of submarines. They left, seeing that she needed no assistance from a bunch of Americans.

From Antibes Hertz brought *Ticonderoga* to Genoa, to haul her for bottom painting, then back to Palma. After being on the boat for several months, Hertz had business to attend to. He left *Ti* anchored in Palma, with a couple of Majorcans aboard and "enough ground tackle to hold a destroyer in a gale." He returned to New York. During the winter *Ti* was hauled at Astilleros Ballester for minor work and in the summer of 1956 Hertz and his crew returned to cruise the southeast coast of Spain, stopping at Cartagena and Almeria, then on to Gibraltar for the first leg of the long, sensuous Tradewind passage back to the West Indies for the winter.

They had to remain in Gibraltar for some days waiting for supplies, some of which were delayed by political upheavals in Algeria, across the straits. (It was a year of upheaval everywhere: the birth of de-Stalinization in the USSR, the crushing of rebellion in Hungary, the beginning of Castro's revolution in Cuba, and the release of Elvis Presley's "Heartbreak Hotel.") While they waited in Gibraltar, Hertz met a Royal Air

Force pilot who offered to take aerial photos of *Ticonderoga* on her 700-mile passage to Madeira, as his periodic training missions were scheduled to go that way. When *Ti* finally did make the passage, however, no aircraft materialized. France and Britain were at that moment replying with bombs to Gamel Abdel Nasser's nationalizing of the Suez Canal; all combat training flights had been canceled in favor of the real thing.

For the November passage back to the West Indies, Hertz invited some friends to join him, including Coast Guard Commander George Downing. (As part of his quest for identity, Hertz would often take active or retired guard or navy officers along on his ventures to add some cachet to the on-deck proceedings.) After a period of unusual calm in the Tradewind belt, *Ticonderoga* had a reasonable passage, making landfall in Antigua. Hertz cruised the islands for the winter of 1956/57 then had the boat delivered to Miami, his homeport. During the passage she had a remarkable one-day run of 264 miles. From her start in Havana the pre-

vious spring, to her berth in Miami, *Ticonderoga* had sailed some 12,000 trouble-free miles in the completion of the first of her several European adventures.

Ticonderoga didn't do much significant racing in 1957, but she nonetheless had one of her most incredible runs in a long history of incredible runs. During a delivery between Palm Beach and Miami, under the guidance of Dick Bertram, she ran 63 miles in a bit over 4 hours, for an amazing average speed of 14.5 knots. She returned to the racing scene early in 1958 (just when the yachting world was mourning the loss, with all hands, of Harvey Conover's *Revonoc*). Hertz entered *Ticonderoga* in a new, quite challenging race that was to start on April 12 at Miami and finish between the breakwaters at the entrance to the Panama Canal. The 1,287-mile event promised a full range of conditions from windward sailing in the Bahamas, close reaching in mid-course, and a long cross-Caribbean broad reach to the finish. The race attracted more than a dozen quality entrants. But at the last minute all but two dropped out and the event was canceled.

Another event that had to be canceled was an attempted revival of the St. Petersburg to Havana Race. The St. Petersburg Yacht Club decided that prudence, in the face of the "unsettled situation" in Cuba, was wise; too many sailors remembered that hail of innocent bullets in the 1952 Batista *coup* and had little interest in confronting the less-innocent munitions of Fidel Castro. The race went to Miami instead, but *Ticonderoga* didn't compete.

Sometime in 1958, after much delay, Rudder Publishing Company finally released Geoffrey Smith's book about *Ti*'s early racing record, titling it *This is the Story of Ticonderoga and Ocean Racing—1937-1952.* Regardless of its ungainly name, the book was a thoroughly researched, if occasionally inexact, little gem (it was Smith who immortalized the erroneous story of *Ti*'s dismasting in the war). Hertz kindly sent Francis Herreshoff six copies of the book; the designer responded with a note of appreciation for

Three principal reasons for the demise of the Havana Race: Fidel, Raoul, and Che.
(Center for Cuban Studies/Osvaldo Salas)

Ticonderoga runs before a zephyr in a great Atlantic swell.

(Mystic Seaport Museum, Inc./Rosenfeld Collection)

Hertz's fine care of the boat, wishing him much continued pleasure with her.

But Hertz's "pleasure" was short-lived; by the time Herreshoff had responded to the gift books Allan Carlisle had once again convinced Hertz to sell *Ticonderoga* back to him. In order to accomplish this unlikely feat, Carlisle promised to transfer some stock to Hertz that, according to Baxter Still, was at the time worth $65,000. Carlisle put *Erivale* into storage and by midsummer 1958 *Ticonderoga* was once again in his capable hands; her first event under those hands was the 1958 Newport to Bermuda Race.

Actually, Carlisle was not the skipper of record for this race either. He found it judicious, for his pocketbook's sake, to charter *Ti* once more for cash; she was sailed by a band of cadets from the New York State Maritime College at Fort Schuyler, the Bronx. With all deserved respect to that fine institution and its many qualified merchant marine graduates, these mariners from the Bronx earned little more than a fervent Bronx Cheer making their way to Bermuda. While *Cotton Blossom IV*, *Windigo*, and *Criollo* were battling for line honors, and *Finisterre* in Class "D" was winning her second Bermuda Race in a row, *Ticonderoga* sailed into oblivion. As scratch boat with a handicap rating of 61.3, she placed 28th out of the 28 boats in Class "A" and 102d of 108 boats in the fleet. And as if that weren't a bad enough entry to Carlisle's lifetime log book, his understanding to purchase *Ticonderoga* from Hertz soon ran into trouble.

By autumn, when *Ticonderoga* attended the America's Cup series in Newport, the stock that Carlisle was to transfer to Hertz had plummeted in value; Hertz reasonably demanded cash instead. To worsen the scenario, Carlisle had brought *Ticonderoga* to Bill Luders' yard for work. Her captain and mate were aboard ready to leave, but there were outstanding bills on her account totalling some $6,000. Carlisle couldn't scratch the money together to pay Luders, let alone Hertz. He contacted the wily Baxter Still and asked for his intercession. Still

Allan Carlisle, while he was still Ti's master.
(Peter Gerquest)

picked up a trusted mate, Frank Dratz, came to Connecticut and somehow settled the Luders bill; the two sailed *Ticonderoga* south to Florida.

They set sail in a fresh autumn northwesterly and were off Norfolk the next day, having done about 300 nautical miles in 36 hours. *Ticonderoga*, so far as the swaggering Still was concerned, was always a "two-man" boat. Still and his pal then brought *Ti* down the Intracoastal Waterway to the Bahia Mar Marina in Ft. Lauderdale. By then Hertz's attorney had instructed Carlisle to pay the balance of the agreed-to purchase price before January 1, 1959, or forfeit the boat. Carlisle couldn't come up with the money. According to Still, Carlisle was so desperate to keep *Ticonderoga* he asked Still to take the boat to the Bahamas to prevent Hertz from foreclosing, which Still refused to do. Somehow, he says, he "came up with the money" to pay Hertz and "took control" of the boat.

Still brought *Ticonderoga* north in the spring of 1960 for cruising charters, and

quickly built a rather exclusive clientele that included a couple of Pan American Airways executives—Juan T. Trippe (the airline's founder and head man) and board member Robert L. Hamill, a Michigan sailor totally smitten by *Ticonderoga*'s charms. That summer, Hamill and his family chartered *Ti* for a Maine cruise when she experienced her closest call with disaster—after her near-tragic launching in 1936 and her hitting the rocks in Blue Hill Bay with Hertz.

Hamill was steering her under power into York Harbor, one of Maine's trickiest anchorages, which is peppered with rocks and lobster pots. As he approached the channel, for some reason he sensed from its silence that the engine had quit. It hadn't. When he tried to restart it, he blew out the starter motor and the engine truly went dead. The swift ebb current drove *Ti* onto the rocks near a large hotel. It was cocktail hour, which provided an intemperate audience to her plight. The impact was so powerful that several planks and a frame were pushed into the boat hard enough to shift one of the toilets off its base. But, so fine was her construction that when the planks sprung out again, leaving the frame cracked, she didn't take a drop of water.

Within an hour the tide dropped and *Ticonderoga* was high and dry on her side; the crew remained helplessly perched on her rail in the gloom. When the flood tide finally floated her again, Baxter Still, a cool and gifted seaman, sailed her down to Boston where he called his old friend Al Grenier. Grenier came out in a launch and towed her to the Quincy Adams Yard. The yard (which had stopped making doors and was back in the boat business) hauled *Ti*, straightened the frame and put a copper patch over the dented planks so Still could sail on to New York. He brought her back to Quincy to have the frame and planks replaced. The incident was all in a day's charter work for Still, and it did nothing to flag Hamill's affection for *Ticonderoga*. In exactly four years he would try urgently, but fail painfully, to purchase her from her next owner.

With days like this in his memory, is at any wonder Allan Carlisle was pained by his final loss of Ticonderoga?

(Mystic Seaport Museum, Inc.)

Allan Carlisle, too, felt pain at not being able to hold on to *Ticonderoga.* "That boat was the great love of his life," Carlisle's son, Allan III, remembers. "Having to give her up was probably the toughest thing he ever had to do." To sense how tough it was, one has to know that long after he lost *Ticonderoga* this final time, Carlisle still couldn't shake off her powerful centrifugal pull; he would remain in her orbit for the rest of his days, volunteering to navigate her whenever he could arrange a berth. When he couldn't race on her Carlisle raced against her, sometimes on a friend's boat, sometimes on *Erivale,* which he took out of storage after losing *Ticonderoga.* Between races he hungrily devoured newspaper and magazine accounts of *Ti's* exploits, living vicariously through other people's words and thoughts. He no doubt looked forward to a day when he could straighten out his finances once more and buy *Ticonderoga* back. To Allan Carlisle, apparently, the expression "final sale" could have no plausible meaning based in reality.

THE GATEWAY
TO FAME

1960–1963

RAY EATON was born in Sydney, Australia. He started sailing in 1960, at the age of thirty-two, when he and five friends helped deliver a 60-foot schooner to California via New Zealand, Tahiti, Bora-Bora, and Hawaii (not bad for a neophyte's test sail). In San Francisco the owner sold the boat to raise cash to start a business; Eaton sold two pints of blood to buy a 1939 Pontiac to drive to Florida. A personable and playful man, an engineer by trade with considerable hands-on electrical and mechanical skills, Eaton met Baxter Still aboard *Ticonderoga* when she was moored at Pier 66 Marina in Fort Lauderdale. Still needed an engineer for *Ti*; Eaton, who had no proper papers, was looking to work for someone who didn't care about his (lack of) status with the immigration authorities. The two had a meeting of the minds. Eaton, however, logically assumed from his magisterial manner that Still was *Ticonderoga*'s owner; surely, as was his style, Still gave Eaton no cause to believe otherwise. Ray Eaton did soon meet

"Big Ti" exits Tampa Bay. (Courtesy of Baxter Still)

the real owner of *Ticonderoga* (the man who helped Baxter Still "come up with" the $65,000 to purchase her from Hertz), an oversized but gentle cattleman from Williamston, Michigan, William T. "Bill" Brittain.

Though Williamston is not a seaport (it is somewhat distant from the waters of three of the Great Lakes), Bill Brittain was a sailor. He was also an exceptional, intelligent man with a brightly checkered life featuring many interests. (One of those interests, as far back as he could remember, was food. Originally from Missouri, in his undergraduate years at the University of Michigan Brittain showed great skill as a student organizer and made some side money in the catering business.) After his graduation he worked for a string of machinery manufacturing and metal-casting firms. When he lost his job at one of them (because he was too aggressive in his zeal to improve operations) he started another company, Universal Die and Casting. It became so dominant in the field that Brittain's company soon gobbled up his former employer's company and, as chairman of the new com-

bine, he took pleasure in cleaning house.

Brittain, however, did not limit his reach to manufacturing. He had his hand in the operation of a fleet of barges and tugs. He managed refrigerated ships that carried bananas and vegetables from Central and South America for a chain of American supermarkets. And he owned a sizable horse-breeding farm that, among its widespread enterprises, supplied galloping stallions and thundering herds for many of Hollywood's western movies (including the "Lone Ranger" series). But Bill Brittain's *prime* interest (no pun intended) was beef: he owned Premier Beef Cattle, an integrated livestock company that raised purebred and commercial cattle and controlled all operations from feedlots to meat packing. He was also President of the Black Angus Association, and one of the industry's most highly respected competitors. Indeed, Brittain was considered by his associates in and out of the cattle, horse, and banana worlds, to be a first-class straight arrow, an absolutely honorable citizen, and very generous. He was also a gentleman who never uttered a profane word,

Handymen Ray Eaton and Baxter Still install a new bowsprit.
(Courtesy of Baxter Still)

Unfortunately, Brittain was diabetic, which somewhat curtailed his participation in distance sailing.

After the purchase, Still brought *Ticonderoga* to Pier 66 to take Brittain and some business associates for their maiden sail. When they arrived, the dockmaster asked them kindly not to return to their berth after the sail because some of the more rowdy young crew had brought a few ladies of the night aboard—not the first (or last) time a glamorous oceangoing yacht had been temporarily converted to a by-the-hour motel, but an unsuitable image for an elegant marina and a no-less-elegant boat. Perhaps the incident led Brittain to rethink his arrangement. In order to give him more responsibility, Brittain offered Still an opportunity to run the boat under charter on a joint-venture basis, to share profits. The two shook hands on it.

Under this program, Still, with fair access to Brittain's exchequer, made some needed changes to *Ticonderoga.* He began by installing a new generator and replacing the worn-out Chrysler engine with a used six-cylinder Nordberg (when that engine soon failed, for the princely sum of $100 he and Eaton scavenged a replacement from an old Chris-Craft motoryacht). They removed John Hertz's cumbersome roll-up mule staysail and altered the mast-gear arrangement (to simplify sail-handling), but added air-conditioning and a powerful stereo system (to no doubt complicate maintenance). Still found some convenient property across the canal from Pier 66 to give *Ti* a safe (hooker-free) mooring; Brittain, a member of the Toledo Yacht Club named her *Ticonderoga of Detroit,* but Fort Lauderdale became her homeport of practice for the next few years.

Ticonderoga's first significant racing under Brittain and the Toledo Yacht Club burgee was in select events of the 1960 SORC. Her performance was little better than middling against some good competitors such as *Tigress, Commanche,* and Pierre Du Pont's *Barlovento:* in the Miami-Nassau Race she was ninth in class; in the Lipton Cup ninth;

no matter how unkind the provocation (making him an unlikely candidate for survival among cattlemen *or* sailors).

Brittain and Still met when Still had *Ticonderoga* moored up the Miami River. Brittain undoubtedly knew of the confused state of *Ti's* ownership and he made an offer to cover the outstanding balance of Allan Carlisle's debt. He bought *Ticonderoga* half as a charter investment, half as a private yacht. Yet in his three years of ownership, Brittain spent a total of only a few weeks aboard,

being quite happy to allow the Ray Eatons and Baxter Stills of the world—men dedicated wholly to knowing, maintaining, and overseeing boats—to operate and race her wherever the wind blew free. Like Allan Carlisle, when he wasn't sailing her, he was content to read about her in the press. Brittain did however accompany the professionals on one or two long passages, and some of the pros sensed that, despite his lack of time, he had a deeply repressed desire to chuck all his businesses and do what they did.

Bill Brittain in one of his rare appearances at Ticonderoga's *helm.*
(Courtesy of Ray Eaton)

in the Nassau Cup sixth. *Ti* was chartered up north for the summer of 1960. In 1961, Brittain and Still raced again in the Circuit, against the likes of John Potter's *Solution* and Ted Hood's *Robin,* both swift new competitors. She fared a bit better than in 1960. In the Lipton Cup she finished second, 59 seconds behind *Barlovento II.* In the Miami-Nassau and Nassau Cup races she took line honors, placing fourth and second overall respectively. The year of 1961 also saw the inauguration of a new race from Miami to Montego Bay, Jamaica. Though *Ticonderoga* did not compete that first year, the event was to play a momentous role in her future as an ocean-racing champion.

After her much-improved performance, Brittain—his landlocked Michigan viewpoint in a state of heady expansion—began to relish the idea of more challenging long-distance sailing. After some discussion with his professional advisors he elected to enter *Ticonderoga* in the 1961 race from California to Hawaii. It was a small step for *Ticonderoga* that within two years would lead inexorably to her ascent to the stars.

Since early in the twentieth century the greatest challenge to long-distance racers had been the Transpacific Race, or Transpac, run in odd-numbered years from Los Angeles to Honolulu and in some even-numbered years

to Papeete, Tahiti. In either case the Transpac would normally assure sailors a jaunty passage in the fresh Pacific Easterly Tradewinds, with a heady (and generally steady) diet of reaching and running conditions. The Transpac, over the years, would thus favor a yacht with a long waterline, billowing sailplan and—as more advanced materials allowed construction of yachts with ever-lower displacement/length ratios—more than a modicum of surfing ability in the long Pacific swells. Later, on the West Coast, a special breed of ultra-light, composite-built surfing "sleds" was developed explicitly for Transpac conditions, many coming from the Santa Cruz area. But in 1961 American

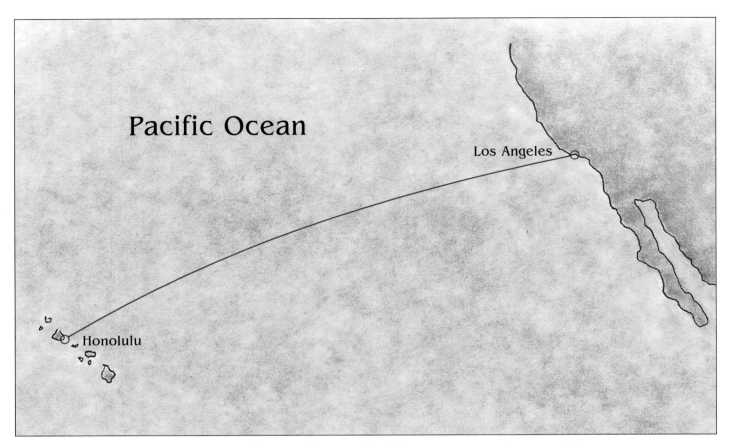

The Transpac is a 2,225-mile great-circle run, and a challenge to navigator and tactician all the way.

(Map: Randi Jinkins.)

ocean racers were still being designed generally to accommodate the CCA or similar rules, which produced hulls with relatively long overhangs that would not develop their maximum sailing lengths until well heeled on the wind. These racers were, in a word, capable of superior windward performance, but didn't have an appropriate hullform for the Transpac's almost perpetual off-wind environment. Harry Noyes and Francis Herreshoff had unwittingly created a New England boat (with a long waterline, relatively low displacement/length, and a big sailplan) that was ideal for Pacific Ocean racing.

Ray Eaton, Baxter Still, and a few hands sailed *Ti* to the Bahamas after the 1961 Circuit and picked Brittain up in Jamaica where he was vacationing. Together they sailed across the Caribbean and transited the Panama Canal. Brittain disembarked and went ahead to meet them later; the boys took a leisurely sail along the Mexican coast, stopping for some pre-race "rest and rehabilitation" in Acapulco. As they approached the

harbor, however, they had a surprise awaiting them: a Mexican gunboat with a .50-caliber machine gun trained on them. *Ticonderoga* was escorted to a dock and impounded by the local constabulary. Apparently, a couple of days before, in Salina Cruz, Still had inadvertently slipped out without paying all of *Ti's* bills and port fees; she was wanted by the Mexican authorities (and it was not for their cruising pleasure).

Still had to go to Mexico City to pay a huge fine. Once it was all sorted out, *Ticonderoga* sailed on to San Diego where Brittain, a member of the yacht club, joined them. Then she moved on to Los Angeles where Robert Hamill, Jr., Bob Hamill's son, joined the crew, along with Allan Carlisle, who came aboard as *Ti's* navigator (he was still hopelessly locked into her orbit). In preparation for the race, Still modified the drive train so that a diver could quickly remove the propeller, the external portion of the shaft, and the strut, to reduce drag and give *Ticonderoga* an added speed edge over the long haul.

Before leaving for the Transpac start off San Pedro, they did just that; they shipped the parts ahead to Hawaii so they could re-install them on arrival. Allan Carlisle used his Hollywood connections to get Dick Powell's son, in his motorboat, to tow *Ticonderoga* to the starting area. At the gun, she set sail for her first time across the rolling blue Pacific. To add to the enormous pageantry of the event, the racers were accompanied by two 318-foot four-masted Japanese sail-training

The removable shaft and strut.

(Courtesy of Baxter Still)

Huey Long's Ondine, *a typical CCA design and a prime competitor in the 1961 Transpac.*
(Mystic Seaport Museum, Inc.)

barques, the *Nippon Maru* and *Kaiwo Maru.*

The fleet started on starboard tack in a fresh, close-reaching breeze out of the WNW that lasted five days, quite unusual for the Transpac, which is usually dominated by easterlies. Under those favorable conditions, *Ticonderoga* (after a poor start) and the M-Class sloop *Sirius II* (ex-*Barlovento*) stepped out in front, and ultimately led the fleet all the way to Honolulu. Although *Ticonderoga's* debut on the Pacific was soon to be capped by a brilliant climax, in order to reach that pinnacle she had to endure some not-so-brilliant valleys. The first minor problem, once she was well offshore, was that Allan Carlisle had trouble handling his sextant, owing to his shaking hands; Baxter Still took the celestial sights and Carlisle was satisfied to do the sight-reduction mathematics. And the weather continued to be unsettled and variable along the course, with intermittent calms punctuated by turbulent squalls. On light-air days, the going was miserably slow and *Ti* could barely squeeze out 60 or 70 miles in some 24-hour periods. When it blew hard, she broke gear and ripped sails, particularly spinnakers, in achieving daily runs well over 200 miles. (One of the more violent squalls dismasted the 50-footer, *Rascal,* in mid-ocean.)

On one dark and stormy night, *Ticonderoga* got caught in a violent squall and the crew tried to drop the spinnaker, one of the few survivors. Shorthanded, the watch summoned Eaton, who was in his bunk, to come to the mast to release the halyard. When he arrived at the windswept foredeck, clothed only in his skivvies, he dutifully reported back to the watch captain that he couldn't possibly follow orders: there was no halyard on the mast. Its winch had been pulled clean off the mast and the pinrail to which the halyard was still belayed had likewise parted; both were hung up aloft under the lower spreader, like a postmodern chandelier. The spinnaker was still flying nicely, but out of control 30 feet in front of the boat at the end of its now-extended halyard. In the chaos that ensued, matters got worse. The crew retrieved the winch and pinrail but lost the spinnaker, which became caught under the boat. Then the spinnaker pole fell on deck and the bow wave rammed it so hard into the main cap shroud it splintered into pieces.

Making the best of a fair sense of general humor, and several shredded spinnakers, the crew converted selected shreds into kites, which they tied to the bow pulpit, much to Still's irritation. He soon begged for a more serious approach to the race and eventually made his point. Despite all the mishaps, after 10 days and a bit over 11 hours *Ticonderoga* finished in Honolulu, well ahead of such luminous yachts as *Escapade, Chubasco,* Huey Long's *Ondine,* and Jim Kilroy's new S&S-designed *Kialoa II.* But *Sirius II,* despite her own broken spinnaker pole and a spinnaker that, like *Ti's,* was dragged under her hull for the last few miles, managed to beat *Ticonderoga* by just 37 minutes after more than 2,200 miles of racing. It was the closest boat-for-boat finish in many years of Transpac competition. Carlisle was so overwhelmed by the thrill of the passage, and by his imminent and oft-repeated departure from *Ti,* that he broke down in tears in the cockpit. His post-race melancholy was cured when he and the crew were treated to a ten-gallon milk can filled with *mai-tais* (imagine if they had won

Despite dragging her spinnaker for miles, Sirius II *finishes first off Diamond Head.*
(Hawaii Maritime Center/Honolulu Advertiser)

overall). Bill Brittain, a rather big man on a rather small island, fell easily into the Hawaiian rhythms and, by virtue of his heft, the locals gave him an affectionate nickname, *Opu Nui* (which freely translates from Hawaiian into Fat Stomach).

The essence of Ray Eaton's analysis of their success was that these Easterners and Midwesterners, in the absence of a reliable weather forecast and having little knowledge of the Pacific, set a game plan and stuck to it. But when *Ticonderoga* was towed triumphally

Carlisle and Brittain (second row, center) lead the celebration of Ticonderoga's *first Transpac.*

(Courtesy of Baxter Still)

into the harbor after the finish, they learned that the game plan of the company that shipped her prop, shaft, and strut had not worked nearly as well. The parts were nowhere to be found. Eventually they turned up, scattered in odd corners of the islands (along with missing gear from other yachts) and they were re-installed. With her power train sorted out *Ticonderoga* was chartered to Robert Hamill and his family for a month of island cruising. They hit no rocks.

When the Hamills were done with their cruise, Still and his regulars did some relaxed island sailing, then high-tailed it back to Florida in time to enter a couple of the 1962 Southern Circuit events. Against new competition from Jack Powell's 40-foot fiberglass yawl *Paper Tiger,* and Ted Hood's new 45-foot steel yawl *Robin,* which together dominated the Circuit, *Ticonderoga* continued her fast ways. In the tricky 400-mile race from

Ticonderoga *had a perfect start in the 1962 St. Petersburg to Ft. Lauderdale Race, which helped her break the record.*

(Courtesy of Ray Eaton/St. Petersburg Times)

Eaton and Still removed the forestaysail boom and reorganized the mast gear.
(Courtesy of Baxter Still)

St. Petersburg around the Florida peninsula to Fort Lauderdale — which had replaced the Havana race — Still could muster a crew of only eight men, at least four short of a comfortable number. The wind was strong, the seas rough, and she broke a lot of gear, including another spinnaker pole (though Still had reinforced it with fiberglass). But,

remembering their poor start in the Transpac, the crew hit the line off the St. Pete Yacht Club right at the gun and *Ticonderoga* went on to finish first in about 50 hours, setting another course record. In the Lipton Cup she was second to finish.

Brittain next wanted to do some cruising, racing, and perhaps a bit of showing off in

his home waters. So in the spring of 1962 he had Still and Eaton sail *Ticonderoga* to the Great Lakes. In New York City they had her spars laid on deck cradles and steamed up the Hudson River into the Erie Canal, across New York State's northern tier to Buffalo, where the masts were refinished in exchange for publicity for the shipyard that did the work. *Ticonderoga* then traversed Lake Erie, the Detroit and St. Claire Rivers into Lake Huron, and sailed in the Port Huron to Mackinaw Race. This popular 250-miler was plagued by the usual Great Lakes biting flies and light summer winds and, as a bonus, a blanket of thick fog. Sailing into a totally vaporous calm one murky night, *Ti*'s frolicsome crew cranked up the volume of the new stereo and played a tape of locomotive sounds into the darkness. This caused more than one beclouded navigator on competing boats to desperately search his chart for a railroad trestle where none of course existed. After placing poorly, despite the wrecking of a few navigator's psyches, *Ticonderoga* sailed the Chicago Mackinac Race and had a good boat-for-boat challenge from the 12-Meter

Mitena. When the wind went very light, the victory went easily to *Mitena; Ticonderoga* finished well down in the fleet.

While *Ti's* crew was jousting with fog and flies up north, more than a thousand miles away to the southeast, over land and sea, the still-vex'd Isles of Bermuda were witnessing the New World debut of a provocative new sailing machine; she was second to finish in the race from Newport. Owned by Cornelis Bruynzeel, a Dutchman resident in Capetown, South Africa, she was designed to a rather advanced concept, by a brainy triumvirate of European naval architects— E.G. van de Stadt of Holland, and Laurent Giles and John Illingworth from England— and built at Lamtico Ltd in South Africa. She was a bit over 74 feet long overall, constructed of a very light four-ply mahogany laminate; she displaced far less than yachts of her size, particularly *Ticonderoga.* In exactly three years, and in another dense fog nearly 6,000 miles to the west of Bermuda, she and *Ti* would share a thrilling rendezvous with destiny. Her name: *Stormvogel.*

After the fruitless lake racing and a bit more pleasant lake cruising, Brittain wanted to attend the 1962 America's Cup races in Newport. Eaton, Still, and crewman Dick Grinnan retraced *Ti's* steps to Buffalo, turned left into Lake Ontario and sailed down the St. Lawrence River. They stopped briefly at the Gaspé Peninsula where, coincidentally, Eaton took a souvenir photo shooting down from the bowsprit. The sky was so precisely reflected in the flat water he later thought he had taken the picture looking up; it was a perfect documentation of the exemplary calm before the storm. The next day, as they sailed toward that exquisite little enclave in the Canadian Maritimes, Prince Edward Island, hurricane Alma's leading-edge winds struck them with sudden fury.

Eaton and Grinnan worked quickly to get the mainsail down, while Still steered, but the 60-knot winds broke every batten in the process. Perhaps as proof that *Ti* was not the "two-man" boat Still asserted she was, both

Dick Grinnan stands guard while Ti *works her way up New York State's canals.*

(Courtesy of Baxter Still)

were exhausted by the time they could furl the sail and set it in stops. *Ti* took off under staysail alone on a screaming rail-down reach, making it through the Straits of Canso and into a safe lee in Port Hawkesbury before the worst of the storm struck. After waiting out the hurricane, the three made their way down the coast to Newport so Brittain and some friends could watch Australia's first America's Cup challenge, in which *Weatherly,* driven by Bus Mosbacher, squeezed out a four-to-one

defense against a faster *Gretel,* sailed by Jock Sturrock. They also had the great privilege of taking Francis Herreshoff out on the water, and to be regaled by his vivid reminiscences. But surely the most memorable event for Ray Eaton took place when Still, steering under power on the edge of the race course, complained to his engineer that he had lost reverse gear on the engine. The conscientious Eaton hopped into *Ti's* Lilliputian engine room, then popped his head out to report

Herreshoff was aboard when Eaton and the crew retrieved Ti's shaft and prop.
(Mystic Seaport Museum, Inc.)

that Still wasn't likely to have *forward* gear either. The shaft coupling had parted and the shaft had backed out of the stuffing box; *Ticonderoga* was rapidly filling with water. Eaton forced a rag in the aperture to stem the flood, then seeing that the shaft was still hanging in the strut he dove over the side and forced the shaft back in with two tackles. When all was done, Herreshoff, who seemed to sense disaster, was quite appreciative.

From Newport *Ti* again wended her way south, staying in Fort Lauderdale for the 1962 holiday season. Ray Eaton left the boat during the winter and flew to Michigan

where Brittain used his good offices (and attorneys) to help him get his "green card," so he might remain and work in the United States without having to look over his shoulder for the folks from immigration. While he waited for this to be accomplished, he took a temporary job in one of Brittain's companies.

Early in 1963 *Ticonderoga* sailed in one of the major long-distance events of the SORC, the 400-mile race from St. Petersburg to Fort Lauderdale. She showed excellent speed, finishing third in a fleet of 25 boats. But she also showed her continued lamentable inability to sail up to her rating. After her handicap was factored in, she placed last among the eight Class "A" boats and 23d overall in the fleet of 25. Around this time, Bill Brittain began toying with the idea of selling *Ti*. She was costing him more than he was comfortable with (he told friends that *Ti's* racing number, "100," had a dollar sign before it). *Ticonderoga* obviously was in need of attention from a man even hungrier for victory than Brittain. That man was very close at hand.

In the concluding event of the 1963 SORC, the 844-mile race from Miami to

Montego Bay, Jamaica, a beamy, voluminous 75-foot cruising motorsailer, *Zia*, was entered in a fleet of otherwise swift racing craft. A yacht on the order of John Hertz's *Tonga*, this lethargic ketch with shapeless cruising sails was described in *Yachting*, with chivalrous kindness, as "leisurely." A day or two before she would have finished the race, at the tail end of the fleet, *Zia's* owner abruptly instructed his crew to furl all sail; he started the engine and motored the remaining miles to Jamaica. This boat owner retired from the Montego Bay race, it is told, because his yacht had experienced a catastrophic electrical failure. With her service batteries drained he couldn't start her generator to recharge the service batteries—the classic Catch-22. He could have sailed on. He chose to motor on, however, not because he was too embarrassed by his poor showing—he was too big a man for that—but because he dared not risk ruining the dozens of steaks he had stowed in *Zia's* deep freeze. This beef-loving Promethean with the Gargantuan appetite and portly motorsailer was Robert F. Johnson, of Portland, Oregon, and Freeport, Grand Bahama. Like Bill Brittain, Johnson was not only eternally hungry for a good grilled steak; he was, more than Bill Brittain, developing an immense appetite to enter, and finally win, some ocean races.

Robert Farrar Johnson—corpulent and jowly to a fault—was a classic teddy bear of a man. This was primarily because he was a somewhat overindulgent man, who consumed food in a manner that would be judged politically incorrect in a more health-conscious era than the free-spirited 1960s. To his great credit, Bob Johnson was also an extremely intelligent, sensitive, and inquisitive man, who hungered for knowledge in many areas of endeavor outside his own. (He once telephoned a good friend at three in the morning to discuss his ideas for converting exhaust gases from the Bahamas' diesel generators into fertilizer, to enrich the islands' fruit and vegetable crops.)

Bob Johnson was also an unassuming

man, quiet and shy to the point of being socially ill-at-ease with people, many of whom mistook his bashfulness for disinterest. He grew more at ease, as surely as the rest of us do, with a drink in his hand, but Johnson was never an abusive drinker; he merely shared his pleasures with others, rarely refusing to buy the next round and participate in it as well. Johnson, in that way and many more, was also a generous man; he cared about people and would willingly help a friend in need, usually with passion and always without fanfare.

Johnson was born in 1912, in St. Louis, Missouri. When he was about twelve, his father, Clarence Dean Johnson, a railroading and timbering man, took the family West in search of a better life. The Johnsons settled first in San Francisco, then by the late 1920s migrated north to Portland, Oregon, where Clarence established the C.D. Johnson Lumber Company and Bob entered the University of Oregon to study engineering (and to become a collegiate tennis champion, while he was still slender). But in the Great Depression, with housing demand falling along with net worths, the lumber business became marginal at best, and Bob dropped out of the university to go to work for his father alongside his two brothers. Clarence and his boys struggled to keep the company alive by building prefabricated housing, an idea that, if only for a few more years, was ahead of its time.

Clarence Johnson died in 1940, on the eve of World War II, and his sons took over the company. But prospects remained poor for the lumber business until December 1941, when the United States went to war and the government had a sudden need for military housing—*prefabricated* military housing. The Johnsons quickly found their order book filled with contracts for administration buildings, barracks, and hospitals along the West Coast. And early in the war they landed the highly secretive assignment to build plywood housing in Hanford, Washington, for scientists and other personnel of the Manhattan Project, who were

Decked out for cruising, with a mighty short rig, Zia was no threat on the racecourse.
(Courtesy of Frank Person)

covertly nurturing the first atom bomb.

After the war the company continued to flourish, as the nation needed more prefabricated housing for American military personnel returning to re-establish their civilian lives. Bob Johnson learned to fly and became a licensed civilian pilot (later buying a twin-engined Cessna for the business). But in the mid-1950s tragedy struck the Johnson clan: Bob's brothers were both killed in an airplane crash while returning to the West Coast from a New York business trip.

Johnson found himself anointed CEO and President of the company, solely responsible for its operation. Within a few years, Johnson, who never finished his studies (but was later granted an honorary degree by his university), arranged to sell the family firm to Georgia-Pacific, the huge lumbering conglomerate; he became a vice president of the parent company. But Johnson was too nonconformist to be just another cog in someone else's great wheel. Around 1960 he resigned from Georgia-Pacific to re-establish

Bob Johnson took great delight in traditional wooden yachts like Groote Beer *(RIGHT).*
(Above: Mystic Seaport Museum, Inc./Right: Rosenfeld Collection)

his independence and created a company to build quality housing. In 1961, with a partner, he founded Grand Bahama Development Company, which built an exclusive apartment complex and service facilities in Freeport, where he also maintained a family home.

As a boy, Johnson had become interested in the sea and ships because his father operated a timber-hauling business out of northern California; his fleet of tugs and freighters were among Bob's childhood playthings. Johnson also learned to sail as a youth, and in his California years he built a small wooden sloop with a friend. For the rest of his life Johnson was an avid sailor; he never found much in motoryachts to attract him. But more than most sailors of his era (who were becoming enamored of fiberglass), Johnson was drawn to wooden boats, those constructed from the material he appreciated best, understood most, and which had, after years of struggle, brought him prosperity.

In the late 1950s, in Florida, Johnson acquired his first ocean sailing boat, the 55-foot *Groote Beer*, which had been built by Dutch craftsmen but used by Hermann Göring, creator of Hitler's *Luftwaffe*, as his private yacht. (Actually, *Groote Beer* should

properly be called a *jacht*, as she was a modern construct of a traditional Dutch *botter*, a beamy gaff cutter derived from old fishing boats, complete with lengthy bowsprit, crooked gaff, and clunky leeboards.) Finding her a bit slow, after a few years Johnson made a charitable donation of *Groote Beer* to the Catholic Church. He then acquired *Zia*, that ungainly ketch-rigged motorsailer with the baggy sails and overfilled deep freeze. (By some inexplicable chance and against all reasonable odds, both *Zia* and *Groote Beer* are said to have fallen off the ways at their maiden launches—exactly as "Big Ti" had done in 1936.)

Ocean racing didn't interest Johnson very much; he was the ideal cruising man. Yet as is every cruising man's wont he did enter a race now and again. According to his cohorts, however, he wasn't a very good racing skipper; he raced not to win, just to experience the sea. He left the sail trim and tactics to others, while he spent most of his energies

sniffing for breeze, piloting, and wayfinding by the stars. Johnson was also a self-taught navigator. He had learned the art by reading many complex books, plowing through, for example, *Bowditch* from cover to cover. But once he became an expert, he developed a humanitarian urge to simplify the process for others. So he wrote and self-published a friendly paperback pamphlet he called *Stars & Spaghetti*. In 8 densely packed chapters

Johnson's gift to navigation lore: Stars & Spaghetti.
(Courtesy of Mark Johnson)

Ticonderoga, *to begin with, was not slow against other boats; she was soon to outrun them all. . . .*
(Courtesy of Baxter Still)

covering a mere 24 pages (and without resorting to impenetrable theory) Johnson unmasked the secrets of sight reduction. As the *pièce de résistance*, he concluded with a wholly unscientific but delectable recipe for his favorite offshore pasta dish.

In his early races Johnson was not a winner; not even close. He entered *Groote Beer* in the 1957 Transpac to Honolulu: she finished last of nine yachts in Class "B" and was more than six days behind the first-to-finish 81-foot *Barlovento;* only *Quascilla,* a 40-footer, finished after her and *Groote Beer* placed next-to-last overall in a fleet of 32. In 1959 he sailed *Zia* in the same race: she was last in

Class "B" and last overall. In 1961 he and *Zia* tried again to find their way quickly to Hawaii: they were 12th out of 13 in Class "A" and 35th out of 41 in the fleet. Apparently sensing that his luck was improving (after all, he wasn't last in the 1961 Transpac) Johnson tried a final time to turn *Zia* into a respectable ocean racer in the Montego Bay Race of 1963, the year he chose unspoiled beef over another awkward finish. (From such dismal regatta results "Yachtsman of the Year" awards are rarely earned.)

But steaks aside, Bob Johnson was no quitter. Regardless of his abysmal early racing record, in many respects he was the perfect

yacht owner. He commanded when he knew what he was doing; he didn't interfere with his expert crewmen when he knew they knew better. He was content to plot courses by sextant and chronometer, direct his ship, and plan meals. All Bob Johnson ever needed, it would seem, was a fine crew and a boat capable of crossing a wide ocean while showing her transom to the fleet. So far as Johnson was concerned, in the early 1960s, that ocean was the Pacific.

That capable boat, as it soon turned out, was *Ticonderoga.* When man and boat met, she would transform Bob Johnson . . . even as he would surely transform her.

GREAT PERFORMANCES

1963–1965

IN *STARS AND SPAGHETTI* Robert F. Johnson described himself as "neither born to the sea, nor born to the plow." He was, in his own words: an amateur tennis champion, logger, surveyor, saw-mill hand, contractor, airplane pilot, plywood manufacturer, saw-mill operator, and amateur cook. Despite the hands-on nature of all those experiences, none would seem to have qualified Johnson to perform sailing feats bordering on the miraculous. But over the next few years he did just that. The first of these feats, although in part political, was his chartering of *Ticonderoga* for the 1963 Transpac.

Johnson knew of *Ticonderoga's* remarkable debut performance in the 1961 Transpac. He also knew generally of her blazing speed potential in a fresh breeze, once her crew could fill her big sailplan and ease sheets. The Transpac, he reasoned, was a race made for *Ticonderoga*: setting spinnaker, spinnaker staysail, main, mizzen staysail, and mizzen totalling more than 6,000 square feet over her 64-foot waterline would make her a

sure threat to CCA maxis whose waterlines were as much as eight to ten feet shorter than hers for the same overall length. Around the time he sailed (and dropped out of) the 1963 Montego Bay Race, Johnson indeed contacted *Ti's* sailing master, Baxter Still, and asked if he was interested in chartering her for the 1963 Transpac. Still was delighted and Johnson happily paid Brittain a $20,000 charter fee in advance. (The fee was that high in part because it included costly racing insurance.) But the charter contract was less than a formal one, which later became the source of a great difficulties.

At first there was harmony between Johnson and Still. Johnson set out immediately to find a sailing master, one who was utterly familiar with the Pacific Ocean — which Baxter Still was not. With so much California talent gathered in Jamaica after the Montego Bay Race, Johnson had his choice. He chose the very best: Bob Dickson. Dickson, a tall, genial Californian, was a true sailing professional; a full-time skipper whose life was given over entirely to the sea and to its mastery, insofar as mere humans can ever hope to master nature. Dickson pos-

sessed great inner calm and enormous Pacific knowledge. Having sailed tens of thousands of Pacific miles he knew almost every Pacific wave by name. Yet Dickson's deep sense of probity caused him to separate his sporting life from his professional one. He didn't generally accept pay to race a boat; he made his living (tenuous as it was) by delivering racing yachts to and from their venues, and delivering cruising yachts wherever their owners wanted to cruise. Bob Dickson's true measure of profit would seem to have come more from the bliss of a passage made good with a reliable boat and a congenial crew, than from a bank account brimming with cash. As proof of that, after he had graduated from university, Dickson had given up a potential career in banking to go sailing. He never turned back, and he never regretted it. (When he hung up his racing boots two decades later, he had sailed more than 200,000 miles and had raced across the Atlantic, 40 times to Mexico, and had sailed an astonishing 24 Transpacs: 20 to Hawaii, 4 to Tahiti.)

Johnson already knew Dickson well, as the two had met in 1959 in Tahiti where

Johnson was cruising on *Zia* after her last-in-fleet Transpac finish. Dickson had sailed there on another boat, but had no interest in sailing back on her. Johnson invited Dickson to sail with him to Honolulu, and Dickson was grateful for the opportunity. Along the way, Dickson taught Johnson, who was then still fairly new to bluewater sailing, some essential safety tricks such as how to run off in a squall. The two developed a warm ocean fellowship.

Unfortunately Dickson had to turn down Johnson's request to skipper *Ticonderoga* in the 1963 Transpac; he was already committed to Baldwin Baldwin's *Audacious*. Dickson, however, thoughtfully recommended that Johnson commandeer his good California friend Danny Elliott, who was also in Jamaica after skippering *Escapade* in the Montego Bay Race. Johnson signed him on. Elliott, like Dickson, started his sailing life as a child, in Alamitos Bay and Newport Harbor, racing Penguins and Dyer Dinghies. He was twice junior national champion in the Snipe class. His father had an old Nicholas Potter Cal 32, which won the 1941 Honolulu Race; when he had a heart attack, Dan campaigned the boat for him. By 1963, when he met Johnson, Elliott was a damned good sailor. He was also a university-trained petroleum geologist with a flourishing oil-exploration business that earned him a comfortable living: he could take time off to race whenever he chose, while the business took care of itself. Like Dickson, but for very different reasons, Dan Elliott also raced as a Corinthian. He certainly needed no inducement of mere pocket money to take time from his business to race; he did it for the diversion. He couldn't say no to Johnson's invitation.

But here is where the sweet harmony between Johnson and Baxter Still began to sour. In preparation for the Transpac, Dan Elliott returned to California to gather a crew of experienced West Coast sailors. Baxter Still (with an East Coast crew that included Ray Eaton) set out to deliver the boat from Jamaica to Los Angeles. (Actually,

Bob Dickson, a helmsman for the history books.
(Ray Eaton)

Eaton and another crewman, Sandy McKenzie, spent part of the time driving a station wagon and trailer filled with new Ratsey sails across the continent, living, as Eaton lamented, on Metrecal because McKenzie was on a diet.) Meanwhile, *Ti* and Still cruised the Mexican coast, stopping in Acapulco and Mazatlan. Once in Los Angeles the East Coast crew worked feverishly to clean *Ti* and get her ready. But days before the start of the

race the first nasty imbroglio ignited between Johnson and Still that almost forced *Ti* to be withdrawn from the 1963 Transpac.

Johnson felt certain that he, as charterer of record, was entitled to have his own man, Dan Elliott, provide all the crew. This would seem logical, as a race across the Pacific demands sailors familiar with its peculiar patterns of wind, current, and sea state—the "local knowledge" that accrues to any boat's

Ray Eaton, who kept Ti *moving.*
(Courtesy of Pat Roberts)

advantage. But a somewhat contrary notion obtained in Baxter Still's camp: he assumed that the spirit, if not the letter, of the charter agreement called for Johnson *alone* to come aboard and that he, Still, would act as sailing master and provide the crew (that was the way many of Allan Carlisle's charters had been run). Still and his regulars already had their sea bags stowed aboard; they seemed to have had the commonly accepted nine-tenths

of the possession law in their favor. As the start approached, the friction between Johnson and Still heated up, and neither would budge. Nor would either let the other take the boat out to practice; *Ti* just sat at the dock awaiting a resolution. At one point, Still offered a compromise: take both crews out for a test sail and pick the best from among the 25 candidates. But by then the hostility between the two camps had reached

a point beyond compromise. Elliott and Johnson refused.

Johnson, who found little in Baxter Still to admire, had made up his mind not to cross the Pacific with him. He sent Elliott on a mission to Ann Arbor, Michigan, to negotiate directly with Bill Brittain. Brittain was feeling quite magnanimous (having just bought a prize steer for about $100,000), and the two sailors met as gentlemen negotiators over cocktails and dinner. They worked out an amicable deal. Elliott and Johnson could take their California crew, so long as they agreed to take Ray Eaton along; he was noncontroversial, a competent sailor, and he knew the boat. Elliott returned to California, but Still rejected the new terms; he insisted on sailing. The only remaining solution (short of an imbalanced contest of fisticuffs between a stout Bob Johnson and a wiry Baxter Still) was a judicial one. The two parties took the matter to a local judge who, two days before the start, decided in Johnson's favor. In Solomonic style, the judge agreed with Brittain and ordered Eaton to sail as well, to provide his unique knowledge of *Ti's* machinery, deck gear, and electrics during the 2,225-mile passage. Although his name later appeared erroneously on the official crew list, Baxter Still was prohibited from sailing.

Baxter Still was utterly dismayed. His crew had worked hard to get *Ticonderoga* ready; to be told at the last minute that they couldn't sail was pretty dispiriting. In his pique he grew absolutely determined to repossess *Ti* as soon as she arrived in Honolulu. He postured and reminded Johnson and Elliott that he would be in Honolulu awaiting their arrival, and would see to it that they paid for every cent's worth of damage, missing inventory, and wear-and-tear, no matter how insignificant. He was not at all placated by the concession to Eaton. Nor was Eaton entirely comfortable with the prospect of sailing more than 2,000 miles with a group he saw as "the enemy." (His West Coast shipmates, in particular the younger ones, were skeptical of *Ticonderoga's*

Ichiban *carried the Transpac's first spade rudder.*
(Hawaii Maritime Center)

islands, as *Ti* crossed into the deep water at the edge of the continental shelf the wind freshened to 25-30 knots out of the northwest and the seas grew higher and longer. *Ti* began to dig her bow into the building Pacific rollers. She would occasionally dive under a big sea and get completely buried, right over the trunk cabin. Perplexed that this was happening in less than whole-gale conditions, Johnson consulted Eaton, asking if it might be prudent to shorten sail. Eaton, unruffled, agreed, casually adding: "She always does that; that's the way we sail her." In view of Eaton's response, Johnson sensed that *Ti* was not only overcanvassed, but that her balance was wrong because she was carrying so much superfluous weight (particularly in her ends), which caused her to pitch excessively into the head seas. Once they shortened sail and settled her down, *Ti's* motion eased; she stopped submarining and began to plunge across the blue Pacific comfortably, if not fleetly, with Johnson setting her on the prudent rhumbline course.

Generally, the wind turned lighter than the Transpac average for the rest of the race, so life aboard was not strenuous. It was made stimulating, however, by the fact that Johnson had catered the race via Pan American Airways' First Class service: he had filled *Ticonderoga's* deep freeze (as he regularly had done *Zia's*) with dozens of frozen meals prepared by Maxim's of Paris, including Cornish game hens, French toast fixings and, of course, his trademark thick and juicy steaks. (Unfortunately, he forgot to get milk, fruit, and cookies. And *Ti* ran completely out of food, water, and Squirt, the crew's favorite soft drink, a full day before she finished in Honolulu.)

About midway in the race, after some spotty breezes, the Pacific Tradewinds finally filled in and *Ticonderoga* began to move. With spinnaker, staysail, mainsail, mizzen spinnaker, and mizzen flying she rose out of the sea, hull shuddering, white water surrounding her from stem to stern. *Ticonderoga* surfed as none of the California critics had expected; they reluctantly became believers

abilities. The nautical "rock stars" of their day, they had already grown accustomed to keener hullforms, synthetic materials, and aluminum spars. In view of *Ticonderoga's* archaic nineteenth-century shape, ponderous double-plank-on-frame construction, raked wooden masts, and low-aspect sails, they sneered that she couldn't get out of her own bow wave. They sardonically baptized her "The Bugeye Ketch.")

The 1963 Transpac was raced under the CCA Rule rather than the Transpac Rule, which were quite similar. *Ti's* rating was 58.1, well below the scratch. (One of the entrants, *Ichiban,* carried the first spade rudder in Transpac history, a harbinger of things to come.) *Ticonderoga's* crew of California

doubters, with Eaton as their captive vassal, had only one day to get to know the boat; they didn't even try out most of her sails. To enhance her speed, as Still had done, just before the race Johnson had the propeller removed from the shaft. *Ticonderoga* was towed to the line off San Pedro on the traditional Transpac starting day, the Fourth of July. The gun went off and the fleet of 32 yachts headed southwest.

Despite their skepticism, in truth the crew had no idea what to expect of *Ticonderoga's* behavior in the Pacific. It wasn't long after the start that they learned more about her, not all of it pleasant. After sailing 50 or 60 miles westward, short tacking in light winds to get clear of the offshore

The "Bugeye Ketch" finishes first in the 1963 Transpac. She is only hours from having a new owner: Bob Johnson.
(Courtesy of Baxter Still)

and began sailing her with determination. And *Ti* returned the favor by clicking off daily runs well over 200 miles, walking away from her nearest competitor, *Audacious.* So exhilarated were the crew that several days into the Trades the watch captains joked with the race committee over the radio (yachts would report their position in a daily roll call) that they had just found her winch handles and light switches. Ray Eaton remem-

bers, more seriously, that they were "absolutely thunderstruck" by her performance. So was he.

Johnson, too, was euphoric. His ocean strategy allowed them to carry the same spinnaker the entire way, and jibe only three times along the course while other yachts jibed often (*Audacious* logged 22 jibes). As a result of his unbounded enthusiasm, the story is often told that halfway to Honolulu

Johnson raised Brittain in Michigan on the radiotelephone and offered to buy *Ticonderoga* "as is, where is, for $50,000." Brittain apparently turned him down, but did not necessarily shut the door completely. Neither Ray Eaton nor Danny Elliott recall the conversation, so some observers felt that the story was apocryphal. Baxter Still also claims that it didn't happen, because he says Bill Brittain was extremely loyal to him and would have informed him of it immediately, which he did not. But Mark Johnson, Bob's older son, who sailed with his father often and on this race as well, assures the world that the call was indeed made.

The truth is that Johnson, so intrigued by *Ticonderoga* before the race, had negotiated the charter to include an option-to-buy clause, exercisable within five days of the Transpac finish. By making the call, Johnson (who knew that Brittain was looking to sell) might well have wanted to jump the gun to assure his inside track against other offers before he came ashore. In the end it didn't matter, though the absence of contractual clarity and open communication among the parties soon caused two more consummately farcical confrontations between Johnson and Still.

The purchase option notwithstanding, Brittain would not necessarily have welcomed that mid-Pacific call from Johnson. As far as he was concerned, he had already sold *Ticonderoga* to Bob Hamill, that most loyal of charter clients. Apparently, while Johnson

was racing to Hawaii, Hamill made Brittain an offer, substantially higher than Johnson's $50,000. Brittain was apparently so certain that Johnson would not meet the price within the five-day grace period, that he verbally accepted Hamill's offer. Hamill was equally certain he had clinched the deal (he invited some friends to meet him in Honolulu after the race, for a Hawaiian Island cruise on his new boat).

Call or no call, sale or no sale, what is irrefutable about these events is that on this race *Ticonderoga* proved to be no dormant *Groote Beer* or lethargic *Zia.* She behaved as Johnson had wanted her to: magnificently. She stood up well to the freshening Trades and moved liked a train. By contrast, in the same weather conditions one of her chief competitors, *Novia del Mar*, took a tremendous spinnaker knockdown and lost her life raft and seven bags of sails overboard (some of which her crew miraculously recovered when they sailed back to California). In the Molokai Channel, in the last 200 miles to the finish, *Ticonderoga* surfed continuously.

She opened the gap with the other leaders, carrying her huge blue-and-yellow main spinnaker and black-and-yellow mizzen spinnaker to full advantage. During one breakneck stretch of a bit over an hour Johnson calculated her average speed at 14.8 knots. When *Ti* crossed in front of Diamond Head light—a brilliant blue-white beam marking the line—she was first to finish, having sailed the course in 11 days, 6 hours. This was 5 hours better than in 1961, but not near the record of 9 days, 15 hours set by the 98-foot ketch *Morning Star* in 1955. She was followed in about 7 hours by *Audacious*, then by three other Class "A" yachts: *Kamalii, Orient* and *Astor.* That she was dropped to second in class on corrected time by only an hour and a half to *Orient*, a yacht she had to give more than 19 hours to, did not matter to anyone, least of all Johnson.

Once ashore, Johnson was even more determined to buy the boat. He and Elliott managed with great difficulty to track Brittain down—he was away from his office on business—to officially exercise the option. As a favor, Elliott handled the negotiations for Johnson and Brittain settled on a price of $85,000. Johnson wired the balance to Brittain's account to complement the $20,000 charter fee. Johnson was now the owner of a twenty-seven-year-old wooden ketch: lock, stock, and bathtub.

At five in the morning Hawaii time, Johnson, Elliott and the crew were indulging in a celebratory party in Waikiki. Once the deal was made over the telephone, Johnson put the receiver down and announced to the wasted multitudes: "I just bought *Ticonderoga.*" The unruly mob had a few more drinks to express their satisfaction. Later in the day Johnson suggested that they all trundle down the road to share in the glory of his new boat. When they arrived at *Ticonderoga's* dock, they observed a group of men busily at work on the boat—washing down, drying out sails, polishing brass, and tossing out trash. Johnson put out his arms and said *Whoa!* to his crew. He directed them to covertly park their bottoms on *Constellation,*

Johnson (in straw hat) leads his California crew in the first-to-finish gala.
(Courtesy of Ray Eaton)

Herreshoff in The Castle, where Johnson and Elliott had an audience to discuss Ti's reconstruction.
(Mystic Seaport Museum, Inc.)

which Eaton declined, too spoiled by the glories of sailing *Ticonderoga.* When Hamill was informed by Brittain of the sale, needless to say, he too was devastated. But, he still owned a 60-foot Rhodes motorsailer, *Mirror,* and he graciously offered Eaton a job as her skipper. Eaton accepted. Bill Brittain and Bob Hamill were good men, solid and true.

Johnson registered the boat as *Ticonderoga of Lahaina,* after the Lahaina Yacht Club, of which was a founding member, and where he often kept *Zia.* The club, on the island of Maui, is an institution of modest facilities— little more than a bar and restaurant—set in an old Hawaiian whaling port. It was proof (if any were needed) of Johnson's lack of pretense. Once the sale was done, Danny Elliott flew home. Johnson sent *Ticonderoga* back to California in the hands of another professional, Bill King (owner of a Herreshoff "S" boat) and began immediately to consider ways to make her more competitive. But he didn't plan to do so in a vacuum. Within days, on July 26, he wrote to Francis Herreshoff at The Castle in Marblehead. He reintroduced himself (having written the designer only one prior letter, to order some brass cannons), and thereby initiated a long, friendly, and memorable correspondence between the two that lasted until Johnson's death.

In that first letter, after wryly recalling the "innumerable difficulties with the former owner and Baxter Still," Johnson lamented *Ti*'s condition, made note of the extra weight she carried, and described her interior and outfit. He then asked Herreshoff's advice on how to make her faster. Johnson proposed, rhetorically, to completely strip her inside: to remove all partitions, plumbing, fixtures, ceiling, wiring, floors, and engines. By weighing everything as it came out, and replacing only what was essential, Johnson believed he could lighten *Ti* by as much as 16,000 pounds. (A substantial portion of that reduction, Johnson said, would be represented by the huge anchor winch, oversize anchors and chain, built-in bunks and thick upholstery, giant freezers and other galley

moored nearby, to watch in rapture as Baxter Still and his merry crew, quite unaware of *Ticonderoga*'s sale to Johnson, made her ready to return to the mainland. Johnson and his men sat close by for hours, stifling laughter as they watched Still's crew scrub the interior, fold sails, and get the boat spruced up. When they were finished, and *Ti* was immaculate, Johnson marched over, introduced himself as the boat's new owner, thanked

Baxter Still for his noble volunteerism, then ordered him off his boat. This was not, to say the least, a cohesive moment in their already fragile relationship.

Baxter Still returned to Florida. He managed to acquire *Escapade* and put her into charter (nothing like that Hawaiian humiliation could keep a good wharf rat down). Brittain graciously offered Eaton an engineering job in one of his Michigan firms,

gear, the original bar and trappings, and, of course, that ultra-cosmopolitan bathtub.)

Johnson also intended to move the galley amidships, to improve the weight distribution, and remove the enclosed private cabins and replace them with five bulkheads to better divide the interior into a forepeak, a sail stowage space under a larger hatch, an enclosed stores area, an open midships sleeping area, and a navigation and communication office aft where he could "write a letter and pay a few ships bills." He also asked Herreshoff's advice on pipe berths, hammocks, plastic drawers, an airline oven, small freezers, a 6-kW Onan diesel generator, and a small 55-hp diesel engine (powerful enough to get *Ti* in and out of a dock or keep her moving in a dead calm). All of Johnson's thoughts were directed toward making her "as light and simple as possible," and as fast . . . .

Herreshoff replied promptly, approving generally of Johnson's planned changes, endorsing the lighter interior and smaller engine, and urging an improved prop-shaft coupling (to prevent a repeat of the Newport incident, where it came apart and nearly sank the boat beneath him). To allay Johnson's expressed fears about structural weaknesses, he recommended that he test *Ti's* bronze keel bolts, and inspect her most vulnerable structural elements: the bobstay anchoring plate, bronze hanging knees, steering gear, rudder hangings, and forestay deck attachment. He offered to send Johnson a complete set of 30 drawings of the boat (a $1,000 package) for copying costs only. And he concluded with a complaint about *Ti's* measurement certificate, which he believed to be erroneous. (He was convinced that a fair, meaning *lower*, rating would improve *Ticonderoga's* chances of winning "more than many thousands of dollars' worth of improvements." He was reiterating his old grievance against yachts designed to circumvent rating rules, which resulted in a rating bias against many other hullforms, in particular *his* hullforms.)

Even after the exchanges of multipage letters, Johnson's thirst for knowledge of

Ticonderoga was not quenched. He and Elliott flew to Marblehead to meet with Herreshoff at The Castle for further discussions. Once face to face, Herreshoff emphasized that, first, Johnson ought to return *Ti* to her proper lines—he was still rankled about her sitting very low in the water by virtue of the weight of Harry Noyes' many luxuries. He was also emphatic with Johnson that he not go ahead with the plan to add bulkheads to stiffen the construction, as the hull, he warned, "needs to torque a bit." They discussed enlarging the tracks, blocks, and other deck fittings. And Johnson asked Herreshoff's thoughts about adding Dorade deck ventilators, of the type Olin Stephen introduced on his 45-foot yawl, *Dorade* (which gave the vents their name). Herreshoff, never one to mince words about his younger rival, replied with an ungracious, expletive-filled, but decidedly undeserved comment on Stephens' lack of originality.

After the meeting, Elliott flew back to Newport Beach, an exclusive enclave south of Los Angeles, where *Ti* was moored at the Donaldson & Dittmar boatyard; Johnson returned to Grand Bahama. Before they parted, however, Johnson grabbed a pencil and the handiest thing he could find to write on—a brown paper bag—and sketched for Elliott the interior layout he wanted. On the bag he also specified pipe berths large enough to accommodate Don Vaughan, *Ticonderoga's* fullback-size winch grinder. That paper bag became Elliott's sole guiding document for the tens of thousands of dollars worth of work he was about to supervise in California. ("A guy who would spend that kind money on a boat," Elliott later mused, "then draw the redesign plan on a paper bag, has got to be some special kind of guy!" Bob Johnson *was* some special kind of guy.)

Before the reconstruction Johnson had the sailplan updated by Kenny Watts, a local sailmaker, and had Watts and Lowell North's loft build the new sails: mizzen and Genoa staysails; two spinnaker staysails; medium spinnaker; mizzen spinnaker; large reacher; "windfinder"; No. 2 jibtop; and Genoa.

(When informed of the changes, Herreshoff bellyached a bit about the Genoa, which he still insisted *Ticonderoga* never needed.) Including the new sails that Baxter Still had put aboard for the charter and a miscellany of her old sails, *Ticonderoga's* inventory expanded to 30 bags.

At Newport Beach, three crews worked around the clock, in shifts of eight hours. A team of carpenters gutted *Ticonderoga*—one could stand inside at the rudder post and have an unobstructed view to the stem. They installed ¾-inch plywood partitions. They built an enormous forward hatch to ease sail handling and provide for belowdecks stowage (prior crews had to lash spare sails on deck). They cut the taffrail bulwarks back, moving the gilt dolphins eight feet aft to accommodate longer Genoa tracks on the main caprail, which they fixed with 20-inch lag bolts through to the sheer strake. (The extra strength was needed because *Ticonderoga's* gear had been designed by Herreshoff to carry the load of stretchy Egyptian cotton sails, but her new inventory of Dacron sails had far less stretch, thus far greater pulling power.) The crew built new blocks. Carpenters cut away some of the keel aft, restoring it almost to Herreshoff's original drawing, to make *Ti* more maneuverable and reduce her wetted surface. They replaced the heavy gasoline engine that Baxter Still had installed with a small four-cylinder diesel, and they set a small generator forward.

The new plan reduced *Ticonderoga's* interior to a minimalist's dream. The galley was moved aft into the saloon, to starboard: it had a small refrigerator and freezer, and three gimballed platforms to hold simple plug-in electric cookpots; there was no fixed range. To port, the dinette was backed up by a chart table for Johnson to reduce his celestial sights and plot his positions. Forward, one step down in the waist, where the cabins had been, pipe berths were installed along the bare hull, four per side, adjustable to offset three angles of heel (*Ti* was probably the first ocean racer equipped with adjustable pipe berths). A spare pipe berth was set in

Johnson expanded Ticonderoga's inventory to include specialty sails and a huge overlapping Genoa.

(Gunnar Anderson)

the sail locker. The interior results were unusually Spartan for a day when the CCA was cultivating more comfort and safety in offshore boats. To conform with the rule, however, the crew enclosed the head. (Johnson's only concession to luxury was, of course, a small bar in the galley. During a race he never denied his men a cocktail, or a couple of glasses of wine with dinner, so long as the alcohol had no effect on their performance.) The team continued to work on this 24-hour schedule until Johnson came

aboard and saw that they had reached a point of fully diminished returns. He declared the work complete, paid the carpenters, and sent them home. In all, the concerted effort reduced *Ticonderoga's* weight by about 11,000 pounds, not quite Johnson's target of 16,000, but surely a notable achievement. It also resulted in a better distribution of the weight: when Johnson bought her she had been down eight inches in the stern and up four inches in the bow from her design waterline, which increased her stern drag and

severely curtailed her performance. When Johnson relaunched her she was down only three inches in the stern and up three in the bow, a substantial improvement. During the work Johnson also discovered the molded ballast that John Hertz had added aft in the keel (2,500 pounds of lead set in a cutout) and he would remove it on *Ti's* next haulout to set her even more closely to her lines. Overall, the big net gains Johnson effected by all this work were in *Ti's* light-air performance, her downwind speed, and her surfing

Ticonderoga slides into Acapulco after her less-than-dramatic debut in her lightened condition.

(Courtesy of Bob Dickson)

ability in a breeze. Who could ask for more?

Johnson elected to keep *Ticonderoga* in California for the rest of the winter of 1963/64. After a good tune-up and some local day races around Newport Beach and Catalina Island, in February 1964 Johnson entered *Ti* in the 1,500-mile San Diego to Acapulco Race. It is abundantly clear that he had high expectations for his "new" *Ti*, with visions of line honors and even a first overall dancing in his head. To gain further advantage, Johnson acquired a radar (allowed in the Acapulco Race for the first time). The unit, which he bolted to the trunk cabin, gimballed rather stiffly, so it had to be continually hand-adjusted to the heel angle. Though other owners protested (because they didn't have Johnson's foresight) their protests were denied. They needn't have concerned them-

selves: *Ticonderoga*'s primitive radar ceased functioning on the second day out. The miracle of the microchip was still around the corner.

The race started in fresh reaching conditions, *Ticonderoga*'s kind of weather. But for some unknown reason, instead of staying with his competitors, Johnson took *Ti* on a flyer and she fell far behind the leaders, including Jim Kilroy's S&S-designed *Kialoa II*, with Carleton Mitchell and Olin Stephens in the afterguard. As she crossed the Gulf of California in a 30-knot wind slightly abaft the beam (carrying balloon spinnaker, overlapping staysail, main, mizzen, and a small mizzen staysail), five helmsmen hit 15 knots or better, and she occasionally sustained peaks above 17 knots. Over one 24-hour period *Ti* logged 249 miles, for a 10.4-

knot average. (It was during this time of solid winds and rolling beam seas that the crew beheld what Herreshoff meant by the hull's "torquing": *Ti* flexed so much they could put a wooden pencil in the gap between a partition and the hull as she rolled to one side, and the pencil would be snapped in half as the gap closed when she rolled back to the other.)

In six days *Ti* did manage to catch up with the leaders, but as soon as she had them in her sights the air went light and she fell behind again, never to catch up. She was third to finish, behind *Sirius II* and *Kialoa*, fourth on corrected time in her class, and a middling tenth overall. Being a straight shooter, Johnson blamed his wrong-headed tactics for her poor showing. Despite the results, though, he was pleased with *Ti*'s performance; he knew his improvements had made her faster and more agile.

Johnson now set his heart immediately to the west, to Tahiti, entering *Ticonderoga* in the 3,500-mile Transpac. He was now so confident about *Ti* that he publicly expressed his expectation that she could break the record of 18 days, 18 hours held by *Morning Star*. He told intimates that if *Ticonderoga* had her breeze (and he made the right tactical choices) the record was hers for the taking. He cockily wrote to Herreshoff of his plans. Herreshoff responded with advice for Johnson to leave the mizzen staysail behind for the Transpac. (The rules now measured its area, and Herreshoff thought it would raise her rating. And he felt it would add to the strain on *Ti*'s rig and slow her down by

causing her to heel more.) Johnson ultimately ignored this bit of fatherly advice. Nevertheless, Herreshoff said a prayer for his success. In July 1964, Herreshoff's prayer, written in Marblehead, was answered far away to the west, in Papeete, Tahiti.

Bob Johnson never got much attention when he sailed *Zia*. But with *Ticonderoga* (like Allan Carlisle) he became the center of attention; fine sailors (and many of dubious talent) flocked to race with him. He had his choice of the best. On big boats of that era the professional skipper and mate were usually on the owner's payroll; sailing masters like Dickson and Elliott were not the skippers, coming along unpaid for the racing. The rest of the crew usually raced as ama-

teurs as well, but might be paid a lowly wage of a couple of dollars an hour in port, to do varnish and whatever. Danny Elliott took charge of *Ti*'s racing and Johnson sat back and let him do it. But no matter how serious they were about racing, *Ticonderoga*'s crew always had good times on the boat and ashore. They were comrades in arms, never squeamish about drinking, and wherever they went they caroused and ate meals together as a brotherhood. They sought and conquered local women, as sailors throughout history have done; they took the odd woman along for a passage when Johnson went home to his family or off to do business. They adopted a *Ticonderoga* song; they bought a hot-air balloon with TICONDEROGA emblazoned on it, and used it when they cruised along the Pacific coast. (Once, as they neared the finish of a race, they made ready to tow Danny Elliott high above them in the balloon. They scrapped the plan, however, when they realized they would be disqualified by the race committee for not having the same crew aboard as they started with.) *Ti*'s crew obviously spent a lot of money on their fun, some out of their own pockets, much more out of Johnson's, nearly all of it frivolously and often to his dismay. They were truly modern seagoing musketeers.

One of the handful of men who formed the nucleus of *Ti*'s fun-loving crew under Bob Johnson was Peter Bowker. Bowker was born in Manchester, England (not exactly a world yachting capital). He served in the Royal Navy in the war, learning to sail on a 27-foot Gunter-rigged boat. After the war he did some sailing in Australia; when he moved to New York City, where he held various jobs, he sailed on Long Island Sound. In 1959 Bowker got mad at his airline job and quit. Just in time, a friend asked him to take his 40-footer to Florida, where they put her in charter and split the income. In December 1959 Bowker did his first "distance" race, from Miami to Palm Beach; this was followed by a Southern Circuit, a Bermuda Race, a transatlantic to Sweden, and a bit of European cruising. He's messed around with

Ti soon fell in among the big boys, such as Jim Kilroy's Kialoa II.
(Mystic Seaport Museum, Inc./Rosenfeld Collection)

121

boats ever since, gaining a grand reputation as a skilled sailor, competent navigator, and, most important, a valorous offshore cook.

In 1964 Baxter Still asked Bowker to join him on *Escapade* for the Bermuda Race; at the same time Danny Elliott invited Bowker to sail *Ticonderoga* in the Transpac to Tahiti. Bowker chose *Ti*. It was a brilliant choice. Johnson also invited Ray Eaton (there never was animosity between them after the 1963 fiasco). But Eaton was still working for Robert Hamill, and would continue doing so for several years. He declined. What an event he missed!

Ticonderoga sailed the 1964 Transpac with six other yachts; Dan Elliott was sailing master, Bob Dickson and Joe Guthrie watch captains, Bob Johnson navigator, with help from an ex-Navy man, Frank Powers, who took backup noon sights to figure *Ti*'s daily runs. On June 20th, after two postponements for lack of wind, the race finally started off San Pedro in frustrating drifting conditions, which kept the boats in sight of the Channel Islands and the spectator fleet for what seemed an eternity. The light, variable wind, mostly in the southern quadrant, lasted for several days. Despite Johnson's earlier confidence, *Ticonderoga*'s crew quickly gave up any notion of matching *Morning Star*'s record-setting passage (which she had sailed in fresh winds all the way, with a spinnaker set and drawing over the entire 3,571-mile great-circle course). When the wind finally freed for *Ticonderoga*, they did manage to set spinnaker and mizzen spinnaker and work out to an early lead. But, at that point Johnson's most optimistic projection of *Ti*'s elapsed time for the course was nowhere near the record.

As a diversion from his discouragement at averaging little more than 100 miles per day, Johnson tried to contact the cruise ship S.S. *Monterey*, where his son Mark and his new wife Dotty were headed for a Tahiti honeymoon. Eventually he did raise the ship, but in the continued slow going it didn't cheer him much. Even after *Ti* sailed into an easterly ground swell, which normally precedes the Trades, the crew was frustrated by wind that

stayed flat for several days more. With no boats in sight and an overcast sky that denied Johnson his sun sights, their position was uncertain. After a week, however, they calculated by monitoring the roll-call that they were ahead of the fleet by 80 miles or more—some small compensation for the agonizingly slow pace.

Then *Ticonderoga* entered what the crew believed to be the Pacific Tradewinds. They set a reaching spinnaker and *Ti*'s speed picked up to better than nine knots—the promise of 200-mile days had finally arrived. But as quickly as the promise was made, about 1,500 miles out of San Pedro they sailed into the Doldrums, slatting about once more in windless rainsqualls for two days, making little headway. Then suddenly, as though a switch had been flipped, on June 30th the catspaws became ruffles, the ruffles wavelets, the wavelets waves, as the wind sprang up fresh from the ESE at 25 knots. The Trades at last! *Ti* began hissing along on a close reach at 11 knots, her rail wet with salt water for the first time in the ten days since the start.

On July 2 *Ti* approached the Equator after a glorious 240-mile day; she was by now 270 miles ahead of her nearest competitor, *Novia Del Mar*, the scratch boat. The breeze remained strong after *Ti* entered the Southern Hemisphere and, allowing for the changing length of day as she made more southing, *Ti* carved a two-day run of 530 miles, for an average of better than 11 knots, which Johnson proclaimed as some sort of record for a 72-foot sailboat. She had subsequent daily runs of 230, 240, and 252 miles. Encouraged, Johnson began to recalculate their progress and determined that, despite the early slow going, *Ti* now had a slim chance of breaking *Morning Star*'s record. He egged his crew on.

But, as the wind grew stronger and boatspeed increased, a grotesque set of events befell *Ticonderoga*, trouble enough to distract the crew from their best performance. Reacting to the boat's roll, new mercury switches Johnson had installed began turning

the interior and running lights on and off at random, disturbing the off-watch in their berths as well as the watch on deck. As though that weren't enough, the electric toilet's mercury switch began to flush it with each roll of the boat as well. Worse yet, unknown to the crew, a yard worker had inadvertently connected the emergency battery into the ship's main circuits. As the service batteries ran down from all this added consumption, the emergency battery went dead with them. There was no voltage to fire up the generator; they couldn't charge the batteries . . . or flush the toilet.

After much effort (in order to fend off a constant bucket brigade), Elliott managed to re-start the genset manually, and the distraction faded. By now *Ticonderoga* was in fresh spinnaker conditions, running ahead of the record pace. When the breeze went forward, the crew doused the spinnaker and set the reacher, big staysail and, against Herreshoff's advice, the mizzen staysail. It didn't slow her down and the blistering pace continued. When *Ticonderoga* passed Tikahau, in the Tuamotu Archipelago, she had been out just 16 days; with only 200 miles to sail to the finish she not only had a clear shot at breaking *Morning Star*'s 18-day, 18-hour record, but it seemed she might break the mythic 17-day barrier as well, an incredible prospect after a drifting start.

Alas, the wind went light in the lee of the Tuamotus, and *Ti* could barely maintain six knots; she needed 31 hours to sail the last 175 miles. She finished 17 days, 7 hours after leaving San Pedro, averaging 8.6 knots over the bottom. She broke *Morning Star*'s course record by a stunning 35 hours. She was knocked down just one peg, to second place overall (and by only a few hours) to *Rascal*, a 50-footer to which she gave more than 90 hours on handicap. Though the 17-day barrier had eluded her, she broke the unofficial non-yachting record run of 17 days, 10 hours set in 1893 by a French Navy patrol schooner, *Papeete*. In honor of that amazing feat, at the award-giving party the admiral of the French navy base in Tahiti

Johnson hauled Ticonderoga *in California for more refitting.*
(Gunnar Anderson)

presented *Ticonderoga* a special commendation (but only after consulting with Paris to confirm *Papeete*'s time). The 1964 Tahiti Race was a prime example of how everything comes together perfectly on an ocean racer—a wooden, twenty-eight-year-old ocean racer. *Ti*'s Tahiti record stood for 30 years.

In Tahiti, Johnson and Elliott had a final falling-out in a relationship that was already withering. For some time, Johnson had felt that Elliott was spending too much of the yacht's budget on unnecessary items (such as monogrammed napkins and hot-air balloons). But the break came over the subtleties of running the boat: Elliott wanted to bring some Tahitian girls aboard; Johnson, though not a moralist, was displeased because his son Mark was there on his honeymoon. In grand style, Johnson and Elliott went to *Novia Del Mar*'s owner, John Scripps, of the Scripps-Howard newspaper syndicate, for an unbiased opinion. (Though neither was an attorney, Johnson and Elliott apparently approved of arbitration as a civilized method of sorting things out.) Naturally, Scripps came down in favor of his fellow owner. Elliott took some of his cronies and left. Bob Dickson assumed command; with no disrespect to Dan Elliott, a superb sailor, *Ticonderoga*'s best was yet to come.

After this triumph *Ti* and her deserving crew cruised around Polynesia for the remainder of the summer, boisterously enjoying their success in Paradise. Along the way they met the three legendary American career drop-outs who owned a vanilla planta-

tion, the Bali Ha'i Hotel in Moorea, and another hotel in Raiatea. Over appropriately blended libations, the gang organized a race from one hotel to the other, with rather rigorous rules. Starting from the Bali Ha'i Hotel bar, at the gun each crewman had to chug-a-lug a large *mai-tai,* then swim to his respective boat; with all aboard they would set sail for Raiatea. The boat whose crew was first to anchor, swim ashore, then down another king-size *mai-tai* at the other hotel's bar, was the winner. There is no record of the results (but in light of the special demands of this challenge, one can only hope that someday all ocean racing might be so painstakingly structured).

Francis Herreshoff was naturally thrilled at the news of *Ti*'s smashing performance in the Tahiti Race. He applauded Johnson and the crew, and reminded them that *Ti* was nearly thirty years old and that the old timers say she is "the last good looking yacht in existence." But he also suggested that the winner, *Rascal,* was what he scornfully called an "out-of-sight" racer (one whose sail area is measured with her foretriangle only, but when her crew is "out of sight" of other boats they deceitfully bend on unmeasured sail). It was an unambiguous dig aimed at skippers who cheat offshore, gratuitous but not far off the mark.

When *Ti* returned to California at the end of 1964 Johnson hauled her once more to complete her refurbishment. The crew refastened and recaulked the bottom and topsides planking, with the result that for many months she didn't take on a drop of water. They refinished her with new polyurethane varnish. They removed the lead ballast plug from the keel, which raised her stern and put her back on her lines. And they improved the arrangement to remove the propeller and strut before a race. Though Johnson had planned to enter the annual race to Mazatlan, to test the changes, he dropped out in favor of a Mexican cruise with friends and family. But he couldn't resist sailing *Ticonderoga* along with the fleet to test her speed. She started well after the gun to keep

The record-breaking schooner Atlantic, *the only non-clipper-bowed vessel in Herreshoff's Speed/Length study.*

(Mystic Seaport Museum, Inc. /Rosenfeld Collection)

clear of the racers and passed most of the boats rather quickly. Along the way *Ti* had a single day's run of 226 miles, an astonishing feat considering that it was sailed in rather light airs. Later, under working sail on a close-reaching fetch between Cabo San Lucas and Mazatlan, *Ti* covered 195 miles in just over 19 hours. During that time she overhauled a beautiful wooden Abeking &

Rasmussen 12-Meter sloop named *Soliloquy,* 72 feet on deck, which was leading the fleet. Her sailing master, Ray Wallace, was astonished at *Ti's* overtaking him; he raised hell with his crew, hoping to sharpen them up and get the Twelve going. But to no avail. *Ti* bore away in *Soliloquy's* lee and quickly passed her, sailing into Mazatlan first. Of course the locals thought that *Ti* was racing

and gave her the gun, much to the chagrin of Wallace and his crew, who were treated as Johnny-come-latelies. Bob Johnson was more than pleased to be greeted by fireworks, even if they were undeserved. After Christmas in Acapulco, the Johnsons left and *Ticonderoga* was delivered to St. Petersburg, Florida, in time to sail the first event of the 1965 Southern Circuit.

Bob Johnson was not terribly sanguine about *Ti*'s ability to capture silver in around-the-buoys races. He did believe, however, that she would acquit herself laudably in long-distance events and he was particularly eager to sail the Montego Bay Race to atone for his wretched showing with *Zia*. Assuredly, Johnson had developed a new zest for the ocean-racing life (a life difficult at best for men of average size, but particularly unkind to a man of his material *avoirdupois*). Ocean racing is not for the faint, the fearful, or the flabby. It is a life of discipline and dedication: of forced wakefulness when the body cries out for sleep; of spray and wind that turn hands to driftwood; of sleeplessness in a bunk, dampness in dry weather, chilliness in summer; of darkness at noon; of hunger after a meal. It is a life spent in defiance of gravity, using muscles the skiing crowd has never heard of; a life spent in constant, wearying attention to sails, compass and helm; a life spent sitting in water on the world's most callous perch—the weather rail. Ocean racing is an arm-wrenching fight against a vessel's helm, a back-wrenching fight against undersize winches, a gut-wrenching fight against seasickness that often makes strong-willed men want to die before their time.

But the ocean-racing life is a wondrous and worthwhile life when the speedometer is pinned, the spray is flying, the boat is in harmony with wind and sea, and your mates are the best. It is a life, obviously despite his size, that Bob Johnson found alluring, once he came to believe in *Ticonderoga*. By the same token, Francis Herreshoff had also come to believe that *Ticonderoga* was fast. His files overflowed with letters and articles extolling her speed, proof to him that she was a day-sailer to confound the racing machines. As proof of *Ticonderoga*'s speed to the rest of the world, Herreshoff tabulated her best speed runs along with documented high-speed runs of six larger vessels: *Champion of the Seas* (a 284-foot clipper ship); *Cutty Sark* (a 212-foot clipper); *Henrietta* (a 107-foot yacht); *Yampa* (a 134-foot yacht); *Endymion* (a 137-foot yacht); and *Atlantic* (a 187-foot yacht). The tabulation included the date and location of the run, the time and distance, the average speed, and a calculation of each passage's speed/length ratio (an indicator of how close a vessel comes her theoretical top speed, which is limited by her waterline length). Needless to say, Herreshoff's tabulation forcefully demonstrated that *Ticonderoga*'s speed/length numbers exceeded all the others, implying that she was the fastest vessel ever to float.

SOME NOTABLE RUNS UNDER SAIL

Decimal Point in wrong place ↓

NAME OF VESSEL Master or owner	L.O.A.	DATE	LOCATION OF RUN	TIME & DISTANCE	AVERAGE SPEED	SPEED LENTH RATIO Velocity devided by √ of length of vessel
CHAMPION OF THE SEAS (Clipper) Alexander Newlands, master.	284'?	Dec 12 1854	On voyage between England and Australia	24 hours ~ 465 N.M.	19.4 K	11.5 ★ see below
CUTTY SARK (Clipper) George Moody, master ?	212'	?	?　　?	48 hours ~ 725 N.M.	15.1 K	10.4
HENRIETTA (yacht) James Gordon Bennett owner. Capt Samuel Samuels master.	107'	? 1866	Running toward the Eastward in the trans-Atlantic race of Dec. 1866	24 hours ~ 280 N.M.	11.6 K	11.2
YAMPA (yacht) Chester W. Chapin owner Captain Eldridge	134'	? 1888	In north Atlantic.	24 hours ~ 284 N.M.	11.8 K	11.1
ENDYMION (yacht) George Lord Day owner Sailing master not known.	137'	June ? 1900	Sailing toward the Eastward when making the trans-Atlantic record that stood from 1900 to 1905	24 hours ~ 266 N.M.	11.1 K	10.4
ATLANTIC (yacht) Wilson Marshall owner. Charles Barr Sailing master.	187'	June ? 1905	Sailing toward the Eastward when making the present trans-Atlantic record during the Kaiser's race of 1905.	24 hours ~ 341 N.M.	14.2 K	10.4
TICONDEROGA (yacht) W.L. main Cdr. U.S.C.G.R., sailing master John Hertz, owner.	72'	Dec 12 1956	On voyage between St. Tomas, Virgin Islands, and Miami, Florida.	24 hours ~ 264 N.M.	11. K	13.0
TICONDEROGA (yacht) Robert J Johnson, owner Daniel W. Elliott jr. sailing master	72'	June 1964	On Race from California to Tahiti.	48 hours ~ 530 N.M.	11 K	13.0
TICONDEROGA (yacht) John Hertz jr., Owner. W.L. main Cdr. U.S.C.G.R. master.	72'	Dec 12 to 15 1956	On voyage between St. Thomas, Virgin Islands and Miami, Fla.	72 hours ~ 667 N.M.	9.25 K	10.8
TICONDEROGA (yacht) John Hertz jr., Owner. Richard R. Bertram, Sailing master	72'	Oct 20 1957	Palm Beach, Fla. to Miami.	5.0 hours ~ 63 N.M.	12.6 K	14.8
TICONDEROGA (yacht) Robert J Johnson, Owner. Daniel W. Elliott jr., Sailing master	72'	June 1964	On Race from California to Tahiti. Ticonderoga was then 29 years old.	17 days 7 hours ~ 3,571 N.M. This is a record for a sailing vessel over this course.	8.6 K	

★ This record was taken from the book *Five Hundred Sailing Records of American Built Ships*, by Carl C. Cutler. But Capt. Arthur Hamilton Clark in the book "*The Clipper Ship Era*" says on page 278, in speaking about the Clipper "Lightning," the phenomenal run of 436 miles in 24 hours, at 18.2 knots, which entitles the "Lightning" to the proud destinction of being the swiftest ship that ever sailed the seas." (On this day Lightning's Speed Length Ratio is 11.2) On page 282 Capt. Clark says, "in speaking of the Clipper James Baines "ship going 21 knots with main skysail set." This appears to be the highest rate of speed ever made by a sailing vessel of which any reliable record has been preserved" (This would be a Speed Length Ratio of 12.2)

Herreshoff tried to prove that Ticonderoga's *Speed/Length was superior (though his decimal points belong one place to the left).*

(Courtesy of Fran MacKenzie)

Herreshoff represented this as the first scientific documentation of her extraordinary character. He sent copies of the table to interested parties, including Johnson and one or two of *Ti*'s past skippers (one of whom had surely sparked the research by inquiring if her clipper bow—like Samson's hair—was the unique source of her uncommon power). Herreshoff confirmed that all the boats on the table (except *Atlantic*) had clipper bows (*Atlantic*, he said, had other speed-giving qualities, notably her captain, Charlie Barr). He maintained that it was not the clipper bow itself that gave a boat noteworthy speed, but that clipper-bowed boats were usually long on the waterline and had an easy entrance and run. Herreshoff added, in promoting *Ticonderoga*, that the other boats had only one high speed/length run, whereas *Ti* had many (he documented five).

But such comparisons were ambiguous then, as they are now, and they were one of the more illusory aspects of Herreshoff's self-promotion. The comparisons neglected to note that yesteryear's clipper ships needed a gale of wind and all sail set to reach their theoretical hull speeds of 18 or 19 knots, whereas a yacht like *Ti* might attain her 10-plus knot hull speed in less than 20 knots of wind. Also, under ideal conditions, *Ti* was able to surf well beyond her hull speed, but the larger vessels had no hope of surfing beyond theirs. In simpler terms, a small boat attains hull speed more readily, and if Herreshoff had bothered to include a dinghy in his table its speed/length numbers would have made *Ticonderoga*'s seem low. Beyond that, the clippers bore the enormous burden of hundreds of tons of cargo, while *Ti* did her best racing stripped out to around 50 tons of displacement. Yes, commercial sailing ships often competed (recall in 1866 the incredible 16,000-mile race from Foochow to London among five tea clippers, in which three arrived within a span of two hours). But clipper-ship racing was based on the quest for profit, not mere trophies, and these ships were of a vastly different character from the yachts that came after them.

This false aggrandizement was, in its time, akin to placing the 60-foot catamaran *Stars & Stripes* on the pedestal of America's Cup winners for its immoral (not immortal) defeat of a 100-foot New Zealand monohull in 1988; or awarding a gas-turbined, jet-driven planing speedboat the "Blue Riband of the Atlantic" for crossing from New York to England more swiftly than the fully laden passenger liner S.S. *United States.* It is a useless game, and it fails to serve history. In *Ticonderoga*'s case, it did an injustice to the portfolio of her true greatness: that she was generally the swiftest among yachts of her size, and even swifter than some larger ones.

Still, after receiving the table, Johnson succumbed to its blandishments and recounted to Herreshoff details of the 1963 Transpac spinnaker reach, in 30-knot winds, in which she averaged 14.8 knots over a distance of 17 miles, and which he believed was *Ti*'s fastest extended run to date. Her crew at the time agreed with Johnson that this was probably the fastest they had ever gone (or hoped to go) in a displacement sailboat. That agreement was not destined to last very long.

Ticonderoga's SORC debut under Johnson, in early 1965, was not half bad. These were fortunately the peak years of the Circuit; within a decade or so confusion over measurement rules would lead to a decline in interest in traditional handicap racing and a fragmentation of the ocean-racing fleet. Approaching her twenty-ninth birthday, and still very much made of wood, *Ti* had to compete with a new generation of aluminum and fiberglass yachts whose design was founded strictly on the rating rule (and its loopholes). Many of these yachts consequently stood a good chance of overtaking *Ticonderoga* in the computation of corrected time after a race. Surprisingly, few could yet overtake her where it truly counted to Bob Johnson: between the start and finish.

In the 108-mile St. Petersburg to Venice Race *Ti* had a fierce challenge from *Escapade. Escapade* executed a better start, but *Ticonderoga* caught up to her within eight

miles. *Ti* made a few feints as if to pass to windward, forced *Escapade* to sail high and broke through her lee. During the night, in a breezy close reach, the two held close until *Ti*'s crew felt overcanvassed and dropped the main with the intent to tuck in a reef. *Ti*'s speed immediately increased from about 9.5 to 11 knots and she began to edge away from the other boat. The crew, fearing a change to her perfect balance, kept the main furled until they rounded the next mark 35 miles away. *Ti* was first to finish, 28 minutes ahead of *Escapade.* She set a new elapsed-time record; she was third overall, nine minutes behind the winner.

In the 400-mile St. Petersburg to Ft. Lauderdale Race, which swings around Florida from west to east and skirts the jewel-like Florida Keys, Ray Eaton (the "enemy" in the 1963 Transpac), took time away from *Mirror* to rejoin *Ti.* Again it was a boat-for-boat race with *Escapade.* In light winds, *Escapade* led up to Rebecca Shoal until a front came through. *Ticonderoga*, under spinnaker, mainsail, and mizzen spinnaker, took off at 12 to 13 knots. When she reached around to the Atlantic side of the Florida peninsula the wind went light again, and headed her. But during the night it picked up again to 30 knots, veering more to the east, perfect close-reaching conditions. *Ticonderoga* covered the last 60 miles from Alligator Reef to the sea buoy at Fort Lauderdale in 4 hours, 15 minutes (with a bit of help from the Gulf Stream). The last part of the leg was simply wild. The seas were tremendous and the crew often felt that *Ticonderoga* came clear out of the water when she surfed. She was first to finish, an hour and a half ahead of *Escapade.*

Eaton, who had been on *Ti* in this race in 1963 (when she broke gear, including her spinnaker pole), deemed the 1965 conditions rougher. But he found that, as *Ticonderoga* was now lighter and more agile, she sailed better. Johnson's work to put her in trim had reduced *Ti*'s pounding in the choppy seas. His reduction in her displacement had affected an improvement in her ballast

A classic of mismatched Speed/Lengths: the 1988 America's Cup between a monohull and a catamaran.
(Mystic Seaport Museum, Inc./Rosenfeld Collection/Stanley Rosenfeld)

ratio, making it easier to keep her on her feet; she sailed rail *down*, but rarely rail *under* as she had before. To assure her trim, the crew did not let her get overcanvassed, reefing the main rather than reducing headsails. She sailed faster than ever.

The 85-mile Miami to West End (Grand Bahama) Race, in a fresh easterly, was a beat at the start, then a close reach to the finish. The same thing happened as in the previous race. Under shortened sail *Ticonderoga* led the fleet all the way and finished first, nearly two hours ahead of the second boat, but her handicap cut her down to fourth overall. Her rating was still an impediment, but after 25,000 miles aboard, Johnson felt he was just learning how to sail his boat.

The fourth race of the 1965 Circuit was an unofficial one run by the Lauderdale Yacht Club. Each year the race was governed by a varying screwball rule, such as a requirement to set all spinnakers sideways. This year the rule required each yacht to be crewed half by women. *Ti*'s gruff Californians pleaded honorably to the race committee that they didn't know enough Florida women, so the yacht club promised to provide them (at no charge). On the morning of the race a swarm of eager, suntanned ladies awaited them at the dock; *Ti*'s equally eager men helped them aboard with a chivalrous flourish. The race course was windward/leeward; it was blowing "stink." The crew put all the women on the weather rail and assigned one man to choreograph their movements during tacks, jibes, and other maneuvers. To everyone's supreme delight, *Ti* was First to Finish, First in Class A, and First in Fleet. But Johnson took greater joy from the successful brush with his old pal Baxter Still, who was now campaigning the 12-Meter *Anitra*. When *Ti* beat *Anitra* handily to the weather mark (an unlikely occurrence in a battle between a beamy ketch and a slim Twelve), Still figured it was all over; he peeled off and sailed for Miami with his tail between his legs.

But in the next race Still got his revenge. The 25-mile closed-course Lipton Cup started in a puffy gale of 40-knot winds

gusting to 50. *Ticonderoga* was five minutes ahead of *Escapade* at the windward mark, with *Bolero* close behind. But *Ti* rounded badly, lost some distance and Johnson elected to cover *Escapade* while *Bolero* and *Anitra* split tacks and found a favorable shift. *Bolero* went well ahead. Another foul-up at the second mark put *Ti* further behind. On the last leg she made up some distance, finishing behind *Bolero*, fifth overall. Then, as if her screw-ups in the race weren't bad enough, *Ti* ran aground in Biscayne Bay on her way back. It was not one of Bob Johnson's better days.

In the Miami-Nassau Race *Ticonderoga* missed breaking her own record officially by only 32 seconds, beating *Escapade* by 1½ hours and *Bolero* by 2 hours. She also showed her more modern competitors, with their fin keels and separate rudders, that stability and good tracking were her specialty when the breeze was fresh and free. But there were circumstances that militated against her setting the record. First, as she led the fleet on the run to the finish off Hog Island light, a cruise ship, the *Bahama Star*, rudely crossed her layline so that passengers could get a

good glimpse of this famous yacht. This forced the crew to jibe twice to get around the ship. Second, Johnson appealed *Ticonderoga*'s official elapsed time because he claimed (and other skippers agreed) that the race committee's clock had a two-minute error. According to the official radio clock *Ti* had actually sailed the course 1 minute, 30 seconds faster than her record of 19 hours, 35 minutes. The Bahamians turned down Johnson's appeal, claiming that *Ti* already held the record, so why would Johnson want to bother so much to claim it again? *Ti* won Class "A"; she was eighth overall.

The 31-mile Nassau Governor's Cup, usually a windward-leeward event, turned out to be a reach-reach event, perfect for *Ti*. She led the fleet all the way, beating rivals *Bolero* and *Escapade* by about 20 minutes, but losing on corrected time to Bill Snaith's *Figaro*, to whom she had to give a whopping 43 minutes in a race she finished in just over 3 hours. Johnson was offended (again) by the inequities of the handicapping, but was more exasperated (again) at the race committee. He was convinced that *Ti* had broken her

Ti won the 1965 Lauderdale YC race with a gaggle of females on her rail.
(Courtesy of Bob Dickson)

Ticonderoga, *reaching sails perfectly set, finished first and broke* Bolero's *record in the 1965 Montego Bay Race.*

(Courtesy of Bob Dickson/Jamaica Tourist Board)

own record for this race as well. The Bahamian committee refused to concede. Though they confessed that they did not know what the record was, they assured Johnson that *Ti* could not have beaten it anyway. Johnson and his crew felt that in both races the Bahamians had closed their eyes to *Ti*'s successes because Bahamian sailors (including Bobby Symonette) had been aboard during the original record-setting passages and the committee didn't want to erase their names from the books. The politics of sailing, Bahamian style.

The last race of the 1965 Circuit, the Montego Bay Race, was nothing less than a romp for *Ticonderoga*. This race has one of the ocean's most spectacular courses. It leaves the Miami high-rises to cross the Gulf Stream to the northeast, usually on a beat into easterlies, then reaches down Providence Channel, enters deep water between Great Abaco and Eleuthera, skirts the shoals along the Atlantic shores of the Bahamas, runs down toward Hispaniola's west end, turns right into the Windward Passage between Cuba and Haiti, then roars on a lusty run in the unrestricted winter Trades on a beeline to the finish on Jamaica's northwest corner.

In the 1965 race *Ticonderoga* and her competitors started in a squall and as the

Bob Johnson (in print shirt) and his merry crew relish their victory in Jamaica.
(Courtesy of Bob Dickson/Jamaica Tourist Board)

was also able to take First in Fleet and First in Class "A." A blistering "September streak" to remember.

Johnson was ecstatic, as he had every right to be. He was also embarrassed at the awards ceremony, after accepting the three main trophies, at having to climb the dais a fourth time to accept the navigator's trophy. Johnson felt deeply about his commitment to sailing. He thought that owners are generally not expected to be navigators, and he wished that someone else could have gotten the trophy. But he felt just as deeply that if he couldn't navigate, he wouldn't want to sail or race at all; if he had to get someone to do it for him, he would miss something important. So Johnson the navigator graciously accepted the fourth trophy.

Back in his Oregon office Johnson wrote Herreshoff an eight-page, single-spaced letter reciting *Ti*'s triumphs and heartbreaks in the 1965 Circuit, commenting particularly on her not taking much water even when she was sailed hard in these events. He devoted the remainder of the letter, however, to testing Herreshoff's interest in designing a scaled-down "Little Ti" of about 31 feet for his son Mark, who was then twenty-seven years old. The "Little Ti," Johnson wrote, would have to qualify for SORC racing and be just as pretty as her big sister, to be built of diagonally laminated spruce covered by fiberglass.

Herreshoff responded that he had already fulfilled several requests for smaller versions of "Big Ti," including the 33-foot *Araminta*, with a rather tall ketch rig, and the 36-foot *Nereia*, which Herreshoff had done at the request of *Rudder* (and whose plans were sold through the magazine). When Johnson asked if the addition of a centerboard to "Little Ti" would make her more weatherly ("Big Ti" suffered from excessive leeway) Herreshoff discouraged the idea owing to what he saw as its expense and nuisance value. But he did take another shot at the late, defenseless Harry Noyes: he blamed him for *Ticonderoga*'s leeway because Noyes wanted her to have extremely shoal draft.

crew attempted to tie a reef in the main the reefing clew ripped out of the sail. They were forced to go across the line under Yankee, staysail, and mizzen only. But again, and no longer to their surprise, they found great speed without the mainsail set. Soon, *Ti* passed *Ondine* to weather; without her mainsail she had found new pointing ability as well. When the crew double-reefed the undamaged part of the sail, *Ti* overtook the leader, *Maradea*, a new 60-foot fiberglass yawl. While a couple of crewmen feverishly sewed the sail, *Ti* squeezed her lead out to several miles by the first turning mark at Great Isaac. But in the light airs *Maradea* regained the lead and kept it until, tacking in a better breeze down the Atlantic side of Eleuthera, *Ti* passed her. Despite her lead, at that point *Ticonderoga* was 20 hours behind *Bolero*'s pace when she set the record in 1963, and she was closely followed by two smaller boats to which she had to give about 15 hours on handicap; at that point there

seemed to be no chance of beating them on handicap, much less breaking the record. (It was somewhat akin to a baseball slugger trying to break Roger Maris' 61 home run record entering September with only 30 homers. There just aren't enough days.)

But then the wind backed to the northeast and freshened, turning to *Ti*'s favor. Within half a day she was ahead of *Maradea* by 17 miles; in another day she opened the lead to 56 miles. At Cape St. Nicholas, Haiti, the crew jibed from a port-tack reach to a starboard-tack broad reach and set primary and mizzen spinnakers before the 25- to 30-knot Trades. *Ti* flew; between occasional lulls, her helmsmen saw lots of 14s, 15s, and 16s on the knotmeter. She sailed the last 270 miles in 27 hours, and was first to finish. What is more, after lagging so far behind the record pace, she broke *Bolero*'s record by an incredible 12 hours—having made up 32 hours over a distance of 600 miles. When the wind went light for the rest of the fleet, she

One of Herreshoff's Ticonderoga *miniatures: the 33-foot* Araminta.
(Benjamin Mendlowitz)

After their sweet success in the SORC, which ended in April, Johnson's crew of regulars piled their gear aboard once more and pointed *Ti*'s bows toward the sunset, through the Panama Canal, up the Mexican coast to California, to prepare for the 1965 Transpac to Honolulu. They could not have imagined what fate held in store for them. If the schooner *America* gained all her global fame on the basis of one 60-mile, around-Cowes race in 1851, then the 2,225-mile Transpac in 1965 might well be seen as the race that put *Ticonderoga* on the map. The World Map. She was already celebrated in the yachting

press and in yachting circles; her name was pronounced regularly in bars and clubs from Falmouth to Forty-Fourth Street. But the 1965 Transpac was so incredible, so fabulous (*pace* Cecil B. De Mille), that the name "Big Ti" quickly spread to the front pages of the general press and was soon spoken in bars as far from the sea as the golden corn fields of Iowa and the purple hills of Tuscany.

The Honolulu Race is a clear shot in the Tradewinds from Los Angeles to the island of Oahu. Some Californians say that the trick to sailing a boat to her rating is to follow the 1020 isobar line, thus to remain in

fresh reaching winds all the way. Others will prescribe sailing a couple of hundred miles south of the 250° 30' rhumbline into the more favorable currents. All agree, however, that near the finish one must approach the island of Molokai on port tack, overstand the layline and sail by the lee for a time, jibe at the ideal moment, pick up the fresh windshift on the other side of Molokai, and head straight for Honolulu at all possible speed.

In 1964, before the Transpac to Tahiti, Johnson had expressed high public confidence in *Ti*'s ability to break that record, and she did. But he had not been very certain

Only 2,225 miles to go: Ticonderoga *executes a perfect start in the 1965 Transpac*
(Gunnar Anderson)

about surpassing *Morning Star*'s record of 9 days, 15 hours in the Honolulu Race—he truly believed it couldn't be done. So did everyone else (once the record was printed in the official history of the Transpac, it was subsequently referred to as "unbreakable"). So as the start of the 1965 Transpac approached neither Johnson nor his crew talked much about the record. They did talk animatedly about beating their four top maxi rivals: *Kialoa II,* Jim Kilroy's speedster; *Audacious,* an old rival; *Stormvogel,* that three-year-old from South Africa that few people knew much about; and Ken De Meuse's 83-foot schooner *Serena,* one of the fastest boats in California, with Dan Elliott aboard as sail-

ing master. Because of Elliott's presence, beating *Serena* boat-for-boat took on the highest emotional priority for Johnson and his eager crew.

Hawaii had become a state of the Union not quite six years before the running of the 1965 Transpac. With regular airline service from the mainland, and cruise ships calling, the glorious archipelago that towers lush and green above the Pacific Ocean was fast becoming more than the mere 50th of the United States; it was one of the hottest island tourist attractions on earth. Still, any contact with events on the mainland was greatly appreciated by the citizens of these

remote islands. So it was not unexpected that Bob Johnson's friend John Barkhorn, who lived in Honolulu, greeted him a day after *Ticonderoga*'s Transpac finish and told him that he had already sent L. Francis Herreshoff clippings from the Hawaiian newspapers of the race results. What those newspaper clippings couldn't convey to Herreshoff (or anyone else) was the inspired action at sea that incited Bob Johnson to baptize the 1965 Transpac "The Great Ocean Race." Like the race itself, Johnson's title was perfect.

The "Great Ocean Race" started on July 4, 1965. In a fleet of 55 boats, a light breeze, and amid waters churned up by

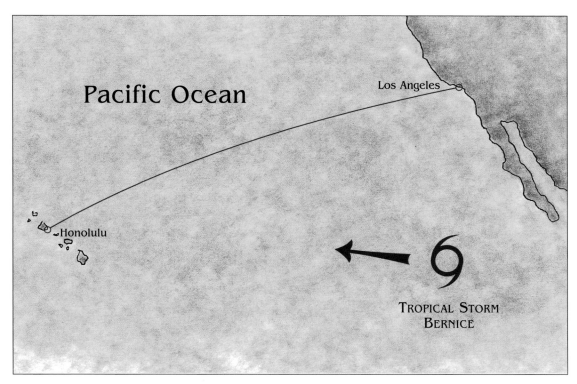

The 1965 Transpac fleet had a fateful rendezvous with Tropical Storm Bernice.
(Map: Randi Jinkins)

5,000 spectator boats, *Ticonderoga* had a superb start. But she lost the momentum almost immediately in the spectator fleet. Then she fell in a hole and was dead in the water for over an hour. Some small boats passed her, and *Rascal,* that pesky 50-footer, was close aboard. No way to get to Hawaii first, no way to break a record. Once the leaders cleared Catalina Island they confronted intermittent fog, drizzle, and continuing light breezes.

The slow early going promised to make the 1965 Transpac a long race. But the situation was aggravated by a dubious weather forecast. Over the Fourth of July weekend a tropical depression had formed off Mexico's west coast; once it hit open water it deepened and was named Tropical Storm Bernice. Normally, these systems (which the Mexicans call *chubascos*) roll off Central America, swing briefly out over the Pacific, then curve back to the mainland, often striking California. As expected, Bernice did initially move westward: on July 6 a Tiros satellite picture put its center several hundred miles southwest of the tip of Baja California, about a thousand miles from the Transpac fleet. But Bernice

did *not* curve back; it became only the third *chubasco* in this century to continue on a westward track. It set a perfect collision course with the Hawaiian Islands, and a likely one with the Transpac fleet.

During the first day of the race the lead changed hands several times among *Stormvogel, Serena, Kialoa II,* and *Ticonderoga.* But, after a handful of sail changes, *Ti* worked her way well offshore, found a fresh, if not a reefing, breeze, and took the uncontested lead. She began plowing smoothly along under 1.5-oz. spinnaker at a rock-steady ten knots. Johnson saluted his fine crew by having Peter Bowker whip up a grand steak dinner for the first night out. After a couple of days of this blessed steadiness, some of the crew found the going a bit monotonous, and were lulled into relative inaction. But on the third day they recognized *Serena* abeam to weather. They sprang to action and watched as *Serena's* crew did the same. The boys on *Serena,* through Dan Elliott's urging, repeatedly changed sails in an effort to find the right combination to take advantage of her taller rig to squeeze ahead of *Ti.* But the more they changed

worse it got; they gradually left the big 83-footer, and Danny Elliott, in the distance. They didn't see *Serena* or Elliott again until *Serena* arrived in Honolulu, long after *Ticonderoga* had finished.

The next day, July 7, they saw close astern the easily distinguished mark of another competing boat: the big red-white-and-blue spinnaker of *Stormvogel* (her owner, Cornelis Bruynzeel, had his spinnakers made into curvaceous versions of the Dutch flag). The crew trimmed up, kept sharp and, as with *Serena, Ticonderoga* pulled slowly ahead, eventually putting *Stormvogel* over the horizon as well. And with some relief. Before the race Johnson had heard credible rumors along the waterfront that under the right conditions *Stormvogel* was capable of higher speeds than any sailing vessel ever launched. She had been meticulously built of light, laminated wood in South Africa by Bruynzeel who, like Johnson, was in the plywood business. *Stormvogel* was more than two feet longer on deck than *Ti,* though not on the water, with tall aluminum masts and a slender fin keel like a Star boat's; she had the shape of speed, and the agility to use that speed well. And she was 30,000 pounds lighter than *Ticonderoga. Stormvogel* (Storm Bird) had every good possibility of beating *Ti* under most conditions, and certainly under the surfing conditions that obtain in the Pacific Ocean.

After a few days at sea, with *Ti* still in the lead, participants received a radio warning that placed Tropical Storm Bernice about 1,000 miles due east of Hawaii, moving westerly at 12 knots on a heading that would take its "eye" just north of Honolulu. The warning, however, did not come as a total surprise to *Ti's* savvy crew; reaching along on starboard tack they had felt, then seen, the telltale cross-swell rolling in from Bernice's churning anti-clockwise winds. When *Ticonderoga* was about halfway to Hawaii Johnson suggested that they jibe to port tack to make some southing in order to converge with the storm, a day's sail away, and enter its northern quadrant to pick up its strong easterlies, which would reinforce the Trades and push *Ti* straight for the finish. Johnson and his watch captains discussed the prudence of the move (one does not always sail deliberately into a storm with impunity). But after Peter Bowker proclaimed that it would be easier for him to remove the ice cream from the freezer on port tack than on starboard, they jibed to port.

Johnson hit it right on the money. Although Bernice had just been downgraded to a tropical depression, its cyclonic flow, combined with the winds in the southern quadrant of a massive high-pressure system sitting off Northern California, produced gale-force winds heading straight for Hawaii. The crew was carrying the 2.2-oz. spinnaker, but in no time it looked ready to blow out, so they changed down to a 4.0-oz., 60-percent storm spinnaker, with a full mainsail and no mizzen. Even with that relatively small area set, the hull rose out of the water and began to fly. Only the most experienced helmsmen were allowed to take the wheel in these stormy conditions. *Ticonderoga* stayed atop wave after wave, surfing impulsively. She rode each crest, soaring at dizzying speeds, steadily hitting 16 to 18 knots; occasionally, she would "lock in" to a wave and the needle of her Hermes-Triton speed indicator would jam hard against the limit at 20 knots. As she rode the crests, water flew off her bow as off a PT boat, and she would throw up a huge roostertail 150 feet astern. Once in a while, when it seemed she could go no faster, *Ti* would slide down the forward face of a wave so fast that she'd send a huge V-shaped bow wave 18 or 20 feet in the air, from amidships, then oversail her spinnaker, which became plastered against the rig. When she would finally break off the crest, and settle into a trough, she was smothered in a rush of green water and white foam. She was screaming along at such breakneck speeds that Johnson couldn't properly say whether this was surfing or not; he just knew it was fast. At this point he began to think, with good reason, that his crew was behaving "like maniacs, like dope addicts." They had become addicts, surely, but to no other substance than that most potent of human drugs: adrenalin. (And they were not alone. After the first light-wind day, all four leading boats had only one 24-hour period in which they sailed less than 200 nautical miles.)

Then, at the peak of the maelstrom, during that preposterous marathon with wind and sea that *Ti*'s crew had deliberately chosen for themselves, all hell broke loose. *Ticonderoga* was boiling along at speeds in the high teens with Dickson, who had amazing powers of concentration, at the helm. Nevertheless, a roaring gust filled the heavy spinnaker and it blew to shreds, leaving only its two luff wires. Unable to set the lighter 2.2-oz. spinnaker, which would surely blow apart as well (and which they needed for the finish), the crew made ready to hoist the big No. 1 Genoa jib, poled out as a replacement for the spinnaker. With the winds now slightly north of east, however, Dickson wanted to get back on starboard tack first, to take a more favorable heading, then set the Genoa. He called for a jibe, a tricky maneuver in these rough conditions. When all crewmen had rehearsed their roles and reported they were ready, he put the helm over to bring the stern through the eye of the tempest. As the boat turned, the stern crossed the wind and, as expected, the main boom snapped over. As was not expected, however, the gooseneck fitting broke loose from the mast and the mainsail ripped from leech to luff about halfway up.

Disaster was everywhere. With no spinnaker, no Genoa, and now no mainsail— *with no sails set at all!*—*Ti*'s speed dropped precipitously (though she could still maintain five knots under bare poles). The crew quickly set a jib, forestaysail, mizzen staysail, and mizzen and got the speed back to 11 knots. While a couple of crewmen jury-rigged the gooseneck, and Bowker and John Rumsey set about stitching the mainsail with their portable Singer, the foredeck crew set the Genoa on the pole and hoisted a second jib wung-out. The speed rose to the high teens again. But, as Murphy's Law always dictates in these reckless conditions, the motion got worse. Without a stabilizing sailplan *Ticonderoga* rolled and yawed terribly in the long Pacific waves. As a result, one of the jibs would now and then come by the lee, quickly collapse, then fill violently again, the noise heightening a drama that surely needed no heightening. After one particularly energetic roll, the poled-out Genoa collapsed then suddenly re-filled with such a violent lurch that it sheered the top several feet of the spinnaker pole track off the mast. The piece of track, along with the spinnaker pole bell and car flew into orbit and fell overboard into the gray Pacific; the pole, hanging from the topping lift, swung free and flailed wildly until one end miraculously jammed between a halyard and the mast, stopping it from inflicting further damage. With no mainsail and no pole for the Genoa, *Ti* was at the mercy of the waves, but Dickson never lost his self-possession. He kept steering for Hawaii, steering for the finish.

Unfazed, these extraordinary seamen remained in control of themselves, their emotions, and the boat. They strapped the main gooseneck hardware back to the mast and rigged a "charm bracelet" of cable clamps, spare jib-track cars, and shackles to hold the spare spinnaker pole to the mast. With so many hands doing repair work *Ti* was quickly running out of crew as well as options. With the pole back on the mast, they were still hesitant to put up the 2.2-ounce spinnaker, so they set the Genoa without the pole and reached up a bit to keep it in trim, make good speed, and regain their composure. In this semi-crippled condition *Ticonderoga* covered more than 250 miles during an astonishing 24-hour period, half of it without her mainsail, which Bowker and Rumsey at last stitched together, then helped hoist and reset. Finally, on the evening of July 11, one week after the start, Bernice more or less dissolved; the wind eased to 20-25 knots and went aft. They were able to square away on a good heading and set the 2.2-ounce spinnaker (but the foredeck crew stayed well clear of the jury-rigged pole, lest the improvised fittings explode as well). Just

as everything seemed to have settled down, early on the morning of the last day, July 13, 1965, a new, more threatening menace arose from the sea: it was a dark image that no one could have anticipated, no one, that is, except Bob Johnson.

With an occasional break in the heavy cloud cover, Johnson had been able to get a sun sight or two in the morning, de-

termining that *Ti* was on a good heading toward Koko Head and the finish. But after *Ti* had sailed more than 2,300 logged miles from Los Angeles and was seemingly quite alone on the gray roiled sea, about 75 miles from the finish a blinding squall came through. As it cleared, and the light returned, the crew spotted a big red-white-and-blue spinnaker, somewhat resembling a Dutch

flag, emerging from the mists to leeward. *Stormvogel!*

It was impossible. The crew believed that *Ticonderoga* was far in the lead, certain of that because for several days Johnson had told them that they were several hours ahead of the nearest boat, *Stormvogel.* How could she now be just a few hundred yards to leeward? They knew Johnson to be a meticulous navigator; they had to assume either that he had made an egregious navigation blunder (not very likely) or that *Stormvogel's* navigator had been misrepresenting his position in his radio conversations, as was sometimes done by more resourceful men.

No one dared assume that it was Johnson who had been dissembling; he was too straight a guy. But Bob Dickson, an astute navigator himself, knew that Johnson's numbers weren't adding up. He confronted the skipper, aside, to see if he had made that blunder. He learned otherwise: for the past few days Johnson had been reporting in casual radio conversations with the yacht *Dexter*, and telling his crew, that *Ti* was 35 miles ahead of *Stormvogel*. He knew well that *Stormvogel* was close, just beyond the limit of visibility in the fog and storm, breathing down *Ti's* neck. He figured that by misstating *Ticonderoga's* position, which *Stormvogel's* navigator would monitor, he could demoralize *Stormvogel's* crew. Thus, if they believed they had an insurmountable distance to make up only a few days from the finish, they wouldn't push the boat so hard and would be satisfied with securing second place. His subterfuge was exposed.

Both boats were under spinnaker now. When *Stormvogel's* crew saw *Ticonderoga*, however, they dropped their spinnaker and began reaching up, in order to challenge *Ti* to a boat-for-boat race they felt they could win. They also had to avoid pursuing a risky course alone (*Stormvogel's* navigator was indeed uncertain of his position). From that moment on, the two boats heard a new "gun," and a new race was on, without a race committee in attendance but with plenty of hard-working witnesses.

As she came up *Stormvogel* showed great speed, gaining bearing on *Ti;* alarmed by a superior boat coming at them, *Ti's* crew knew they had to do something smart. Dickson suggested that the only logical strategy open to them was to sail well up to weather,

and hope to find room later to set the spinnaker and use their longer waterline to advantage on a run. Once they both squared away *Stormvogel's* shorter waterline would limit her speed. They set the reacher, doused the chute and headed up about 15 degrees; *Stormvogel* followed, reaching up higher and approaching *Ti* at phenomenal speed, passing astern of her within 100 yards. Once *Stormvogel* was to weather of *Ti*, she bore away to a parallel course.

At that moment *Ti's* crew had another powerful shock, but this time a rather pleasant one: as *Stormvogel* came close aboard they saw that she had no main boom or mainsail; she was carrying a large Genoa jib set free on her mainmast where the mainsail should have been. Her boom had broken earlier, but Bruynzeel had apparently discouraged his crew from doing jury repairs because, with *Ticonderoga* 35 miles ahead, there was no value in their exhausting themselves to make up an impossible deficit. They didn't trouble to repair the boom. Johnson had won the psychological race.

But there now was the real race to contend with. Dickson suddenly thought they had a chance. He reached up higher, in fear of *Stormvogel's* superior speed. Again she followed, but she didn't have a reacher on, just a double-head rig; *Ti* had more sail area, so *Stormvogel* lost some ground. The wind was up again, to 30 knots now. With the heavier air, even under her shortened canvas, the lighter *Stormvogel* would close the gap quickly in the puffs, only to fall back in the lulls. It was touch and go like that until *Ticonderoga* was able to bear away to set her 2.2-oz. spinnaker and go for the jibe point; her long waterline would then do all the talking.

Stormvogel's crew headed up, this time in order to work well enough to weather of *Ticonderoga* to reset their own spinnaker and take advantage of the wave pattern. They were seeking the ideal angle to ride synchronous waves—the sailor's equivalent of the surfer's "Banzai Pipeline"—on which to surf past *Ticonderoga*. As the yachts approached Molokai Channel, the wind piped up to 40

knots, quite normal for that stretch where the air funnels between Molokai to the south and Oahu to the north. Up to weather, once she found her best wind and sea angle, *Stormvogel* bore away for *Ticonderoga*. The seas were mountainous. Both boats were surfing, with spray flying from their bows. *Ti* never fell below 11 knots; on the waves she hit 14, 16, 18. *Stormvogel*, hitting spurts over 20 knots, regained some lost ground. But through it all *Ticonderoga's* crew kept her straight on a heading to the finish, while *Stormvogel's* crew repeatedly tacked downwind in search of a better rhythm, a better groove. She was sailing faster than *Ticonderoga*, yes, but she was covering greater distance. The question was: Which would prevail, speed or distance? When she came down from her windward position for the last time, she had her answer. After all that brutal work *Stormvogel* had fallen several hundred yards astern of *Ticonderoga*. At that point Chip Cleary, the watch captain, asked crewman Skip Allan if he wanted to steer to the finish. Allan, a fine California sailor, felt he didn't know the boat well enough; he deferred to Dickson (it was the only time Allen turned down the helm in his ocean-racing life). Dickson remained at the wheel for the last 35 miles, enduring more than two hours of wearing concentration and cruel physical stress.

At Koko Head, with six miles to go, *Ticonderoga* was a half mile ahead. Dickson calmly prepared the crew for one more maneuver: the final jibe to the finish. It was dark now, nearing midnight, and *Ti* was sailing steadily at 12 knots. With all the crewmen in position, their hearts pumping fiercely, Dickson rehearsed them carefully then gave the command to jibe. He turned the boat. As *Ti's* sweet transom and flowing nameboard were shown broad and full to Aeolus, the god of the wind, the trimmer overhauled the mainsheet, the foredeck crew tripped the pole to free the guy from its jaws and called for the topping lift to be slacked so the pole would dip and swing under the headstay. *Ticonderoga's* topping lift was set on an old reel

The approach to Koko Head, Oahu, the final turning mark to the finish at Diamond Head.

(Phil Uhl)

winch (Baxter Still had used it for the Genoa halyard). The mast man released the winch brake but the pole refused to budge. As happens *always* with reel winches under pressure, the wire had sprung and jammed between the reel and the housing. As *Ticonderoga* came though the jibe the mainsail snapped over but the pole remained frozen high above the foredeck. In 30 knots of wind, in a miserable roll, Dickson kept the spinnaker flying without the pole, sailing behind the enormous sail without letting it break, while the rolling became more miserable without the pole's stabilizing effect. And *Stormvogel* was roaring over Dickson's shoulder.

Suddenly, after no small amount of shouting, kicking and cursing, the reel winch let go and the pole came crashing down, falling to the weather side; its outboard end was caught immediately in the boiling bow wave and it slid viciously aft along the rail until it smashed against the shrouds, nearly splitting in half. Thinking instantly, Dickson called for more spinnaker trim; he headed up to make *Ticonderoga* heel in order to get the pole end out of the water to take the pressure off; it was about to snap like a matchstick. The crew quickly hauled the pole end on deck, snapped the new guy into the jaws, raised the pole, and squared away. Jibe complete!

Bob Johnson later wrote of that frightful moment: "I have great admiration for the aptitude and precision of the America's Cup sailors. They are artists. But we are in a different business. Accomplishing a dip-pole jibe at night in 30 foot seas, 40 knots of wind, with a 3,800 square foot, 2.2-ounce Dacron spinnaker is not exactly child's play. Add to this a 30-year-old-ketch with a bowsprit that takes the man on it under water, a rainsquall, jury-rigged spinnaker hardware to replace the regular spinnaker pole gear that ripped right off the mast three days before, and the sum total is a situation that comes under the heading of amateur sport and offers security somewhat less than a foxhole in South Vietnam. A professional seaman wouldn't attempt it. Good sense and the union rules wouldn't permit it. . . ."

Being no union man, after settling on the new jibe, Dickson had the crew briefly set a reacher and he headed *Ti* up 25 degrees, using that waterline to finally pull away from *Stormvogel.* Then he bore away for the finish. In the inky haze, intermittently illuminated by Diamond Head's light, *Ti* closed on the line with *Stormvogel* now more than a thousand yards behind. At the finish, yachts had to leave the flashing-red Diamond Head buoy to starboard. But there was one last problem for *Ticonderoga*'s valiant crew. As they approached the line they could see not one but hundreds of red lights flashing in the pitch-dark night. Hearing of the electrifying boat-for-boat race taking place at their doorstep, local folk had assembled into a huge, bobbing spectator fleet around the finish line. Many of the boats' red port running lights, low on the water, were rhythmically being occulted by the choppy sea; they all looked like red navigation flashers, making it nearly impossible to pick out the real one. With *Stormvogel* still bearing down, it was panic on deck until they did pick it out. One man was assigned to do nothing but stare at and point to it for Dickson to follow, like tracking a man overboard, until *Ticonderoga* passed the buoy by a few feet. *Stormvogel* crossed 5 minutes, 48 seconds later. In addition to the spectator fleet, several thousand people were gathered ashore watching the finish. Automobiles were parked with their lights on; every piling, dock and boat was filled with cheering people trying to see how a twenty-nine-year old clipper-bowed yacht with gilt scrollwork, dolphins, and trailboards could beat a modern, sophisticated composite-built boat two-thirds her weight. And beat her she did. (Six hours later, in another thrilling boat-for-boat finish, *Kialoa II,* with a broken spinnaker pole, roared

Ti cuts through Diamond Head Light's beam, marking the finish of the 'Race of the Century.'
(UPI/Corbis-Bettmann)

THE FINAL CURTAIN

1965–1971

AT A DINNER given by the Transpacific Yacht Club, one of the Transpac Race sponsors, Commodore Ralph Phillips made this unequivocal declaration: *"Ticonderoga* now holds more elapsed-time records than any ship in the world and, in fact, probably more than any yacht ever built." *Ti* had climbed to the summit of ocean racing, and it would have been reasonable to assume that she had few peaks remaining to conquer. If you had made that rash assumption in the summer of 1965, you would have been wrong. Dead wrong. *Ticonderoga* had thousands of miles of hard-fought challenges and a number of incredible races ahead of her. But her appearance in the 1965 Transpac would not only be her last in that race, it would also be the last Transpac won by an old timer; a new breed of modern sleds was sailing over the horizon, armed to conquer.

Fresh from his Transpac win, and still feeling the impact of all that broken gear, Johnson had *Ticonderoga* sailed back to

'Big Ti' sails in California waters.
(Gunnar Anderson)

Newport Beach for more work. He replaced much of her rigging. He replaced the single spinnaker pole track with three separate tracks, and outfitted *Ti* with three poles, so the crew would never have to perform another one of those hair-raising, life-threatening dip-pole jibes in the midst of a gale-ridden sea. He increased the size of all her gear and fittings. As far as Bob Johnson was concerned, *Ticonderoga* had broken everything she was going to break and she was never again going to be handicapped by gear failure. He replaced some sails and added more heavy spinnakers. He generally refurbished her. Then *Ti* was sailed up to San Francisco for the Big Boat Series, a four-race event for first-class ocean racers.

As might have been expected, the crew's inevitable post-Transpac letdown, and some of *Ti*'s old frailties in racing to her handicap around the buoys, combined to place her ninth overall in a fleet of 14 boats. Her one saving grace was that boat-for-boat she beat them all except *Kialoa* and *Baruna*. That included the new S&S yawl, *Jubilee*, with a stellar crew of America's Cup sailors from the

12-Meters *Columbia* and *Weatherly* (with an afterguard of Olin and Rod Stephens). The other "overall" saving grace for the series was that it was won by a very pretty 55-foot sloop named *Vixen*. *Vixen* had originally been designed as a yawl named *Persephone* for William Strawbridge of Philadelphia. At the time of the Big Boat Series of 1965 *Vixen* was twenty-eight years old, one year younger than *Ticonderoga*. She was the only yacht ever designed to the CCA Rule by a curmudgeonly East Coast naval architect who otherwise refused to recognize the rule: L. Francis Herreshoff.

In the autumn of 1965, during a respite between races, Johnson brought *Ticonderoga* to California for some more work. This time, however, as a further precaution against gear failure, he had both masts unstepped and stripped of all metallic parts. Every item was x-rayed for cracks and casting flaws, and replaced where necessary. Then in early 1966, approaching her thirtieth birthday, *Ticonderoga* joined many of her California friends again to race to Acapulco, an event

Germania *(ABOVE) and* Audacious *saw lots of* Ticonderoga's *transom in the Transatlantic and Skaw Races.*
(Mystic Seaport Museum, Inc./Rosenfeld Collection)

Swedish, and Norwegian yacht clubs; the responsibility for setting the course and running the race rotates among them. This year the Royal Danish Yacht Club was celebrating its 100th anniversary, so it assumed its turn to run the race. The Danes laid out the course to start north of Copenhagen, off Elsinore (Kronborg) Castle, the fabled setting of Shakespeare's "Hamlet." It ran across the Kattegat to Skagen, then on the Skagerrak to Kristiansand, Norway, turned east toward Oslofjord, then south along Sweden's western coast, and back across the Skagerrak to finish at Skagen Harbor. The total distance was about 360 nautical miles.

Ticonderoga's top competitors again were *Germania VI* and *Audacious.* The weather was terrible for the fleet of 179 boats. After the start in a very light-air southerly, the breeze reversed itself and turned into a howling north-northwesterly, making it a hard beat into a nasty, short chop. Facing all that windward sailing, and knowing how her mainsail slowed her down in a blow, the crew set a plan of balanced small sails: No. 3 jib, working staysail, storm trysail, and mizzen. And rather than sail high in a vain attempt to keep up with the more weatherly competition, Johnson elected to foot off for speed, even if it meant sailing a longer distance to

Norway. Once she settled down, her heeling and leeway under control, *Ticonderoga* moved along comfortably at about ten knots, leaving all the small boats behind. Soon, however, the wind increased to more than 50 knots; it carried away *Ti's* masthead anemometer and radio antenna. The sea got so rough that at least five boats lost their masts, one boat was sunk, and 97 boats were forced (or volunteered) to run for shelter and retire.

Germania and *Audacious* sailed higher than *Ti,* of course; and their crews ignored her, assuming she was no threat. They tacked as necessary in a boat-for-boat race all the way to the windward mark. Yet, despite the superiority of these two boats, they were out-foxed by a practical skipper. While they tacked in rough water—which widened their tacking angles and reduced their speed made good—*Ti* sailed on one long starboard-tack fetch and soon found the smooth water in the lee of the Norwegian shore. Once in the lee, *Ti*'s crew set the mainsail again and they short-tacked close in along the coast, rounding the weather mark and reaching off for Sweden. A half hour after rounding, they made out *Audacious* and *Germania* still beating; both rounded the weather mark well more than an hour after *Ti* did.

Nobody on the two 73-foot windward-going boats could believe their eyes; in their zeal to match race they had overlooked one 72-foot factor. Off the wind now, and in strong favorable currents, *Ticonderoga* picked up time on the run down the coast of Sweden and more on the reach across to Skagen. She was first to finish, 3 hours, 40 minutes ahead of *Audacious*, and 3 hours, 53 minutes ahead of *Germania*. No other boat finished until 14 hours after *Ticonderoga*. So great was her margin over the survivors that she held her time to win the race overall on handicap; she was the first American yacht ever to do so.

Johnson was frankly surprised at this result. He knew *Ti* could do things that no other boat could do, and he knew that she had to be sailed differently from other boats. But, even considering other stunning triumphs, he hadn't expected such a decisive victory. Nor had he expected her to suffer so much abuse—she had a broken generator and bilge pumps, damaged headstay, and ripped sails. Johnson took her to Copenhagen for repairs. He flew to meet his wife for some well-deserved time off in London's fine restaurants and fancy shops. But his holiday was cut short when the crew called him back: the King of Denmark was scheduled to hand out the trophies at the awards dinner and it would have been an insult if he missed the event.

After the Skaw Race, Johnson treated his gang to some time ashore in Gothenburg,

Bob Johnson and his Skaw Race trophies.
(Courtesy of Mark Johnson)

Sweden. Then, with Ramona aboard, they took a leisurely cruise, heading southwest, across the eastern reaches of the North Sea. In rough weather they sailed past the low, sandy German East Frisian Islands (the real-life setting of Erskine Childers' haunting novel, *The Riddle of the Sands*), through the canals and locks of Holland, and on into the intricate waterways of Amsterdam. The Johnsons and a few stragglers did a bit of touring, taking in museums, canal trips, and good food in this most lovely and humane of world-class cities. On the sentimental occasion of *Ticonderoga*'s thirtieth birthday—August 10, 1966—Johnson took a few moments aside to contemplate the total mileage she had logged since he bought her in Hawaii. Excluding much daysailing, he calculated she had covered more than 50,000 nautical miles in just over three years. He was pleased with that record, and took pride that *Ticonderoga* shared with *Ondine* and *Storm-*

vogel the distinction of being one of the most traveled racing yachts on the scene.

He shared that news in one of his typically long, cordial letters to Francis Herreshoff, narrating the year's events, offering his amazement that a thirty-year-old yacht would be capable of such stellar performances against modern racing machines with "aluminum and plastic hulls, aluminum spars, rod-rigging, high-powered bicycle winches, etc." Johnson was, of course, correct. *Ti* was proving Herreshoff's now almost redundant contention that a boat not designed to the rule could still be as fast as (or, better yet, faster than) those designed to the rule.

From Amsterdam *Ticonderoga* headed for Rotterdam, Oostende on Belgium's North Sea coast, and across the Channel to Cowes. *Ti*'s crew always had good times cruising, with or without Johnson. Everywhere they went the boat was recognized and treated as the celebrity, the showpiece, she was. And local folk, sailors or not, welcomed her and treated them as heroes. Everywhere they went it was diverting, and warm, and comfortable. Everywhere, that is, except the hallowed turf of the Royal Yacht Squadron. Despite *Ticonderoga*'s worldwide fame and the unequivocal prowess of her crew, when they arrived in Cowes, on the Isle of Wight, they were denied entry into the headquarters club. It is not certain that they were rejected because they wore the wrong blazers or the wrong striped ties, or if they simply wore no blazers and ties at all; it is known they were a rough and honest bunch of characters whose oil was deemed immiscible with the salty water of England's yachting upper crust. Happily, the other, more empathetic Cowes clubs welcomed them with open arms, big hearts, and well-stocked bars. On balance, nothing was lost (and cheerio to stuffiness).

While the Johnsons toured the Continent, *Ti* sailed to Lisbon (stopping in Cherbourg to duck some miserable weather, and being mistreated by French authorities). In Lisbon she was hauled for a paint job, then she sailed to Majorca. In October

Johnson called Bob Dickson, who was in charge, with instructions to bring *Ti* immediately to Grenada for haulout and work: he was anxious to have her home. Over Johnson's objections, to avoid the hurricane season, Dickson waited a month, using the time to advertise for a couple of women to join his delivery crew (Dickson always tried to take female companions on his non-racing passages, and he was certainly not alone in that desire). When the notice came out in a local newspaper there was a line of lovely Spanish volunteers around the dock. But Dickson didn't take any of them: Ramona Johnson was more austere than her free-spirited husband and she objected to such (universal) practices.

Ticonderoga stopped in Gibraltar, Madeira, and the Canaries, and from there headed across the Atlantic. Once she arrived in Grenada, and the work was done, the pace slowed accordingly. The Johnsons cruised the Caribbean during the winter of 1966/67. Little by little, many of *Ti*'s more mature and experienced crewmen, foreseeing little action, scattered to the four winds and committed to campaigning other boats. *Ti* was left with a less discriminating crew, not particularly versed in the gentle art of yachtsmanship. They quickly developed a dishonorable image for themselves and gave the boat a slightly off-color name throughout the islands. Johnson didn't like the vibrations he was receiving. It was too late to put his best East Coast crew together in time to sail another SORC, so he planned rounding up some of his old California mates and hauling out of the Caribbean in the spring of 1967 to return for more West Coast racing, and another Transpac to Honolulu. He had a novel incentive this time. The California Yacht Club had invited *Stormvogel* and *Ticonderoga* to sail a match race. It was a relatively new event, pairing a modern and a classic yacht, which had been sailed only twice (by *Kialoa II* against *Columbia*, and *Chubasco* against *Narragansett*).

Johnson was pleased by the invitation but he postponed his acceptance for good reason:

Jamaica beckoned. Before he made his mind up about heading west, he entered *Ti* in the 1967 Miami to Montego Bay Race, his great East Coast obsession. Though he tried once more to round up his best regulars, several, including Peter Bowker, had found other commitments. Bowker and the others would regret having accepted berths on other boats. The 1967 Montego Bay Race turned out to be one of *Ticonderoga*'s most glorious of her many glorious performances.

The are moments in this sporting life when the energy of the universe suddenly focuses with perfect timing for an individual or team to reach beyond the norm and smash through to victory. Who knows where this energy comes from, or how it is focused. "Broadway" Joe Namath experienced it when his New York Jets took Super Bowl III from the superior Baltimore Colts; Mark Spitz experienced it in the 1972 Olympics when he won five gold medals for swimming. We know that history often records these sporting events in the same reverential tones it reserves for the miracle of birth and the tragedy of death. Humanity hungers for such triumphs in a world bereft of much inspiration, and when they occur they can momentarily suppress the cares and woes of a populace otherwise distracted.

It is no arrogation, then, to add *Ticonderoga*'s 1967 Jamaica Race to the annals of such triumphs, and to try to document it here. But, like countless ocean races, it is difficult to reconstruct just why this race was such a triumph. This is because an ocean race—in which a baker's dozen stalwart men sweat and strain in concert, 24 hours a day over a span of several days, to squeeze the last ounce of speed out of a great inert machine—takes place wholly out of view and earshot of the public. Mark Spitz and Joe Namath performed their magic before worldwide television audiences of millions. But ocean racing, particularly in American waters, is not a spectator sport. *Ticonderoga*'s crew, like the crews of a thousand racers before and since, performed at sea—out of

sight of shore, in the black of night, in days bedimmed by squalls—with no television cameras, Klieg lights, microphone booms, or "color" commentators to render a blow-by-blow description for the masses. They just bent to their tasks as a team, as a family, making their abbreviated log entries serve as the only record of their achievement, until it was over. When it was over, the rest of the world knew the story of the race only by its statistics—who finished in what place—not by its noble, moment-to-moment athleticism.

In this respect, ocean racers are like scuba divers breaking the surface after a magnificent reef dive below. They can only share the magnificence of the deep among themselves; even the best photographs won't do. Thus the public can never know the joys, fears, tastes, smells, routines, and satisfactions of trimming sail, steering by instinct, navigating by the stars, being awakened from sleep, eating dull food, and facing cold spray, day and night, for the sole purpose of finishing as swiftly as possible (thereby bringing an end to adversity, even as it terminates fellowship).

If the 1967 Montego Race, which started on March 20, was such a triumph—and certainly it was—it is only fitting to let Bob Johnson describe it, briefly, as he did in a letter to his dear correspondent, L. Francis Herreshoff:

> A good ship is a living thing, every sailor knows that. And if a ship has a heart, the Big Ti has one. She started to move and in 24 hours passed the whole fleet ahead of her. Then some gear broke and she fell behind the leaders with less than 25 percent of the race left. She had no chance left to win on the handicaps, but she had to be first. Like a racehorse, she put on her final stretch drive as the wind buil[t] up the seas longer and bigger. She swept past the leaders and into Montego Bay 2 ½ hours ahead of the next ship, but 18 hours behind her time of two years previous. She was leaking badly and had

Cornelis Bruynzeel gave Stormvogel *a bowsprit in time for the heavenly match race that was never to be.*
(Hawaii Maritime Center)

broken gear. She had given one final great performance . . . ."

One final great performance. Mighty words indeed. And prophetic words as well. After that thrilling first-to-finish, if not record-breaking, run to Jamaica, Johnson faced a dilemma. He had planned, after the race, to have Bob Dickson sail *Ti* to California for yet another Transpac and the made-in-heaven match race with *Stormvogel.* (He had learned that Cornelis Bruynzeel, in preparation for the match, was adding a small bowsprit to *Stormvogel* to increase her foretriangle and make her more competitive. Johnson knew it would be a battle as great as in 1965.) But two glaring realities forced Johnson to change his mind and not send *Ti* to California: *Ticonderoga*'s troublesome leaks, and his growing obsession with building a new boat.

In Montego Bay Johnson met up with his trusted offshore cook and fellow offshore navigator, Peter Bowker, who had sailed to Jamaica on another yacht. He asked Bowker to deliver *Ti* to Freeport; she was coming home. Bowker organized a crew and set out. Rather than sailing northeast, into the teeth of the Trades and the vicious head seas and currents that funnel through the Windward Passage, Bowker took the quartering breeze and headed northwest, sailing for the Yucatan Channel's strong north-running currents to pick up the Gulf Stream in the

ed its flat surface to the sea and my knees would involuntarily bend, the deflection was so enormous. It was fairly hellish and fairly grueling, and certainly damaging to the boat. And they wondered why her sides didn't fall clean off after Montego Bay. *Ticonderoga* wasn't built for racing. She was a daysailer. For those who have sailed aboard her there is no other vessel that compares. She certainly occupies a special place in my life."

Eaton was speaking for himself. He was speaking for many people. He was speaking for the world.

Ticonderoga was now nearly thirty-one years old and had well over 100,000 miles under her keel, half of them with Bob Johnson. Despite his sentimental attachment to the old girl, he knew that she was no longer a serious contender for silver. She had won all those races, broken all those records, and held as many as 30 at one time (some of which may stand forever because the races are no longer run). There was surely no way *Ti* could handle yet another SORC of potentially destructive round-the-buoys racing. Even if he had been inclined to spend the small fortune needed to put her right, *Ti* might not stand a chance against the growing new breed of lighter wooden-boat killers being built to faster, rule-driven designs.

It was in no way an indication of a loss of his deep affection for *Ti* that Johnson was looking to a new ocean racer; it was surely the sense that it was time to move on to a boat more in tune with the times, a boat that was, if possible, even more competitive than *Ti*. Indeed, for months his crew had seen him sketching ideas, testing notions for a lightweight sled capable of winning the Transpac. Johnson didn't much care about winning on corrected time; he wanted to get across the finish line first (and he jealously hoped to break *Ticonderoga*'s records before a sled owned by another man did). But before moving on, Johnson had to dispose of *Ticonderoga* in some proper way. He informed the crew, through Peter Bowker, that they were free to find new decks to race on; *Ticonderoga*

Ticonderoga's most glorious racing days were over. . . .
(Gunnar Anderson)

was staying at Spencer's indefinitely. (He then offered to navigate for Cornelis Bruynzeel, on the improved *Stormvogel* in the 1967 Transpac; his offer was graciously accepted by Bruynzeel out of mutual respect and admiration.)

Johnson's first thought, after learning that *Ticonderoga* was being held together only by benevolent water pressure and unspoken prayer, was to place her with a broker in order to sell her. But to a man who loved her so profoundly, that seemed risky: it might have placed *Ticonderoga* in the hands of someone who did not appreciate her, respect the nobility of her past, or minister to her needs as they would surely arise. And the equally problematic prospect of a buyer's having immediately to make an enormous investment in *Ti*'s structural salvation, let alone

her cosmetic renewal, would have discouraged the most ardent wooden-boat lover (even Allan Carlisle, had he known of her availability).

An alternate solution, always available to wealthy yachtsmen, was to donate *Ticonderoga* to a worthy not-for-profit institution and take an appropriate write-off against taxes (as Johnson had done with *Groote Beer*). It would seem a proper way to remove her from the cruelty of the marketplace, at least temporarily. (In most cases a donated vessel would be used for a year or two by the recipient, then quietly sold for cash. It was a way of creating a philanthropic fund for the recipient, while protecting the donor's tax benefit.) Johnson thought immediately of placing her at the celebrated Mystic Seaport Museum in Connecticut;

there she could be refreshed, preserved, and shared appropriately with the world. But when he offered her to Mystic, the museum directors replied, with heartfelt regret, that they didn't have the requisite funds to properly rebuild and maintain her.

After consulting with local yacht brokers, Johnson elected to donate *Ticonderoga* to a little-known institution, Nova University, in Fort Lauderdale. Nova had an active oceanography department that was mapping surface and deep-sea Gulf Stream currents in the waters between Miami and Bimini. (For that purpose, Nova's oceanography director, Dr. William Richardson, had developed an air-dropped buoy that released a dye to photograph surface currents, and a buoy that transmitted ocean data to satellites.) The university's development office had spread the word through local brokers, of whom there are legions in south Florida, that the laboratory needed yachts, workboats, and fishing vessels for its offshore work. The donation to Nova was a natural fit in Johnson's eyes, and in the spring of 1967 it was arranged by Bob Fisher, the legendary yacht broker (later president of Northrop & Johnson).

On June 7, 1967, at a gala press conference at Spencer's, Johnson handed *Ticonderoga* over to Warren Winstead, Nova's president. In a speech filled with pride, Johnson sang *Ti*'s praises as having held more elapsed-time records than any other yacht in history, and having broken many of lesser importance. In thanking Johnson, Winstead acknowledged how important *Ticonderoga* was to yachtsmen throughout the world; he vowed that she would be used appropriately and that the university would gain the greatest possible benefit from her.

As was not unusual for *Ti* (whose stardom had bedazzled yachting writers as much as Marilyn Monroe's had bedazzled gossip columnists) the press coverage of her gentle retirement was filled with some of the same journalistic bombast that accompanied her brilliant years of racing. It was largely inspired by a university press release devel-

oped by Johnson out of Herreshoff's self-promoting speed/length table. The release recalled that a hundred years before, the schooner *Henrietta* had won the "Great Ocean Race" of 1866, from Sandy Hook to the Isle of Wight, with a slower average speed than *Ti* did in her race to Denmark. It also repeated Herreshoff's ill-suited comparison to the clipper ships *Flying Cloud*, *Red Jacket*, *Cutty Sark*, and *Thermopylae*, concluding with the fallacious logic that, with only occasional bursts of speed beyond 20 knots, *Ticonderoga* was generally faster than they were and deserved some special recognition for being so.

After the donation ceremony, most of the ballyhoo was repeated by factually challenged journalists writing mostly for uninitiated readers. One headline writer got it right,

however, sentimentally naming the story "Big Ti Retires A True Champion." That put *Ticonderoga* in her correct place in history, on the correct pedestal: not jammed among the enormous *Thermopylae* and *Cutty Sark* of yesterday, but sailing beside the ocean-racing giants of her day such as *Stormvogel*, *Morning Star*, *Baruna*, *Dorade*, *Robin*, and *Finisterre*. The greatness of "Big Ti" was that she was capable of beating yachts of her size, many at a time, and that is where her fame justly lies. She was no deeply laden clipper ship hell-bent for profit; she was just a light clipper-bowed ketch with a sweet set of lines and an unmatchable turn of speed.

It seems appropriate here, having extinguished the flames of overstatement, to ask the inevitable question about this great yacht:

Nova ultimately found little use for Ti in its motorized oceanography fleet.

(Nova University)

Hetairos, one of Bruce King's several modern classics modeled after 'Big Ti.'
(Tim Wright)

Why *was* "Big Ti" so fast? Francis Herreshoff might have replied with something elegant, thoughtful, and correct (as he did in the 1950s):

> Take a model like *America*, cut away her deep forefoot, give her a little fuller deck line forward, put her ballast all outside, give her a smooth bottom, light spars and cross-cut sails, [and] she will leave our modern racing freaks of the same sail area hull down in a few hours.

And, he might also have concluded, as he did elsewhere:

> Now, if you own a yacht that is handsome and liked by both experienced and inexperienced people, and it is the only boat left practically that has the romance

of the sea about her, and then if she turns out to be the fastest sailboat for her speed/length ratio that has ever been recorded—you have something to be proud of.

Yet, it is not appropriate to find the reason for *Ticonderoga*'s speed solely in Francis Herreshoff's subjectivity. We need a more objective answer to the question, one that can be documented by the modern scientific tools of computer calculations, velocity prediction programs (VPPs), and polar plots. For that answer we turn to a naval architect, Bruce King, who (like Francis Herreshoff) is an artist first, a designer second. A Californian transplanted to Maine, Bruce King has built a successful career designing yachts based on the classic model, borrowing from

the Herreshoff idea, but extending it into modern forms and materials. Beginning in the early 1980s King drew such clipper-bowed beauties as *Whitehawk* and *Signe;* then he turned to creating spoon-bowed classics such as *Alejandra,* echoing yachts designed to the International Rule, with lovely overhangs and narrow beams. From his vantage point, King sees *Ticonderoga*'s performance as being the result of Herreshoff's clear intent, coupled with a bit of luck. King writes:

> *Ticonderoga*'s remarkable ocean-racing performances were due largely to her waterline, which was approximately 10 feet longer than mainstream yachts built to the 73-foot Bermuda Race limit— yachts such as *Escapade, Baruna,* and *Bolero.* These were all beautiful, highly

developed yachts, representing the style of the day; their owners and designers were interested in optimizing upwind perform-ance, which, to their credit, they did. But *Ticonderoga*'s superiority was off the wind, particularly in strong winds: so much ocean racing is sailed off the wind, it takes a lot of windward work to make up for that added 10 feet of waterline.

We are told that *Ticonderoga* was not designed with racing in mind. I'm uncer-tain therefore whether Herreshoff's dimensioning her to the 73-foot limit is significant. But, in some ways *Ticonder-oga* was the sled of her day. With long waterline and lower displacement/length ratio she performed like later sleds such as *Windward Passage* and the Santa Cruz 70 (designed with entirely different shapes from *Ticonderoga*'s) particularly for downwind races such as the Transpac.

To accomplish a more compelling study of *Ticonderoga*'s speed potential, Bruce King digitized Herreshoff's lines drawing and cre-ated an offset file. For a valid comparison to a competitive contemporary yacht (not a clipper ship) he digitized the lines of *Escapade*, a mainstream S&S design of the day. King ran both yachts through the Aerohydro Velocity Prediction Program, which generated polar plots over a range of true wind speeds from 5 to 25 knots in 5-knot increments. King's VPPs bore out the hypothesis that Herreshoff had proclaimed years before. Comparing the plots, King observed that *Ticonderoga* is superb off the wind, but not very good sailing upwind (owing primarily to her lack of draft):

Ticonderoga's short keel doesn't provide much lift; she makes considerable leeway. *Escapade*'s keel draws a few inches less than *Ticonderoga*'s. But *Escapade*'s center-board, when fully lowered, increases her draft by a factor of 1.8 (to 13 feet); the board functions as a more efficient lift-ing surface, reducing her leeway and pro-ducing less induced drag. As a result, *Escapade* is able to sail about 8 degrees

closer to the true wind than *Ticonderoga*. *Escapade* is faster upwind in any wind speed; her increased efficiency is enough to overcome the effect of *Ticonderoga*'s longer waterline.

Bearing off a few degrees, however, the speed curves cross (except in light air). In 5-knot winds *Escapade* remains slightly faster, mostly a function of sail-area/wetted-area. However, reaching

in 10-knot winds and higher, *Ticonder-oga* is clearly faster. With a strong breeze of 20 to 25 knots, the speed difference in-creases to about 1 knot, the stuff of elapsed-time records.

This is the view of Bruce King the naval architect, the scientist, the technician. But Bruce King the artist must also be heard from here, as *Ticonderoga* is a creature of

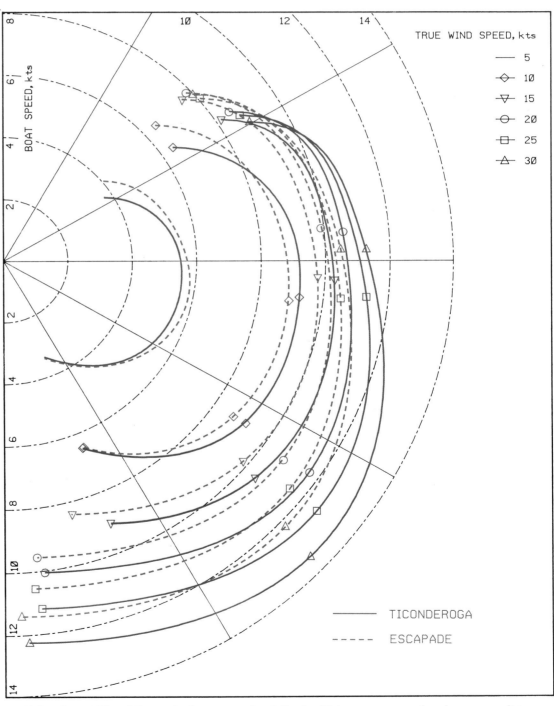

Polar plots of Ti *and* Escapade *demonstrate forcefully that* Ti *has superior speed under most conditions.*
(Bruce King)

many more facets than mere reaching speed and polar plots. She is a creature of acknowledged loveliness. On this subject no designer could speak more eloquently than King:

> *Ticonderoga* stands out among all yachts like a C-major triad against a background of white noise. From her high clipper bow, with flaring topsides, hollow waterlines, and upturned billet, she exudes an air of stately pride, blended with a touch of defiance. From her quarter, her beautifully sculpted transom (crowned by wraparound taffrail and caps) presents as pretty a stern as one can imagine.
>
> With a full deckline forward and spiral sheer, a pronounced powderhorn effect is visible from many vantage points, increasing her visual excitement, particularly when contrasted with modern yachts with computer-generated "plane-curve sheerlines." *Ticonderoga's* racing celebrity, combined with her beauty, has developed her persona into mythical proportions. What makes her so intriguing, though, is not just that she set records, but that she did it with so much style, something sadly missing from present-day ocean-racing yachts.

As it turned out, once she was safely in Nova's arms, *Ticonderoga's* generally poor condition militated against her being used for oceanographic research, or for much of anything else. Like Mystic, Nova simply had no budget for a major refit and subsequent maintenance. *Ticonderoga* remained on Nova's roster only until the autumn of 1967, when she was sold without publicity to the Robodor Corporation. A Manhattan-based company, Robodor was owned by Robert S. Robe of Oyster Bay, New York (a lifelong sailor and former teacher of history and French) and some of his friends. They operated a small fleet of quality yachts in the Caribbean, and managed private yachts for charter. Abruptly, America's most noble, most beloved racing yacht, holder of so many ocean-racing records, entered the crewed (if

Robert S. Robe, who dared to take Ticonderoga *off the racing circuit and put her into charter.*

occasionally *crude*) charter game as one of Robodor's flagship attractions. There was no other way to keep her sailing.

Robert Robe acquired *Ticonderoga* through Bob Fisher, after meeting him in the summer of 1966 while sailing in the New York Yacht Club cruise on his 55-foot S&S yawl, *Magic Carpet*. Robe got a bargain, purchasing *Ticonderoga* from Nova for $30,000. But Robe's paying-out days were just beginning. He turned *Ti* over to Spencer's in-house designers and carpenters, and hired Henry J. Davis, skipper of Carleton Mitchell's *Finisterre*, to oversee a major rebuild. The yard removed all the planking below the waterline and did some repairs to her keel backbone. The fifty-odd broken frames were sistered (new frames were set beside the old

ones, which were left in place). They replanked *Ti's* underbody from garboard to waterline, but kept her original topsides planks and bulwarks. They lifted her decks, removed the extensive rot, and replaced the teak planking.

Spencer's also gutted *Ticonderoga* inside. They discarded Johnson's pipe-berths and replaced them with a three-cabin charter layout to make maximum use of the space. Forward of the saloon to starboard they built a double cabin and head, and to port two smaller cabins with a single head between them. They moved the galley forward to the mainmast, and left the remaining space forward for captain and crew. In the saloon to port Spencer's installed settees around a new dining table; to starboard a big freezer, ice-

Ticonderoga *at Spencer's, in full dress for her entry into the charter trade.*
(Mystic Seaport Museum, Inc.)

maker, and bar. At the base of the companionway they built a large bin to stow an emergency life raft and a supply of wine (granted, an odd combination, but not unexpected for a charter yacht with properly ordered priorities). In areas where painted and varnished wood had warmed the Noyes family in the 1930s, Spencer's now installed the coolness of 1960s white Formica. Though it was not classic, *Ticonderoga* gained an efficient, Howard Johnson motel interior—modest in its simplicity, client-resistant in its materials, and commercially correct.

Spencer's also installed a new GM 4-53 engine, a 12.5-kW generator and 6.5-kW backup, a water desalinator, and an air-conditioning system. They revarnished the old spars, and reinstalled the old standing rigging. (*Ti* had been partly stripped of gear in anticipation of Johnson's building a new boat, so Robe had to replace much of her electronics, running rigging, deck fitting, and a few sails.) Robodor gussied *Ti* up, gave her a new corset, so to speak, to prevent "middle-age spread"; they daubed on some new makeup to disguise the old girl's aging. She could now lift her skirts and dance once more, but to a very different drummer. The work was completed in about six months; it cost Robodor well over $100,000 to convert *Ticonderoga of Lahaina* into a charter yacht with a still-great name, *Ticonderoga of New York*. It gave *Ticonderoga*, in the company's view, a new image (insofar as Formica could replace wood). But the new image was certainly not entirely deferential to the mem-

ory of that other great name: *Tioga of Marblehead.*

Ticonderoga was relaunched on March 23, 1968; Mrs. Robert Robe repeated the honors that little Hope Noyes had done nearly thirty-two years earlier. Six weeks later, on May 9, 1968, the year of the second American Revolution, the first man to rebuild *Ticonderoga*, John Hertz, Jr., died of a heart attack in Miami Beach. He was just sixty. He left a legacy of some considerable sadness, loneliness, and alienation in his wake, but also one of profound, uplifting generosity to his beloved *Ticonderoga* and his few close friends (Dick Bertram, who remained close to Hertz until the end, has on the wall of his living room a half model of *Ticonderoga* with the dedication: "To Dick—The greatest sailor of them all—Affectionately, John"). Somehow, despite the chaos of his troubled days, Hertz had a great heart filled with abundant energy and unfaltering love, all of which this erratic man showered upon his few trusted sailing companions and on *Ticonderoga*, setting a precedent that would inspire future owners to give her several more leases on life as she inevitably aged. In just a few years one of those owners would vow to preserve *Ticonderoga* for at least 50 more years. And he would, as it will soon become clear, succeed.

Robodor signed on Henry Davis as *Ticonderoga's* captain. After her shakedown, he and a crew set out to deliver her to the Virgin Islands for her first charter, joining stablemates *Pride of Cockaigne*, Robe's *Magic Carpet*, and other venerable wooden craft (including *Bolero*, which Robodor managed for racing). Alas, on the way south *Ticonderoga* bumped a reef along Puerto Rico's pleasant shores—Davis, seemingly, had not fully cultivated an immunity to the bottle. Robe sent Brian Coen, his general manager, to meet the boat in St. Croix to sort things out. Under Robe's instruction, Coen took *Ticonderoga* over with the intention of returning to New York as soon as he found a replacement for Davis. It never happened, and Coen stayed aboard; at least he escaped New York's harsh winter.

A transplanted Englishman, Brian Coen had become involved full-time as a yacht captain when he was hired by Robodor to run *Bolero.* He came from a heavy background in military and civilian transportation: Cunard ships, Canadian Air Force planes, and chartered jets. Coen ran *Ticonderoga* under charter for Robodor for the next two seasons. He operated out of St. Thomas and the British Virgins at first, eventually sailing down island to Grenada, which then became *Ti's* main winter base.

With her renown among sailing cognoscenti and vigorous promotion from the New York office (run by a gracious manager, Peggy Hooker), Robodor had little trouble booking *Ti* into a pretty full season. A thoroughly romanticized but very affecting promotional film made by another Robodor sailing professional, George Sustendal, made the booking road even smoother. It became quickly obvious to Robodor that lots of people had heard about *Ti's* racing reputation and knew how she had rewritten the record books. They apparently wanted to charter her just because she was "Big Ti." (But business wasn't hurt by the fact that Robodor could also honestly advertise *Ticonderoga* as the only air-conditioned charter boat in the Caribbean.)

The winner of the 1967 SORC was George Moffett's *Guinevere.* Bob Johnson was impressed by her performance, but more impressed by the unfettered spirit of her designer, Alan Gurney. He asked Gurney to design a replacement for *Ticonderoga* (no easy assignment). Based on lengthy discussions, Gurney produced a ketch-rigged, 73-foot "dinghy," with a shallow, flat canoe body modeled somewhat on Bill Lapworth's Cal 40. Johnson built her himself of frameless, triple-laminated diagonal spruce planking, in a shop he set up under a tent along the beach on Grand Bahama. He used local laborers who had rarely seen a maxi, much less built one. This new boat excited him. But Johnson

felt it would never give him the satisfaction he had with *Ticonderoga;* nor by virtue of its modernity could it possibly be as beautiful. He named her in honor of that stretch of windblown ocean between Haiti and Cuba, where the sea is rough, the current swift, and *Ticonderoga* nearly fell apart. He named her *Windward Passage.*

Johnson went on to great glory with *Windward Passage.* He launched her in late 1968, sailed her to Florida, and made her immediately into a tough competitor. She had several boat-for-boat duels with another fast maxi: *Blackfin.* In the spring of 1969 *Windward Passage* came to California, and in July Bob Johnson realized one of his greatest ambitions: He and *Passage* broke *Ticonderoga's* elapsed-time record in the Transpac to Honolulu, a dream come true for Johnson (even if it had to be at *Ticonderoga's* expense). But, the race committee penalized *Passage* two hours after hearing a protest filed by the skipper of a smaller yacht, *Espirit,* over an infraction at the start. This erased both the record and *Passage's* first-to-finish. *Blackfin* won the honors. Johnson angrily vowed never to sail the Transpac again. He didn't, but for two reasons: he was a man of his word, and his days were numbered.

The estrangement between Johnson and Danny Elliott lasted from the end of the Tahiti Race of 1964 until they bumped into one another in September 1969 at a club bar in northern California where Johnson was attending a family reunion. As men of great depth and compassion, after five years they patched up their old differences quickly over a drink. A few hours later, Johnson, still grossly overweight, still smoking against medical and friendly advice, suffered a massive heart attack. He died on September 16, 1969. *Windward Passage* continued to win races in the hands of his sons Mark and Fritz, who dedicated their greatest triumphs to their father's memory.

Johnson replaced Ti *with another record-breaker,* Windward Passage, *designed by Alan Gurney.*
(Mystic Seaport Museum, Inc./Rosenfeld Collection/Stanley Rosenfeld)

In a letter dated two years before he died, Johnson informed Francis Herreshoff that *Ticonderoga* was being put into charter after being refurbished for $100,000. Herreshoff responded in disbelief that Robe could even find $100,000 worth of repairs to do, because, he said, *Ti* had cost just $70,000 to build ($84,000 with her sails and his commission). The fallible memory still at work. But Herreshoff warmly concluded with a comment of pinpoint accuracy: "I also am extremely pleased that you have appreciated her beauty, for almost everyone else has been so brain-washed that they think the rule-cheating tubs are beautiful."

The month Bob Johnson died, Robert Robe picked up his correspondence trail with Herreshoff. Intending to replace some of *Ticonderoga's* inventory, he dropped a note asking for her sailplan. He also informed Herreshoff that he was having a model made of *Ti* that he intended to bequeath to the New York Yacht Club. (Ironically, Robe loaned the model to a New York men's haberdashery for display purposes; it disappeared and is no doubt decorating some retired executive's den.) Herreshoff responded by offering him a somewhat used blueprint he was willing to part with it "at a reduced price of $10." Despite his generosity, Herreshoff was not enamored of the notion that *Ticonderoga*, no longer in Johnson's capable hands, had been reduced to a stable horse running as a yacht for charter.

Ah, chartering! A sweet-scented breeze breathes life into your sails. Your well-found ketch reaches easily across scintillating blue waters. Fragrant hot coffee at sunrise. Crisp, choice snacks at noon. Cocktails in the evening. A cooler filled with beer all day. Footprints left in the sands of timeless beaches. An evening dip, in a placid lagoon, under cerulean skies. Drinks and cheese in the cockpit. Broiled grouper ashore. A seductive hot shower. The loom of the Southern Cross. Gentle sleep lulled by rhythmic swells. Night-blooming jasmine. No muss. No fuss. No maintenance.

But who cleans the toilet and clears it of alien objects? Changes the diesel engine's oil? Replaces pump impellers? Rises before dawn to percolate the coffee? Refills the cooler? Rigs the accursed awning? Serves the lunch? Starts the balky outboard? Refreshes the linens? Replaces the towels? Keeps the boat clean and off the coral? Finds spectacular snorkeling or an inn unknown to the guidebooks? Or dives for your lost prescription sunglasses? And who, dear charterer, offers you (without official sanction, formal training, or board certification) counsel on money markets, new novels, quarterbacks, nuclear proliferation, the fate of Bosnia, the World Wide Web, Hollywood's latest, and both sides of a marriage's reckoning? Your charter crew. That's who!

Chartering a yacht is romantic. But only for the guests. For the responsible crew, it is hard work. Yes, it can be satisfying hard work, but it is more likely sheer drudgery. That is notably the case when a yacht is booked successfully, as *Ticonderoga* was under Robodor. During the 1969 season Brian Coen replaced all of *Ti's* standing and running rigging, deck fittings, turnbuckles, and halyards. He then tuned her up. And, as is every charter captain's burden in life, he also "tuned up" her acres of varnish. To his credit, he also added to his crew of two deckhands, Angela the cook, who was assigned to him by Robodor. She did more than cook, however; she soon became Coen's mate (first in the strictly nautical sense, then the strictly nuptial). Together Angela and Brian ran a pretty fine ship and gave clients their money's worth. (*Ticonderoga's* weekly rate of $2,500 was reasonable for the period, but a pittance for a charterer who, as most did, regarded her with awe.)

Brian and Angela fell in love with *Ticonderoga;* they found her beauty exceptional and her speed exhilarating. Though they tended to sail her conservatively to protect the company's investment, they were surprised that, even with her heavy interior, she was incredibly fast. They were able to plan their schedules on the basis of a predictable ten-knot average speed, under sail or power,

no matter where they went. But when Brian took the large generator out of the engine room, to replace it, he noticed that she sat better in the water (Robodor's interior had again sunk her below her design waterline). While waiting for the new generator, Coen discovered that her performance was much improved as well. If he could have found a way, he would have left the generator out altogether in favor of the added speed. But, as is obvious to anyone who has been there, no charter party would tolerate the absence of the many amenities a genset so dependably assures.

Ticonderoga had a full schedule of back-to-back charters with hardly a half-day turnaround between bookings. Her typical itinerary was Grenada to Martinique, and back to Grenada. (On one of those trips to Grenada the Coens adopted a Burmese cat they named, of course, "Ti-Ti.") In the off-season the Coens took *Ticonderoga* to Grenada for upkeep, but it wasn't much of a break for them as they did much of the work themselves. They managed to do twenty-six weeks of chartering per year, about as much as one can expect from vulnerable human flesh and a no-less-vulnerable wooden yacht. *Ti* was so much in demand that Robodor was able to raise her rate to $3,000 per week (including fuel and food, but not liquor). Among *Ti's* earliest charterers was Norton Simon, the philanthropic art collector who, like many others, became a repeat client of theirs. It would appear that *Ticonderoga* made the transition from racing thoroughbred to hire horse rather handily.

But in the spring of 1970, at the end of *Ti's* third winter season in her new incarnation, Robert Robe, his hopes for reasonable profits not realized, became disenchanted with the yacht chartering business. He closed Robodor and put all the boats on the market. Without so much as a blink (or the financial wherewithal) the Coens began negotiating with Robe to buy *Ticonderoga.* It was difficult for them to put a price on her. But, as Robe was eager to clear out of the business quickly, he accepted $70,000, half

Ticonderoga had traded the call of the racecourse for the alure of the green flash.
(Dana Jinkins)

his investment. The Coens borrowed from a Connecticut bank and from friends to seal the deal.

The purchase by the Coens, who were already very attached to her, brought *Ticonderoga* two significant cosmetic alterations. Owing to Coen's British citizenship they logically changed her nameboard from *Ticonderoga of New York* to *Ticonderoga of Portsmouth* (for Coen's English birthplace). And they exchanged her American yacht ensign for a British one — the "Red Duster" appropriate for a vessel of her new registry. Thus, for the only time in her life this quintessentially American yacht sailed under

a foreign flag. As a result of Coen's cheeky, if entirely warranted, flag changing, there were some raised eyebrows and long faces among the crews of the Caribbean-American charter fleet. (But they needn't have been so concerned; *Ticonderoga's* foreign-flag phase was destined to be short-lived.)

The Coens considered *Ticonderoga* their private property and were tempted to sail off with her on their own. With limited funds, however, and facing a tidy debt, they chose the more practical route of remaining in Grenada and continuing to charter to pay down their loans. They picked up where Robert Robe had left off. (After closing

Robodor, Robe returned to his studies, earned a Ph.D. in history, and became the official historian for Theodore Roosevelt's estate, Sagamore Hill, on Long Island.) Robe was out of chartering for good. But he may not have been wise to strike the deal with the Coens so quickly. When Norton Simon heard of Robodor's closing he contacted Robe and offered to purchase *Ticonderoga* at a very fine price. But he called too late.

Another man hanging about the Caribbean at the same time also missed the chance to buy *Ticonderoga*. He was far more persistent, however, than Norton Simon. His name: Ken MacKenzie.

BOAT . . .
SHE SHINE SO

1971–1981

IN 1970, FRASER FRASER-HARRIS owned a house on the south coast of Grenada, where he also moored *Quest*, a stout Stonington motorsailer. In an enticing approach to the luxury charter market Fraser-Harris offered both the boat and the house as a package, a week for each, to clients who wanted to enjoy some relaxed time ashore after relishing active time at sea. The skipper of *Quest*, and the more-or-less manager of the house, was thirty-year-old Ken MacKenzie—dashing, sideburned and, nearly all the time, barefoot.

MacKenzie was an adventurous spirit who had been running boats in the Caribbean for five years. Born in 1940 to a working-class New Hampshire family, as a child he moved to Maine where his father became a machinist at the illustrious Bath Iron Works, which built a mix of commercial and naval vessels. At the onset of World War II the elder MacKenzie joined the Navy, serving in submarines. Following somewhat

Chartering: two weeks before the mast. . . .
(PPL/Alastair Black)

in his father's footsteps, Ken joined the Navy Reserve after finishing high school. In the mid-1950s he did a three-year active-duty hitch as a quartermaster on a destroyer, serving in the Mediterranean, Persian Gulf, Indian Ocean, and Caribbean. By the time he was mustered out MacKenzie had gained his sea legs, but he had few prospects and less money. So he went to California to seek his fortune in the boom and balm of Orange County residential construction.

In driving to and from work on the freeway MacKenzie passed Disneyland twice each day; but not once did he have the time or inclination to enter its sacred grounds or experience its synthetic charm. It wasn't long before his laid-back New England soul found frenetic California life totally disagreeable. After a year or so out of his element, MacKenzie returned to the quiet of Maine, to ricochet between vocations in carpentry, bricklaying, house (and fine-art) painting, picture framing, and insurance sales. Although the insurance game finally earned him a bit of pocket change, its stultifying routine repelled him (as had the

Santa Ana Freeway). MacKenzie broke loose from the allure of the shore to again go to sea, this time on bluewater sailboats.

Until then Ken MacKenzie's sailing resume had very few entries: one high school summer on *Joyant* (a Nathanael Herreshoff P-Class sloop owned by a family friend) and some casual small-boat cruising in New England with other friends. Yet he became bold enough to sign on as crew for a yacht being delivered to the Caribbean—everybody's dream trip. He found offshore sailing so totally absorbing that he knew it had to be his next stock in trade. After a few more illuminating deliveries, in the fall of 1965, at the age of twenty-five, Ken MacKenzie took a skipper's job in the Caribbean on a yacht suitably named *Off Soundings*, running her for two years. Then for a time he sailed *Lord Jim*, one of the Caribbean's most visible charter yachts. In 1968 he moved on to skipper a sturdy William Hand double-ended motorsailer, *Physalia*. That was how Ken MacKenzie met Lucile Frances Shumaker.

A native of Denver, Fran Shumaker came from a family of successful farmers and

The delectable Caribbean scene: vibrant markets, native sloops, deserted beaches, snug harbors, and supremely private bays.
(Dana Jinkins)

yacht masters, crews, clients, even booking agents—were good people, happy people, fun-loving people. One would have thought, from the outside, that profit was the last thing on their minds. The charter fleet comprised almost exclusively high-maintenance older wooden yachts—ketches, yawls, sloops, and schooners with great wooden spars, shiny brass fittings, broad teak decks, and acres of teak and brightwork, with not a hint of Kevlar, aluminum, or *(gasp!)* carbon fiber in view. Crew uniforms generally consisted of shorts, T-shirts, bikinis, deep tans, and calloused feet.

Before the charter business shifted to bloated fleets of fiberglass bareboats catering to parochial clients, crews with encyclopaedic local knowledge could sail willing guests anywhere—drop the hook in the Pitons, Marigot Bay, the lesser Grenadines, within lee-side

bays, or behind weather-side reefs—and nearly always be alone. They could trawl and bring in fish for dinner, or dive over the side for fresh conch or lobster. Colorful markets, with their bounteous fruits and vegetables, had not yet been invaded by hordes of obese, camera-toting cruise-ship passengers seizing their five desperate minutes of souvenir shopping ashore.

It was an ebullient, memorable time for crews and clients, who cherished little more that bright blue skies, clear blue seas, scintillating nighttime heavens, refreshing rain squalls, and omnipresent low-cost grog. Something special would always happen on a charter, even if it was no more than the capricious fragrance of a windshift, a slight variation in the water's hue, or a gentle new rhythm to the sea. It was a bonus to see a rare lunar eclipse not be blocked by tall buildings,

share the perfection of an unearthly gray-pink sunrise, observe the silent rising of Canopus, or get a fleeting glimpse of the fabled Green Flash.

Brian and Angela Coen had owned *Ticonderoga* for one year, not enough time to place their trademark on her. In little time, the MacKenzies did, and as a result of their dogged joint efforts her reputation as an ideal charter venue grew quickly. But, as was normally the case in the male-dominated game of charter sailing, when a couple operated a yacht it was inevitably the man, The Captain, who tuned the rig and set the pace, and the woman who worked the galley. In *Ticonderoga*'s case, with all respect to Fran MacKenzie—who ever remained "too nice" for charter work—*Ticonderoga*'s celebrity grew largely out of Ken MacKenzie's quirky, assertive persona.

Ticonderoga's *charter interior: modest and functional, still cozy.*
(PPL/Alastair Black)

Ticonderoga was in fine shape when the MacKenzies took possession of her, so they made only a few changes to Robodor's configuration—decorating upgrades such as new carpeting, cushions, and hotel supplies. But they ran a different, less urbane, operation than Robodor's. They had no New York office to promote and advertise the boat; they spread the word through a small roster of friendly charter agents (Island Tours in Bequia, the Nicholsons in Antigua) and Robodor's client list, which was generously volunteered. They solicited business through select advertising and tried everything in their power to keep *Ti*'s name in the public eye by promoting newspaper and magazine stories, organizing and sailing races—any publicity for the least occasion. They cultivated their own charisma, and built their own clientele.

But it didn't happen quickly. Under the Robodor organization and the Coens *Ticonderoga* had done as much as twenty-six weeks of chartering each year (the McAllister syndicate had bought her on the basis of that success). But, through no fault of theirs, *Ti*'s bookings under the MacKenzies did not live up to expectations. In the better years they had no more than twenty-two weeks of work;

in poor years, fewer. For their charter work they usually had two crew, a deckhand and a stewardess. They spent summers in New England (except one unhappy one in Antigua), where they homeported in Newport, or

in the Chesapeake. For deliveries to and from the Caribbean they took at least two more crew, usually friends from New England, Bermuda, or the islands.

Winters in the Caribbean the MacKenzies, as their colleagues did, tried to book each charter to begin where the previous one ended, to make the transition easy. But in a pinch they willingly dead-headed the boat because of *Ti*'s reliable speed: as the Coens had learned, she guaranteed a minimum of ten knots under sail or power. Their most enjoyable of dead-heads was from Martinique to Antigua, always a splendid 150-mile reach in the Easterly Trades. After making that passage and others numerous times, they developed that most essential of assets, local knowledge of wind and current, which always heightens the joy and enhances the satisfaction of sailing a well-found boat.

But despite their boundless energy and the constant Tradewinds, life on *Ticonderoga* was not without its down side. The overriding hurdle was her age: maintaining a thirty-five-year-old wooden boat and keeping her from breaking down, while running demand-

A rare moment for Ken and Fran to share in the pleasures of their boat.
(Courtesy of Fran MacKenzie)

ing charters, even on a limited budget, sapped much of the syndicate's income and marginalized its profits. To cut costs, the MacKenzies had to indulge *Ti*, particularly her sails. Still, no sail has infinite life and many had to be replaced. The other, more expensive, sources of *Ti*'s power also failed on occasion. Over the years, because of charter clients' incessant demand for lights, music, hair dryers, air conditioning, hot water, ice cubes, and on-time service, she went through three 15-kW gensets, two smaller ones, and two main engines.

And it began almost immediately. Within the first year or two, at the height of a Caribbean season, Robodor's GM 4-53 engine burned out. The MacKenzies, who couldn't afford to cancel any charters, had to sail her engineless for several months while awaiting the replacement. They sailed in and out of harbors, on and off anchorages and, naturally, from island to island and charter to charter. They even dared to bring *Ticonderoga* stern-to the stone quay in one of their key ports of call, English Harbour, Antigua, using agile combinations of anchor, mizzen, and staysail to position, turn, and stop her in tight, yacht-filled quarters. At the end of that motorless season, as the charter fleet made ready to head north again for the spring, the MacKenzies challenged everybody to a race to Bermuda just for the hell of it. About a dozen boats participated, and when *Ticonderoga* arrived in Bermuda the MacKenzies sailed around the reef-rimmed North Channel into Hamilton, dropped the hook and brought her smartly stern-to at the Dinghy Club, where Ken was a member. Later they sailed back through the reefs, through Town Cut, into St. Georges Harbour where they moored with two anchors and line to a tree, to assure their egress in any wind direction. After visiting friends, they sailed on to Newport.

This ennobling experience led Ken to begin fantasizing about someday chucking

A great escape—the beach at Petit St. Vincent.
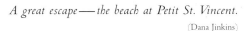
(Dana Jinkins)

Thirsty sailors gather for a jump-up on Shirley Heights, overlooking Antigua's English Harbour. (Dana Jinkins)

the main engine altogether and locomoting *Ticonderoga* forever under sail alone—it surely would have posthumously indulged Herreshoff's disdain for internal combustion. The MacKenzies never realized that fantasy. But no one can deny that the couple enjoyed their boat to the fullest, even with an engine, even if their annual schedule became routine: West Indies charter work through the holiday season and into early spring; fun in Antigua Race Week; a quick delivery north; charter work in New England in the summer (with time out for shipwork as needed); an autumn delivery back to the islands in time for the charter shows and the heating up of the holiday season, *ad circulum, ad infinitum.* With all this time spent in transit, they always needed more promotional material to keep the rest of their time booked as fully as possible, and in the winter of 1975/76 they received some. It came at no cost, but it turned out to be more than they bargained for.

The Rolex watch company contacted them, through its advertising office, and chartered *Ticonderoga* to shoot a product commercial in Antigua. Rolex sent a team down to English Harbour with models, costumes, props, a film crew and, of course, a sampling of his and hers watches. In exchange for use of the boat, Rolex executives offered to splice some of their film to archival footage of *Ti*—including the amazing 8-millimeter sequence of her 1936 launch—add narration and graphics, and produce a promotional film. The shooting went well for a few days. Toward the end of the session the filmmakers asked the MacKenzies to sail *Ticonderoga* outside English Harbour, tacking and jibing back and forth with the setting sun as backdrop, while they filmed her from the altitude of Shirley Heights with a long lens. The Caribbean light grew warmer and softer, and after several passes she sailed slowly by the camera

for the last time as the sun obligingly set.

But something strange happened as the sun dropped beneath the cloud-rimmed sea. Even the cameraman, Ivan Javor, noticed it, thinking it might be camera flare, which would have ruined the film. (Everyone was sensitive to this because another professional filmmaker, Stan Waterman, had done some earlier shooting, and something had spoiled his footage.) The cameraman turned to the Rolex advertising director, Frank Rohr, and in a thick Slavic accent said: "Frank, I think something went wrong. There was a funny green thing in the camera. Do you think it ruined the film?" Rohr, a wise old salt (and a former mate aboard *Ti),* knew otherwise. He rushed the film back for processing. Some days later he spread the word among the score of yachts moored in English Harbour that he was going to show the unedited rushes at the bar of the Admiral's Inn, a favored watering hole for the Caribbean sailing crowd. On the appointed evening dozens of thirsty sailors gathered and a mellow glow quickly spread over the assemblage. Someone hung a clean bedsheet from a rafter as an improvised screen, and the crowd took hastily arranged seats in the lounge. The lights were doused and the film rolled.

For the most part it was prosaic commercial footage—smart people on a sweet yacht having a swell time. Then came the sunset. When *Ticonderoga* made the final pass, and the sun set behind her, there was a collective gasp in the room. *The Green Flash!* Javor's green thing was actually that rare phenomenon sailors hear about all their lives but rarely if ever see. Indeed, most sailors don't even believe it exists and disparagingly attribute it to the viewer's overexposure to demon rum, or to his looking at the world through the bottom of an empty (green) beer bottle. But Javor's green flash was real, and spectacular at that; it became part of *Ticonderoga's* promotional film. And part of her legend as well.

During the years the MacKenzies owned her, *Ticonderoga* encountered eight storms of great intensity offshore. In the autumn of

1971, during their first delivery to the Caribbean, they were clobbered by a gale off Virginia and forced to sail into Hampton Roads for safety. On a later sail to Bermuda, two hours out of Newport it began to blow like hell out of the north. They reduced to mizzen and staysail, and added a double-reefed main the second day. Though *Ticonderoga* was typically overloaded with anchors, chain, and charter paraphernalia, they flew like a planing speedboat, with green bow waves and spray flying through the rigging. For two days Ken could not get a sun line (*Ticonderoga* came equipped with Consolan and Loran "A," both obsolete and useless at the time, so MacKenzie navigated by sextant and RDF). On the third day he calculated they had made good more than 500 miles in two days—shades of the Transpac.

No doubt, the autumn 1973 delivery provided the MacKenzies with their worst weather event. That was when *Ticonderoga* met up with hurricane Gilda. As the MacKenzies prepared to take *Ti* to Bermuda, the first leg to the Caribbean, the storm was stationary over the Bahamas, reportedly dying and downgraded. On a reasonable forecast the MacKenzies and six friends left Newport. But, as can happen with these unfathomable storms, Gilda strengthened, sped north along the Gulf Stream and gathered more energy from its warm waters. With little warning, *Ticonderoga* sailed into Gilda's leading edge. As wind and sea built, the crew progressively stripped *Ti* to a spitfire jib, then bare poles. There was no point in heaving-to, as the MacKenzies had already learned that *Ti*'s cutaway forefoot and bow windage prevented her from staying up in the wind; they ran before it, towing warps to keep their speed and steering manageable.

Within hours the seas were averaging 20 to 25 feet and the wind was screaming in the rigging, blowing spindrift off the wave tops; no one dared look to windward, nor could they breathe in the face of the wind, which they estimated at 80 knots. At one point, as the seas seemed to tower over the boat in every direction, one of the younger crewmen

came on deck and seriously suggested that they spread oil upon the waters, which brought only a moment's black comic relief from the awful tension and fear. Then, with Ken at the helm, and Fran and a young crewman sitting beside him in the cockpit, a rogue wave—a wall of water Fran described as a "big horseshoe"—began to break far away and continued to break until it engulfed them from astern. It pounced on *Ticonderoga* with a roar, swamping her. Ken was pressed by tons of water into the wheel, which split into pieces. Fran and the boy were swept off their bottoms; she was washed along the side deck. As she was pushed past Ken in the cockpit, one of the broken wheel spokes gashed her leg, which she did not know until later. She fetched up along the rail at the end of her safety harness.

The sea buried the boat and filled the cockpit; Ken found himself under water, gasping for breath. He thought *Ti* was surely filling and would sink in no time. He managed to stand up well enough to get his head above water and to see white foam and green water all around him, cascading off the house and deck in every direction. Preparing for the worst, he removed his safety harness to avoid being dragged down with the sinking hull. But then, with a shudder, *Ticonderoga* began to rise, coming slowly from under the enormous weight of water. Only then could MacKenzie see that, as the massive sea had run the length of the deck, all the bagged sails and the Zodiac inflatable, once lashed to the cabin, had broken loose. But all had miraculously fetched up in the bowsprit netting. Nothing went overboard.

Ken opened the companionway door to look below: it was wet, yes, but not filled. One crewman was praying, promising never to use swear words, vowing to do penance by eating a pound of dirt. But *Ticonderoga* was afloat. And she was absolutely fine. After the worst of it, when *Ticonderoga* passed through the storm's eye, the crew hove to for a while to give everyone some rest, to patch Fran's leg, and for Ken to jury a new wheel out of vise grips, hose clamps, battens, duct tape,

In Gilda's wake the crew steered by jury-rigged wheel, keeping an eye out for mountainous seas.
(Courtesy of Fran MacKenzie)

screw drivers and parts of the broken wheel. Then they set sail once more for Bermuda.

The log entries for that terrible day in no way describe the dread of the occasion: *Pooped. . . . Wheel damaged. . . . Fran puncture wound in leg. . . . Towing warps. . . . Eye of the storm. . . . Hove to with trysail. . . . Bermuda.*

Though *Ticonderoga* was a charter yacht now, the MacKenzies raced her as often as they could: Ken personally became the living embodiment of the universal doctrine that whenever two sailboats meet there is a race on—even if it is only on one boat. He zealously raced everything that floated, to show off *Ticonderoga*'s amazing speed. He particularly relished challenging other boats for stakes ranging from cases of beer, to rum, to champagne, depending on how wealthy he thought the owner of the opposing boat was (as a result, *Ticonderoga*'s drinks lockers were nearly always filled to capacity). At the outset, the MacKenzies also thought that chartering *Ti* for racing events might be an attractive proposition for keen sailors, and a satisfying, profitable venture for them. But after just one unpleasant charter experience in Antigua Race Week they chose never again to charter to racing crowds. From then on they reserved racing for themselves and their friends, for no gain other than highly prized earnings measured in amusement and camaraderie.

True, *Ticonderoga* didn't race in the big leagues very much. More often she raced with the stately yachts of her era, generally in cruising classes and non-spinnaker divisions. Indeed, many of the races *Ti* entered were known only to the charter fleet. And, as expected, she did well as long as she didn't have to endure an inordinate amount of windward work. She won the race from Guadeloupe to English Harbour four times, once sailing the 40-odd miles in a bit over 4 hours to set the record. She raced from Trinidad to Grenada and set the record. Joining the mainstream at least once, she did the Marblehead to Halifax race, searching for her old record; in very light running conditions she didn't come close. The MacKenzies' favorite run, however, which they sailed several times, was the Ft. Lauderdale to Key West Race, a manic event whose course closely skirts 150 miles of

Even under cruising sails, Ticonderoga
remains a formidable competitor.
(Courtesy of Fran MacKenzie)

MacKenzie raced anything with sails, so long as it was a classic (like the 10-year-old replica of America*).*
(PPL/Alastair Black)

Florida's coastal reefs and is not for the faint-hearted helmsman or the insecure navigator (many are the yachts that have hit the coral on that otherwise pleasant route). They always sailed to Key West with an ensemble of good friends, had a splendid time on the way, and indulged in a great party ashore.

In the late 1970s, Key West mania led to their sailing with the popular singer Jimmy Buffett, and on another occasion entertaining one of the least likely guests they ever had

aboard: the mildly spastic comedienne Phyllis Diller. A friend of the MacKenzies brought Diller aboard one afternoon while they were tied up in the submarine pen. MacKenzie remembers her as "a real antique, very frail." Regardless of her antiquity, the two sat in the cockpit, drinking beer and trading stories. Then Diller invited the crew to be her guests at an evening appearance in town, where to their surprise they heard a couple of Ken's stories worked seamlessly

into Diller's bizarre routine. Another visitor to *Ticonderoga*, in the late 1970s, who caused a different sort of stir, was Wernher von Braun (the German rocket pioneer who developed the Saturn and propelled America into space). Retired from NASA, Von Braun had grown interested in the question of visitors to Earth from other worlds. He came aboard to inquire of the MacKenzies' interest in a Pacific Ocean charter to search for UFOs and other evidence of such encounters of the unimaginable kind. His visits, however, produced nothing beyond chatter. (Von Braun died in 1977.)

Ticonderoga's charter parties came from all over the map: Ogunquit, Pretoria, Houston, Neuilly, Tulsa, New South Wales, Brazil, and Larkspur (California). Most guests were ordinary folk who signed Fran's guest book with ordinary names: Squire, Fox, Carter, Evans, and Goldstein. The most unusual name signed in the book (besides Herreshoff) was "Mom MacKenzie from New Hampshire, USA." Some prominent figures from the sailing world also signed: naval architect Dick McCurdy; America's Cup syndicate manager Ed du Moulin; and the Jewett clan—Lucy, Fritz, Betsy and George—who often chartered *Ti* in the islands in winter and took her over *en masse* for the America's Cup summers of 1977 and 1980. On those occasions *Ti* was even used as a distinguished tender to some of the American 12-Meter sloops, towing them out to the America's Cup buoy to race, towing them back to Newport to rest.

Earlier, on the MacKenzies' first America's Cup charter in 1974, Ken had an inspiring notion. Seeing the host of fine old yachts assembled for the races—under charter, or with their owners aboard to see and be seen—he envisioned a race made in heaven among this magnificent, disparate fleet. He stirred up excitement for the race, which he insisted would be bound by no rule other than that entrants had to be classics (whatever that meant); there would be no measurements or handicap ratings to confound the issue of boat-for-boat diversion. A few takers sailed the course on a layday between the four-to-nil drubbing *Courageous* handed Australia's *Southern Cross.* Everyone had such a good time they planned to repeat it during the next Cup series in 1977.

The event became a permanent fixture known as the Classic Yacht Regatta, one of a

The 1980 America's Cup defender, Freedom, *seen through Ti's saloon portlight.*
(Courtesy of Fran MacKenzie)

string of races for traditional yachts that begins in early August with the Opera House Cup, off Nantucket, and ends in late September with the Mayor's Cup Race for schooners in New York Harbor. But by the second time the Classic Yacht Regatta was run, the spark of racing sponsorship had ignited the sailing world, and the promotion hucksters from Mount Gay rum, among other corporations, put their covetous hands on the Newport event. What had once been a casually run spectacle created among yachtsman for the pure delight of sailing, was now transmogrified into a formal program with classes, measurement certificates, handicaps and lustrous prizes. It may have gained lots of free rum punches, but it suffered a colossal loss of the MacKenzie-inspired naiveté. That didn't stop MacKenzie from trying again. He planned to challenge classic boats to a major offshore race— Newport to Bermuda, New York to Ft. Lauderdale, wherever—but it failed to materialize. A more intimate match race he had organized against *Victoria,* a *Ticonderoga* clone, was canceled by her owner, John Barkhorn (who had been inspired to build her by Bob Johnson).

But when MacKenzie was triumphant with his racing, he was triumphant. And surely his greatest triumph was the OpSail Tall Ships Race from Bermuda to Newport on the occasion of the United States' Bicentennial, in June 1976. Organized by the American Sail Training Associations, the race attracted the greatest gathering of square-rigged ships since the nineteenth century, accompanied by a grand fleet of smaller yachts. Each entry was required to have a crew consisting of at least half cadets, or trainees. The MacKenzies took a half dozen kids, from locales as far-flung as Australia, the Channel Islands, and Shaker Heights, Ohio, along with Betsy and George Jewett (to bolster the dignity and import of the occasion). At the start of the race, a bit of right-of-way confusion brought on by over-zealous skippers led to three collisions among the big boys: the American *Gazelo Primeiro* struck the Romanian *Mircea;* Spain's *Juan Sebastian de Elcano* rammed Argentina's *Libertad;* and the Italian *Stella Polare* skewered the committee boat. The contretemps put a momentary damper on the proceedings, but once the entangled boats were separated, and the embarrassed wounded attended to, the race

*Feb. 25: General hangover; patronize Rum Dub Bar. **Feb. 26:** Ken challenges commodore New York YC to race. He declines; we beat him anyway. **Feb. 28:** Ken shows film about Ti on Ping-Pong table draped with bedsheet. Backgammon. **March 1:** Jump-up! More backgammon. **March 2:** General hangover. Still more backgammon. **March 3:** Fly home. Tears in our eyes.*

Lest one come away with the impression that Ms. Purdy's precious time in the Caribbean comprised only backgammon and bibulation, she assures that it was not nearly so. *Ticonderoga*, she said, was a gem. And for Ms. Purdy one of the local lads who came aboard *Ticonderoga* during her charter summed it all up perfectly:

Boat, . . . she shine so!

Yes, to the local kids with big eyes and to Canadians hard up for warmth in February, Ken MacKenzie kept his boat shining. But MacKenzie was admired also by his peers (and there is no more critical group). One Caribbean charter skipper characterized MacKenzie as "extremely cordial and generous. You couldn't pass the boat without being hoisted aboard and given a beer. And he was a bloody good sailor, who ran the boat respectably: 'Fourteen-knot MacKenzie' we used to call him, because he claimed never to go anywhere with *Ticonderoga* at less than fourteen knots."

The same colleague, though, also saw the flip side of the MacKenzie coin: "He was terribly opinionated. He ran the boat like Captain Bligh. There were only two ways of doing things: MacKenzie's way and the wrong way. As long as you danced around that and didn't lock horns with him, it was okay. But he lost some friends down there because of that."

Perhaps, in the eyes of at least one other nonobjective observer, the boat she *didn't* shine so. That was Hope Ellen Noyes Smith. Married and in her early fifties, Harry Noyes' only daughter and her husband Walter sailed into Newport one summer afternoon around

At Ti's helm MacKenzie was all seriousness. But, in the bowsprit, . . .
(Opposite: Alastair Black/Above: Dana Jinkins)

1978, tying up at Bannister's Wharf on their cruising sailboat. She was raising horses now (along with llamas and pedigreed Dalmatians) in her Tioga-Coach Kennels, but she had fallen belatedly in love with sailing and was willing now and again to go off with Walter on their sloop and entrust her animals to a foreman (or their children). Mrs. Smith saw *Ticonderoga* coming in to the harbor and began to nervously size her up. In order to gain the assurance to walk over, she downed a martini. Then she popped over and introduced herself to MacKenzie as the little girl who had christened *Tioga* more than forty years earlier. MacKenzie warmly invited her aboard. As she climbed below, her disappointment was heavy. Though she got

along famously with MacKenzie, a kindred spirit, she saw that all the wonderfully rich varnished woodwork of her childhood was gone. In its place she found only utility, Formica and, for her, sorrow.

As the 1970s faded, the charter business turned dismal for MacKenzie and *Ticonderoga*, as it did for most boats. Record-breaking inflation of more than 13 percent and interest rates over 20 percent meant only one thing: there was no discretionary money left in the American family's budget for charter holidays. *Ticonderoga* was costing the syndicate $100,000 a year to operate and maintain, and they were hurting. Out of necessity Ken was running *Ti* on a tighter and tighter

budget, which took its toll on her once-fine condition.

Yet, despite the difficult business situation, and no matter how draining it was on them, the MacKenzies remained deeply committed to *Ticonderoga*; despite high interest rates, they borrowed another $30,000 to keep afloat. Their backers, however, were not as sanguine; they began looking to sell *Ticonderoga* and get out of the charter game. They soon found a prospect in John Scripps, Bob Johnson's Hawaiian "Solomon." Scripps flew down to charter *Ticonderoga* in order to literally take her measure (like Johnson and Bill Brittain he was a large man who needed lots of room).

Scripps, however, had somehow been led by the syndicate to believe that the MacKenzies wanted to sell *Ticonderoga* and knew of his interest to buy; the MacKenzies, on the other hand, were given the impression that Scripps was interested only in a long-term charter, not in making an outright purchase. When he learned how they had all been misled, Scripps, who had no desire to buy the boat out from under the MacKenzies, cordially bowed out of the deal.

The MacKenzies decided it was time for them to gain full control of *Ticonderoga*. They appealed to Fran's father, who helped them finance a buyout of the syndicate. They now owned the boat 100 percent. But that only delayed the day of reckoning. At the end of the 1979 season, exhausted from nine grinding years of charter work and having only debt and callouses to show for it, the MacKenzies threw in the towel. They sent word around the waterfront that *Ti* was for sale. In order to put her in top condition, MacKenzie recaulked the deck (which set off a rumor that he was trying to mask some structural weakness). The couple then waited for the expected avalanche of offers. But there were hardly any inquiries—few people came to inspect the boat, fewer to take a test sail. *Ticonderoga*, despite her great name, re-

Chartering: paradise, if you ignore the accounting.
(Dana Jinkins)

mained on the market for well over a year with barely a nibble.

By the summer of 1981, lying in Newport, *Ticonderoga* was still for sale, and from afar still a beautiful sight. The man who finally focused on that beauty, even from 2,000 miles away in the landlocked city of Boulder, Colorado, was David Edwards. Edwards was born in 1935, in Michigan, but moved to Colorado when he became a pathologist. He operated a clinic in Boulder, supplementing his income through real estate trading and development. Coming from the Midwest, Edwards wasn't a wholly committed sailor. He had done some youthful dinghy sailing in Michigan, but had not gotten his first taste of real sailing until the early 1970s while he was stationed in Germany with the U.S. military. On his return home he bought a 35-foot cruiser and had her delivered to the Virgin Islands. He took an annual holiday aboard with his family and chartered her the rest of the time. He sailed occasionally with friends who had larger boats. His first offshore experience was a 1976 delivery from Florida to Tortola, a tedious, wet, windward thrash that takes stamina and resignation, and should discourage anyone from ever going offshore again. It didn't discourage Edwards.

By 1981 he was looking for a larger yacht. Among his circle of friends was Jim Ryley, a broker in Rowayton, Connecticut. It was Ryley who informed Edwards that *Ticonderoga* was for sale. Despite his limited sailing time and geographic seclusion, Edwards knew *Ti*'s name and a good deal of her history. He agreed to let Ryley pursue it for him. Ryley made an inquiry with the MacKenzies; they too were interested. Edwards flew to Newport to inspect *Ti*; he learned that the asking price was astronomical. He saw that she needed a fair amount of refurbishing so when he returned home he made what he thought was a reasonable counter offer. He didn't hear from the MacKenzies. *Ticonderoga* was also listed with a Florida brokerage that received no decent offers. The MacKenzies were beginning to feel the pressure. As their loan happened to be held at a bank in Denver, where Fran's father lived, the holders of the paper contacted Edwards. Sensing the stress correctly, Edwards offered them $325,000. They accepted.

In September Edwards flew back to Newport to join *Ticonderoga* for the Classic Yacht Regatta, the last time the MacKenzies would sail together in the event they had inaugurated seven years earlier. As has already been established, MacKenzie liked to put on a good show for his charter parties—food, drink, entertainment, not to mention electrifying 14-knot sailing (wind and imagination permitting). For this event, MacKenzie outdid himself. During pre-start maneuvers *Ti* was on starboard tack in about ten knots of breeze; a smaller boat on port tack myopically crossed her bow at close quarters. Just before the collision someone on the smaller boat looked up and cried: "Hey, there's a big boat up there!" To the accompaniment of splintering wood and shouting, reminiscent of her launching, *Ticonderoga* T-boned the other boat's mast with her bowsprit, bringing it down amid a tangle of wire and line.

Fortunately there were no injuries. Most of the damage was sustained by the sloop; *Ti* took superficial damage to her portside caprail, gilded trailboard, and bobstay. When they disengaged, the end of *Ti*'s bowsprit was embedded with splinters from the other boat's mast. It was a messy bit of amusement for all, one that only insurance companies could make right. For Edwards, however, the demonstration sail was a definitive moment: somehow he knew he had bought the right boat. For the MacKenzies, Ken in particular, it was equally transcendent. It ended the epoch of their ownership not with a whimper but a bang.

Fran and Ken returned with Margaret and Trevor, now four and one, to their house in Newport. Days after the deal was set, on an inspiration Ken walked down the street and knocked on the door of an old sailing chum, Peter Warwick. Warwick, a former British Merchant Navy officer, had worked as a surveyor for Lloyd's Insurance before turning professional yacht skipper (he had run *Puritan*, *Cintra* and *So Fong*, among other yachts). Warwick was between jobs. He recalls their conversation proceeding more or less along these lines: MacKenzie: What are you doing? Warwick: Looking for work. MacKenzie: I'm selling *Ti* on Friday. The new owner needs a skipper. Are you interested? Warwick: Who wouldn't be?

That was on Wednesday. *Ticonderoga* was hauled on Thursday, surveyed on Friday, and Warwick was hired on Saturday (with a good reference from Bill Criswell, the owner of *Whitehawk*). On Sunday, Warwick, Edwards, MacKenzie, and a delivery crew left Newport to take *Ti* to Oxford, Maryland, to avoid the approaching New England winter. It was cold, blowing hard on the nose as they motorsailed nearly all of Long Island Sound into a nasty sea. Several people got off on City Island to seek refuge; the rest of the trip was uneventful.

In all her years *Ticonderoga* had few owner/operators: Brian Coen, Ken MacKenzie and (depending on how you define owner) Baxter Still. The other owners had professionals running the boat for them, and those owners acted as skipper only when they were aboard (and in some cases, not even then). Ken MacKenzie lived on *Ticonderoga* for the better part of ten years—longer than anyone else. In that time he could not help but become a part of her, at one with her. He felt her every move through his bare, bruised feet; he knew her every creak and noise in the marrow of his bones; he understood her every capability in his heart. MacKenzie felt he had sailed her well—hard but never pushing her too much, never abusing her. In return she taught him something new every day, and he never stopped learning (he was apparently the only owner to note that *Ticonderoga* was a half knot faster on starboard tack than port). Halfway through his ownership, in a 1976 interview in *Rudder*, MacKenzie expressed his feelings toward *Ticonderoga* this way:

> Every time I spend one minute away from the boat, I feel I'm robbing her of something. I can't stand it. . . . When I first saw *Ti*, I knew this could be the boat for me if she became available.

When Ken MacKenzie put on a show, he pulled out all the stops.

(Benjamin Mendlowitz)

Ticonderoga's halcyon years with the MacKenzies: washed away with time and tide.
(Courtesy of Fran MacKenzie)

What's the sense of owning something if it isn't special and something to be proud of? I went to the wall financially for *Ti,* but I wanted a boat that was ready to go right away. We can take off today for the next island or the next continent. In fact, that's my dream—to take *Ticonderoga* around the world with a charter or company that will understand what she's all about. . . .

MacKenzie never found that charter. Or that company. He never met the group that understood *Ticonderoga* as well as he did. He ran out of money before he could fulfil that around-the-world dream. The aftermath of *Ticonderoga's* sale went beyond MacKenzie's ruined dreams. The partnership that he and Fran had so lovingly established at sea ran its course; they divorced ashore. Curiously, one of the few regrets Ken MacKenzie ever had about his glory years on *Ticonderoga* was that, while he soberly sought all knowledge of the boat, and went to great lengths to find answers to his every gnawing question about her, not one prior or subsequent owner ever had the curiosity or the will to contact *him,* to ask similar questions or share similar knowledge.

After relinquishing *Ti* to Warwick, Mac-Kenzie sailed her only once more, the following spring. He felt that his existence went "downhill" after that. He had to find a new occupation, a new focus, a new essence. Apparently, for the man who had most intimately been a part of this magnificent boat—and despite a household filled with mementoes of her—there wasn't much of a life after *Ticonderoga* for Ken MacKenzie.

A Return to Private Life

1981–1993

WHEN DAVID EDWARDS took possession of *Ticonderoga* his several vocations were doing well. He intended within a few years to put some good money into fixing her up, then keep her for many years more. He hoped eventually to take time away from those vocations for some long-range cruising. But he didn't have much time to use her that first season, so he postponed any major work and had Warwick prepare to put her back into charter.

Warwick had already perceived the telltale signs that, in the last few years, Ken MacKenzie had been forced to run the boat on a shoestring; there were lots of little things to do to get her back into shape. Over the next couple of months, in Oxford and Annapolis, Warwick had the most pressing work done. Then in early December (surely too late in the year for comfort) he left for Bermuda. It was, as he recalls, "a rotten, diabolical trip" into the teeth of a vicious winter storm. He stripped *Ti* down to a spit-

Tranquility, thy name is Ticonderoga.
(Jim Daniels)

fire jib, but soon learned that this was no way to drive her in high winds and big seas; she wallowed. Once he put a bit more sail up she galloped. *Ti* arrived in the Virgin Islands in time for Christmas. Edwards came down for a cruise with his family, as did some of his friends.

With little time to prepare for chartering—they had no advertising, no brochure, and had already lost a good part of the season—the Warwicks (Peter's wife Andrée was his cook) weren't able to get more than one or two charters that first winter. At the end of the season, as was all but preordained, they entered *Ti* into Antigua Race Week. Unfortunately, business up north prevented Edwards from joining them (a motif that would run through most of his ownership). After Race Week, Warwick brought *Ti* back to Connecticut to work on her engine and tanks, and do some cosmetic touching up. He prepared new brochures for the coming winter season. Edwards and his family came from Colorado to cruise New England. Though they enjoyed the sail, Edwards was already seeing gray financial clouds on the

horizon. *Ti* was costing him about $10,000 per month, which was not nearly covered by her meager charter income. He began to have fleeting thoughts of selling her, less than a year after buying her.

Then in the summer of 1982 he was approached by a knight in shining armor from Stamford, Connecticut, Joe Healey. He told Edwards that he was a competent skipper and engineer; he told him he was well connected in chartering; he sang a song of profits, which was sweet music to Edwards' already weary ears. He even convinced Edwards to make him a limited partner, for a small investment, and to turn *Ti* over to him for operating under charter. Edwards abruptly dismissed the Warwicks and they were once again between jobs.

Ti's new master moored her in Stamford, and advertised her in New York City for all-inclusive day charters; with a big banner flying from her mainmast truck, she became a glorified sailing "head" boat. He operated *Ti* on Long Island Sound until the fall, then took her to Florida, where he put her into the Derecktor shipyard, in Dania, for some

friends of the Kennedy clan. When the guests boarded, with Senator Teddy Kennedy very much in evidence, there were some questions of responsibility for bill paying (and sobriety) to be settled. A small fracas ensued and Kennedy accidentally elbowed Jan and knocked her down. John refused to take them sailing. Someone from the clan then intimated that there would be trouble ahead if they canceled; Whitney held his ground. When they sorted things out, as a sign of good faith the Kennedys invited Edwards to the family compound in Hyannis Port. In return Edwards offered the clan a free week on *Ticonderoga* in Maine the next season.

At the end of the second summer, Edwards asked the Whitneys to sail *Ti* to the Caribbean for the winter. With the help of brokers Julie Nicholson, Missy Harvey, and Tina Hinckley, they managed to book a fair charter season. But for the Whitneys, getting there was more than half the fun: because of her incomparable speed, they found ocean deliveries the most stimulating aspect of running *Ticonderoga*. For Edwards, who joined them on the leg from Bermuda to St. Thomas, the thrill was hardly less; in the Tradewinds she never sailed slower than 9 or faster than 11 knots. Later Edwards and his family cruised the Virgins and Grenadines.

Whenever he sailed *Ticonderoga* Edwards discovered more than her still-remarkable speed; he met full force with her legend. Everywhere, from Maine to Grenada, people would approach her with the same reverence as for a movie star or potentate; thousands (it seemed) would claim to have sailed her (thousands, it seems, still do, and nearly all of them were on the 1965 Transpac when *Ti* vanquished *Stormvogel*). At crowded public events, such as Fourth of July gatherings, she would be swarmed by sailors in dinghies trying to get a close look at her—to absorb some small portion of her aura—then return to their lesser boats feeling augmented

Though showing signs of age, Ticonderoga *still sailed like a champion.*
(Robert D. Hagan)

Tom Reardon, skipper of Ticonderoga *after the Whitneys: his enthusiasm knows no bounds.*
(Benjamin Mendlowitz)

(or dejected). Edwards found that aspect of his ownership as thrilling as sailing her on that Tradewind reach from Bermuda.

The winter of 1985/86 the Whitneys operated mostly out of Antigua. But at the end of the season, after more than three years of uneventful, rather routine work, they

developed an itch to get into the charter business on their own. They had recently met a wiry, affable thirty-one-year-old professional sailor, Tom Reardon, who had admired *Ti-conderoga* for six years since seeing her in Antigua (where he had delivered a Swan 47 from California). Reardon was then skipper of *Brigadoon III.* A fanatic surfer from Long Island, Reardon had discovered sailing while he was in high school, doing an occasional "beer-can" race on a friend's C&C 24. He had read about Antigua Race Week and the chartering game, and on the basis of that slim evidence he concluded that sailing was the life for him. In 1977 he dropped out of junior college, headed to California, and between surfing days started hanging around yacht clubs in hopes that something would rub off. Within two years he was a professional. The Whitneys had in fact subcontracted Reardon to take over *Ti* briefly that winter, so he already knew the boat; when they made it known to him that they were planning to clear off *Ti,* he leaped with both feet at the opportunity to replace them.

Reardon was invited to meet Edwards aboard *Ti* in the Virgin Islands on April 1, 1986; he insisted on arriving the day before to avoid the risk of beginning a venture on a day reserved only for fools. His superstitious machinations paid off; Edwards hired him. Skipping Antigua Race Week, Reardon and the Whitneys brought *Ti* north. In mid-May the Whitneys departed with their gear. But they left behind something of infinite value: two years of incredibly warm feelings as expressed by all their charter parties in *Ticonderoga's* logbook. An entry from Alice Lorillard's party says it all: "The trouble with the whole damn trip—it came to an end!"

Reardon moved his bags aboard and immediately began hustling for business, sending out brochures, making calls. And despite a persistent feeling that Edwards was already selling *Ti,* he began booking the coming Caribbean season. When *Ti* was invited to be an escort vessel in the parade of tall ships for the reopening of the Statue of Liberty in June 1986, he brought her down from Maine for the honor, then sailed back for more chartering. In September 1986, a charter was booked by a Florida broker, Louise Bolton (the wife of John Bolton, one of Bob Johnson's *Ticonderoga* regulars). That charter party was headed up by a gifted, amiable, somewhat bald, but ever magnanimous

The 90-foot Whitefin *was Bob Voit's ideal (until he chartered* Ticonderoga*).*
(Benjamin Mendlowitz)

California businessman, Robert D. Voit.

Voit, who kept a comfortable motorsailer in Newport Beach, had been toying with the idea of buying a classic American yacht. He knew of *Ticonderoga's* stature; he had read of, and been thrilled by, her famous duel with *Stormvogel* in the 1965 Transpac. But Voit had never given much thought to owning *Ticonderoga.* The boat that fit his ideal was the 90-foot *Whitefin,* one of Bruce King's modern classics. Through the distinguished Ft. Lauderdale yacht broker Penny Parrot (of

In Blue Hill Bay, Voit began to sense the differences between a true classic and a fine pretender.
(Benjamin Mendlowitz)

Parrot, Parrot, Elfenbein & O'Brien) Voit had already taken a week's charter on *White-fin* in the Bahamas and remained partial to her. Perhaps he saw in the newer yacht the potential for a less complicated sailing life than with an aging one. Fortunately, Jim and

Pat Roberts, two of Voit's very boat-wise friends, knew better. With his interests at heart, and knowing well the subtle distinctions between a new and a true classic, they provoked him into chartering *Ticonderoga* as well. And they came along on the Maine trip

to be quite certain he got the message.

On a particularly chill, foggy Down-East day in September 1986, *Ti* was sailing to Blue Hill, Maine, doing ten knots, with nobody at the wheel. Reardon noticed that the circumstance had not escaped Voit's notice. When they dropped the hook and furled sail, everybody went ashore for sightseeing and to find a bit of warmth before the many Blue Hill fireplaces. Reardon took Voit into town. Now, Blue Hill is one of those magical places that only a callous lout could fail to love; it is miles beyond picturesque, yet never hokey, with small shops, charming inns, unassuming houses, and a plethora of antiques set out in genuinely antique shops. Voit and Reardon went to a local pub and had a couple of beers. By day's end the two developed a rare synergism, so that when Reardon (now confident to the point of cockiness) suggested that Voit might be able to buy *Ticonderoga* (and keep him on as skipper), they agreed to pursue the notion.

David Edwards was finding little relief from the stress of spending money he didn't have. He wasn't sailing much, and the fun had been drained from his ownership; he was also confronting a vexing business mishap at home. Soon after the completion of Voit's season-ending charter, he called Reardon and instructed him to take the boat to Ft. Laud-

erdale, to be near the broker action; he wanted to sell *Ticonderoga*. Edwards contacted Penny Parrot. He had her brokerage write a contract that specifically excluded certain charterers, Voit among them, from a commissionable sale; the paperwork was to be handled by Parrot's son, Jody O'Brien. *Ticonderoga* arrived in Florida in mid-October. Voit soon made Edwards an offer, which privately Edwards considered insultingly low; he nonetheless countered. Voit went silent.

Meanwhile, Reardon showed the boat to other potential buyers, but the interest was surprisingly cool. Voit surfaced again toward the end of December, with Jim Roberts. They arranged a showing with Reardon. Voit was pleased by the inspection, but ambivalent about *Ti's* condition. And he was still not impressed by her mundane charter interior. By chance, lying in a nearby slip was Voit's ideal, *Whitefin*; she too was seriously for sale. Reardon, who had a sense of Voit's needs, insisted that he give *Whitefin* another inspection. When Voit had fully absorbed the inequality of these two very fine yachts, and saw how a true monarch stands up against a

pretender to the throne (even a splendidly realized pretender), he didn't have to think very long. He simply declared: "That was very gutsy of you. You just sold *Ticonderoga*."

Voit called Edwards and offered him $425,000. Edwards did not immediately accept Voit's offer; he was already entertaining offers of $465,000 and $475,000. These offers, however, were from potential buyers who both insisted that Edwards carry the financing; Voit's somewhat lower offer was for cash, free and clear. Edwards was understandably discomfited by the larger offers, as they implied risk to him, and he was in no mood for risk. He and Voit talked some more and agreed on a price of $440,000. But, for reasons that are not uncommon in this age of tax planning and cautious accounting, Edwards was under pressure to close on the sale before the end of the 1986 calendar year. It was December 21 and the clock was ticking. Loudly.

Edwards in Colorado and Voit in California tried to find some time in their busy schedules to close the sale, but they found no open dates in common. Beyond year-end business affairs, both had Christmas and New Year's plans with their families—unchangeable plans. With the seemingly impossible time constraint, the deal appeared to be unraveling before their eyes. But through an oddly fortuitous persistence, both discovered that they were having their family Christmas dinners in Sun Valley, Idaho with reservations at the *same* restaurant. O'Brien hastily prepared the papers; Voit and Edwards met at a Sun Valley coffee shop the day before Christmas and signed.

Bob Voit was the right man at the right time. *Ticonderoga* was fifty years old and in somewhat frail health beneath her valiant exterior. Voit thought he had acquired an outstanding cruising yacht. He did not yet know that he was assuming a massive responsibility handed down by history itself. He was about to commit his heart, his soul, and a not inconsiderable portion of his net worth to *Ticonderoga's* purchase and, more crucially, to her salvation.

His charter of Whitefin *almost led Voit to buy her.*
(Courtesy of Pat Roberts)

Bob Voit assumed a great responsibility, handed to him by history.
(Benjamin Mendlowitz)

Ticonderoga nearly fell apart in 1967 from the unintended effects of Bob Johnson's vigorous, record-hunting navigation. Two decades later, after chartering under four owners and surviving further, equally unintentional, abuse, *Ticonderoga* returned to private life under the caring hand of Bob Voit. But, unlike Johnson, Voit wasn't much interested in racing *Ticonderoga*. Nor, unlike Johnson, was his regard for her driven intellectually by her incredible racing history; it was driven emotionally by what she meant to him, not to the rest of the world. In Tom Reardon's words: "Without the personal passion, *Ticonderoga*'s historic aspect would not have

mattered to Bob Voit—he might just as well have donated money to have someone else take care of her."

Voit certainly had the resources, and the integrity, to do just that. He was born in 1940 into a family whose name, Voit, was synonymous with high-quality sporting gear. The W.J. Voit Rubber Company, a specialty manufacturer, had been founded by Voit's grandfather, William Julius Voit. Old W.J. was principally an inventor, not a businessman; he was far better at formulating manufacturing processes than figuring corporate projections. As a result, he suffered more than one bankruptcy on his road to Utopia.

Eventually, and very famously, he invented Paddleball, a globally popular, simpleminded pastime that set the precedent for such later universal, craze-level amusements as the hula hoop and the pet rock. More significantly, W.J. devised an effective, economical method to cover roughly used sporting goods (basketballs, footballs and the like) with flexible rubber instead of more costly pigskin—making them more durable, consistent, and lively. The demand for such goods became permanent in an age in which synthetics have all but replaced naturals.

Despite W.J. Voit's resourcefulness, however, it took the intervention of his son,

After his initial summer in Maine, Voit invited friends to sail in the Newport Classic Yacht Regatta.
(Benjamin Mendlowitz)

After the work, in April of 1987 *Ticonderoga* went to the Bahamas for a time (she had to leave United States waters to avoid Florida sales tax), then wended her way up the East Coast to Newport. Voit spent some time cruising in the area, sailed to Boston for the Fourth of July celebration, then Maine. Because Voit had invited so many of his friends to enjoy the boat, Reardon found it expedient to just shuttle between Camden and Bar Harbor every ten days or so for a new group to come aboard. *Ticonderoga* sailed the Classic Yacht Regatta in Newport, was hauled in Maine for some minor work, then she headed for the Caribbean in November. During the winter Voit and more friends visited the islands, and in the new year Reardon took *Ti* to Antigua

for two weeks of mandatory varnishing. He sailed her to the Virgins, Antigua and finally on one of those classic booming reaches south to the Grenadines.

When he dropped the hook in Grenada, Reardon noticed something ominous: the caprail was two inches higher at the mainmast's port chainplates than at the starboard. Under the enormous tension of the strenuous port-tack reach, all the chainplate bolts had snapped; the rig was being held up by little more than the knees fastening the covering boards to the bulwarks. *Ticonderoga* was crippled, insofar as vigorous port-tack sailing was concerned. But Reardon managed to maneuver her on a long starboard tack back to English Harbour, Antigua, where he had new fittings welded and the chainplates refas-

tened. The repair was sound enough for *Ticonderoga* to win the Old-Timer's division in Antigua Race Week, in April 1988.

And what an authentic old-timer's event it was. To celebrate his new ownership, with Pat Roberts' help Voit invited (at his expense) seven of the heroes who had sailed *Ticonderoga* in her record-breaking streak under Bob Johnson—John Bolton, Peter Bowker, Bob Dickson, Ray Eaton, Grant Hoag, Pat McGee and Ron Young. Voit thought that having them aboard during an intense race series would afford them an opportunity for a sentimental reunion, even as watching them sail would give him insight into handling *Ticonderoga* better. The seven were each a quarter-century older, so Voit treated them like citizen kings. But he made them work for their trip, and they sailed the hell out of the old girl. Pat Roberts later produced a souvenir booklet for each man, filled with snapshots and a bit of relevant boat history; in appreciation, the magnificent seven chipped in to have the esteemed modelmaker Ken Gardner fashion a half model of "their" boat for Voit.

After the racing, Voit had originally planned to have Reardon sail *Ticonderoga* across the Atlantic and lay her up for the winter in southern France or Palma, Majorca, so he could spend the next year cruising Europe. The chainplate failure, however, gave the major refit a new urgency. Voit suggested having the work done in an Italian yard he knew that had fine woodworkers; Reardon, on the line to oversee the work, was uncomfortable with another language and with Italian mechanical and electrical workers. Inasmuch as Voit also hoped to cruise the Baltic Sea, for a special purpose, they elected to do the refit in England. After Antigua, Reardon sailed *Ticonderoga* to Bermuda and the Azores, making European landfall in Falmouth, England. Then he sailed on to Lymington, to look at the Berthon Shipyard, on the western end of the Solent across from the Isle of Wight, one of the two refit candidates (the other was Southampton Yacht Services, at the other end of the Solent). It was in the Berthon yard that John Munford had his first look at *Ticonderoga* before accepting the challenge of converting her bland charter interior into a glowing classic once more.

Munford, an Englishman whose name had been offered by knowledgeable friends of Voit's and Reardon's (including English-born Brian Coen), was the logical choice for *Ticonderoga's* interior renovation. He is one of the most respected yacht stylists in the business, a discerning contemporary designer who knows exactly what a traditional yacht needs. He had redesigned the interiors for many true classics and designed, from scratch, the interiors for many new yachts in the classic mode. He was at the time completing an exquisite cherry-panelled masterpiece for the rebuild of the J-Class

yacht *Endeavour* at the Royal Huisman Shipyard, in Holland, for her new American owner Elizabeth Meyer. Munford did a survey, took some photos, and returned to his studio in Southampton to begin preliminary sketches for a proposal. But his real design work couldn't begin until *Ticonderoga* was

hauled at summer's end and the entire refit was begun.

From Lymington, *Ticonderoga* traversed the English Channel to Cuxhaven, Germany, then transited the Kiel Canal to Gothenburg, on Sweden's west coast, where Voit came aboard with some friends. There, while

Ticonderoga drifts under a cruising spinnaker in Somes Sound, Maine.
(Courtesy of Pat Roberts)

Ticonderoga *briefly parted the Iron Curtain when she sailed into Tallinn, Estonia.*
(Embassy of Estonia)

Ticonderoga was anchored in the harbor, where she had been anchored only once before after her smashing Transatlantic and Skaw Races in 1966, a speedboat whizzed by her, only to turn on a dime and return because her owner recognized *Ti* from 1966—the mystique had not faded one iota. From Gothenburg they cruised around the waters near Stockholm and the exquisite, birch-covered archipelago between Sweden and Finland, then on to Helsinki, where they remained for a few days. Again, *Ticonderoga's* fame prompted a stranger, a Finn, to saunter up to her at the quay and claim with pride that he had been reading about her with pleasure all his life.

Plainly, Voit was not a typical cruising man. He didn't care to sail into a new harbor or a new nation just to say he'd been there. His wide interests in societies and cultures led him to choose his cruising grounds carefully, and to program shoreside visits for maximum contact with local people. He preferred visiting bars, clubs, or simple restaurants in which to discover the heartbeat of each place (as he had done in his seminal post-college travels). In that spirit he also wanted to renew his brief acquaintance with

the Soviet Bloc, so he elected to take *Ticonderoga* behind the Iron Curtain for her first venturesome continental sally, across the Baltic Sea into Tallinn, Estonia.

The sail from Helsinki to Tallinn was beautiful, beneath clear summer skies and on shimmering blue seas. As they crossed into Estonian waters, though, Voit abruptly realized he was no longer in the West; a sense of foreboding overtook him, perhaps triggered by thoughts of his long-ago burglarized papers. He knew all the ship's documents were in order, yet he still felt he was entering an alien world. When a helicopter with the red hammer and sickle painted on its side overflew the boat, he knew he was back in the East, in the world of guns, boots, and baleful *apparatchiks.*

Although *Ticonderoga* was the first U.S.-flag vessel to enter Tallinn in forty-eight years, which should have been cause for celebration, the bureaucrats treated the crew icily. *Ti* was not directed to a town dock, where she could be seen by ordinary people with whom the crew could connect; she was sent instead to a secured berth among dingy tankers and oily freighters. And the crew had to fill out a mountain of paperwork worthy

of a containership. Voit and his friends were also denied use of the boat to tour around the country, because an absurd cabotage law required them to exit Soviet territorial waters each time they moved to another port. *Ticonderoga* remained secured in Tallinn for a week while Voit, his guests, and the crew were given "official" tours by the local authorities.

Voit, a highly civic-minded person, particularly asked to visit an Estonian school, a farm, and a hospital to see how they functioned under collective command. The authorities impassively obliged by showing the group a school with no students (it was closed for the summer), a chicken-farm film about chickens (but no live ones), and a hospital building (from the outside only). On another day their guide was an Estonian student, who was more forthcoming. They visited the Olympic facilities and witnessed the raising of the Estonian flag for the first time since the war, a harbinger of earth-shaking events to come. Indeed, it was the beginning of the transition to freedom in the East, but freedom was still over the horizon for the occupied Baltic states. (Before leaving Tallinn Voit learned that they had been secretly observed by Russian security while sailing from Stockholm to Helsinki, long before they sailed to Tallinn.)

From Tallinn, at summer's end, *Ticonderoga* returned to Sweden, passed through the Kiel Canal and, after waiting out equinoctial gales in Den Helder, crossed from Holland to Southampton Yacht Services. They had just completed the refurbishment of the 108-foot *Altair.* After an inspection of the facilities Reardon and Voit knew beyond doubt they had found the ideal yard to perform *Ticonderoga's* overhaul. The Southampton experts gave her a thorough going over to verify the work she needed. Initially, besides the new Munford interior, Voit and Reardon assumed that *Ticonderoga*

The spectacular figure of Altair *was well preserved by Southampton Yacht Services.*
(Christian Février)

To rid it of decay (ABOVE) Southampton Yacht Services gutted the hull, then meticulously rebuilt it.
(Southampton Yacht Services, except center right: Peter Chesworth)
(Opposite: Yachting World/Malcolm White)

needed only a new deck and deck beams, sheer strake, covering boards, bulwarks, and some new machinery. Once Southampton's wizards opened her up to prod and peek beneath her skin, however, they found rot running deep into *Ticonderoga's* structure. And many more problems. They advised considerably more work. When all the surveys were completed, the Southampton management team, led by Peter Davies (a former professional skipper), handed Voit their best detailed estimate of the total cost to rebuild *Ticonderoga* properly. Bob Voit was an experienced yachtsman; he'd owned wooden boats. He knew that they can be expensive conveyances to maintain. He was never surprised by an honest shipyard estimate, never surprised by an honest shipyard invoice. The Southampton estimate, however, was higher than any yard bill Voit had ever seen, higher than Giffy Full's estimate of a half million dollars. It totalled 600,000 pounds sterling or some $920,000 in 1988 greenbacks, well more than twice what Voit had paid for *Ti.* He was shocked. Yet, after only a few moments' thought, he proclaimed: *"Let's do it!"*

Southampton commenced the work on *Ticonderoga* on October 1, 1988, and finished it September 9, 1989. In those eleven months they almost completely rebuilt her hull. They removed and scrapped the old deck, plywood underdecking, bulwarks and planking above the waterline, where Spencer's had stopped. They discarded all of the old frames and replaced them with ninety new steam-bent teak-and-oak half frames, which

they sistered to the new Spencer frames. They replaced the bulwarks and twenty-seven of the deck beams, and installed new marine plywood and teak planks on deck. They replaced the entire topsides above the waterline with double-planked mahogany and new bronze fastenings. They renewed the bronze hull and deck reinforcing straps. They built new stainless-steel fuel and water tanks; mounted a new engine, a rebuilt generator, and a new propeller and strut; changed the plumbing, electric control panels, and wiring; installed a new custom deep freeze, new sailing instruments, some new bronze winches, and new mainmast standing rigging; added a few new sails; and they covered her with many (imperial) gallons of fresh paint, clear varnish, and teak oil.

While Southampton's master carpenters and technicians did the hull rebuild, John Munford, whose offices conveniently adjoin Southampton Yacht Services, consulted with Voit and began the transformation of the interior. Voit's brief to Munford was to improve the general arrangement, particularly the saloon and navigation areas, and to redesign the galley, crew area and forecastle, all of which were to be gutted and replaced. Voit also wanted the owner's and guest cabins to be brought in line with the rest of Munford's stately design, which included warm varnished mahogany bulkheads and white-painted panels (farewell to Formica). Munford extended the owner's cabin toilet to include a stall shower, taking the extra space from the captain's cabin (alas, poor Reardon). Voit obtained vibrantly patterned prayer mats from India, which were painstakingly cut into dramatic coverings for the saloon upholstery. Munford also did some important restoration to the deck, including the replacement of what in his gentlemanly British idiom he called a "disgusting piece of Perspex joinery, useful but ugly [Bob Johnson's colossal Plexiglass forward hatch]." When Munford completed the drawings and renderings of every detail to Voit's keen approval, the joiners went to work fabricating and installing the new interior. In the end, *Ticonderoga* looked superb. Voit was rapturous.

In the 1950s Geoffrey Smith wrote that, at her launching in 1936, *Tioga* was all

The deck was totally reconstructed, then John Munford's interior was installed.
(Above & top right: Peter Chesworth/Right: KOS)

Ti made her post-rebuild debut among hundreds of classics at the 1989 St.-Tropez Nioulargue.
(Christian Février)

"white, gold-leaf and pale blue grace." Other than the pale blue, which had long since been abandoned, *Ticonderoga* emerged from the Southampton Yacht Services shed in a flawless suit of white, bright varnish and gold. Although no one but a magician could have anticipated every item of restoration she would need until they had gotten inside her, Southampton's final bill matched their estimate squarely; Voit was doubly pleased. "You start realizing," he commented, "that you don't own a boat like this the way you own an automobile. It's a sort of caretakership, a trusteeship for the future. I had an intense desire, and the resources, to do it right. I'm going to do anything I can to preserve *Ti-*

Reborn, Ticonderoga *is launched, to Voit's delight.*
(Top & far left: Peter Chesworth/Left: John Munford)

conderoga; she can last another fifty years if she's properly tended to. In that sense it was easy to enter the yard for a major refit without considering money. Even if it took twice the time and twice the money, we were still going to do it right."

In his exultation over the successful completion of *Ti*'s rebuild, one of the first things Voit did was to call David Edwards and honor him with a standing invitation to take a week's sail with his family whenever it suited his schedule. Edwards, a man of pride and sensitivity, gave lengthy consideration to the invitation. On one hand, he wanted to accept just to see the old girl in her newly refreshed state. On the other, he felt that a reunion with the new *Ti* might erase the fond, if sometimes troubled, memories he had of the old *Ti*. He never took up Voit's offer.

The reborn *Ticonderoga* sailed from Southampton to Palma, Majorca, for a week's easy shakedown in calm Mediterranean waters. Then she made her glowing debut before the most critical audience of any vintage yacht's life: the aristocratic owners, professional crews, international press, touring gentry, and all-knowing hangers-on who gather in Saint-Tropez in early October for *La Nioulargue. La Nioulargue,* the most magisterial sailing party in the world, is the annual meeting of classic yachts that closes the summer season on the French Riviera with a varnished, brassy, overcanvassed splash. Motoryachts are banned summarily from the minuscule harbor; the clubs, bars, hotels, cafes, and restaurants of Saint-Tropez cater willingly and exclusively to the sailing crowd, just before retiring for the winter. For one

vivacious week the world's finest surviving sailing yachts—many well over 100 feet long; some nearing 100 years old—race against one another in deadly earnest and with a keen sense of history. With stalwart hulls, towering rigs, miles of rigging, and acres of golden sail, these lovingly maintained, splendidly sailed yachts constitute a living museum and a breathtaking maritime legacy upon which history's door must never close.

Ticonderoga's dazzling return at the Nioulargue placed her center stage in that great pageant of gilt-edged nautical treasures. She caught the eye of every passerby in the crowd as they jostled along the quay to gaze at her and snap photos, despite the gunwale-to-gunwale presence of such Titans as *Altair, Orion, Royono,* and *Puritan,* which dwarfed her in size but not in sheer radiance. Bob Voit generously flew Bob Dickson and Ray Eaton to France for the week of racing; Peter Bowker, on another boat, joined them for a one-day reunion sail. Dickson, sailing her for only the second time in thirty years, was proud of the old girl and her new outfit. He gazed tenderly around her deck, his keen blue eyes admiring Southampton's handiwork, and proclaimed wistfully: "She looks similar, maybe fancier with a bit more chrome. But, on deck she's the same: The rig hasn't changed. The shape hasn't changed. The feeling hasn't changed."

At the finish of the race, after several hours thrashing about in a frisky Mediterranean Mistral *(the wind that makes you crazy!),* Voit was breathless: "They couldn't have sailed her better. When she's sailing right there's no better high. And it's complete with a hangover: I don't get back into the real world for a day or two after sailing *Ti.*"

Bob Voit had found, bought, rebuilt, and reintroduced his classic yacht to the world. And she blew his mind, like a drug, in 25 knots of wind.

Grand schooners run before the afternoon breeze to the finish in St.-Tropez Bay.
(Christian Février)

Voit and companions visit Istanbul (TOP), *and meet quaffers of homemade brew in Bucharest.*
(Courtesy of Robert D. Voit)

After Voit's Saint-Tropez high, *Ticonderoga* was given some time off to winter at Villefranche, outside Nice. In early spring she sailed to Rhodes, then Istanbul where Voit joined her. Again, his knowledge of political geography and current history produced some unusual cruising grounds for the summer of 1990. He chose to sail deeper behind the Iron Curtain into the Black Sea, to Bulgaria, Romania, and then Odessa, in the heart of Soviet Ukraine. In advance of the trip, Voit had his secretary apply for letters of invitation to local yacht clubs and the necessary crew visas—mandatory for a visit to the USSR. But she failed to get a visa for the yacht itself, because the Russian application forms had no such category; it caused substantial problems throughout the cruise, beginning in Bulgaria.

When they sailed into the port of entry they managed to bluff their way into local approval, but only after they were set upon by a horde of officials from immigration, customs, and health who thoroughly disrupted their space. Voit, by an unhappy coincidence, was suffering the effects of some bad food or water. Just as the health inspectors asked Reardon, the captain, if there were any sick people aboard, Voit couldn't check himself from disgorging over the rail. The *apparatchiks* raised a woolly eyebrow or two until Reardon assured them it was merely a case of *mal de mer*. They approved the entry permit.

After some brief touring, *Ticonderoga* sailed to Constanta, Romania, to the yacht harbor, which was characteristically encircled by military guards. As in Bulgaria, after a bit of fussing and fuming, the bureaucracy grudgingly allowed them entry. Leaving the boat in the harbor with some crew aboard for security, Voit, his companion, another couple, Reardon, and his stewardess took a train up to Transylvania, going second class to meet the real people and observe Gypsy life firsthand. Wherever they went, in fact, they tried to find student hangouts and off-beat bars to get some insight into people and events. They found the adventure frightening at times (in Bucharest they learned that some students had been shot in Ceausescu Square a few days earlier). But they never sensed they were in personal danger. (And they found no small amount of solace in the ability to buy quart-size jars of fine Russian caviar for about $25.) Reardon in particular found these forays into the East fascinating: "They weren't about boating; they were about culture. One of the beauties of traveling with the boat, however, was that no matter where we were—taking long side trips for several days at a time—when we came back to the boat and went below . . . with our watermaker, it was home."

From Constanta they navigated about 30 miles up a narrow stream, then entered the terminal reaches of the heroic Danube River, about 2,800 kilometers from its source in Germany's Black Forest. They motored down a fork, through lovely lake country, then back to the main stream, with Soviet Moldavia to port, Romania to starboard. Nearing the river's mouth, they checked into the Moldavian side to get clearance for Odessa, where they had been invited to stay at the yacht club. Once again their papers were rejected, but the *apparatchiks* called ahead to the club and *Ticonderoga* was granted a temporary stay, so long as she remained on the Moldavian side of the river. With dirty smokestacks and oil refineries belching grit on that side, but clean, inviting Romanian fields on the other, *Ticonderoga's* party ignored the authorities and anchored across the river alongside graceful overhanging trees and in view of shepherds tending their flocks.

It was early July; the days were long and languid. They had a nice dinner with good wine. As they all relaxed in the cockpit in the quiet of evening, a gang of Romanian soldiers in a horsedrawn cart broke the silence with assertive shouts from ashore. Finding counter-shouts useless, Reardon and one of his crew (an Australian bloke who spoke Russian), went ashore in the inflatable (not easy for Reardon who had a chipped bone in his foot and was on crutches). When the Romanians saw the crew's papers they told

Ticonderoga slips into the harbor of Constanta, Romania.
(Courtesy of Robert D. Voit)

them to leave. They left. Anchoring downriver until a gale passed, they sailed out into the Black Sea and on to Odessa. When they arrived at the yacht club their papers were again deemed out of order; they were quarantined for three days before being allowed ashore. As Voit had found in his backpacking days, life behind the Iron Curtain was not as diverting as Soviet spin *doktors* would suggest.

Ticonderoga left the Soviet sphere after three weeks, returning through the Dardanelles and the Sea of Marmara into warmer Greek waters to face the less prickly menace

The market in Odessa offers charm and fresh fruit.
(Courtesy of Robert D. Voit)

of the Hellenic civil service. While she was crossing the Aegean in August (as Saddam Hussein's elite Republican Guard was invading sandy Kuwait) a faulty casting in the mizzenmast runner snapped, as did the mizzenmast; for the remainder of the summer *Ti* sailed as a sloop. From Piraeus she sailed around the fabled Peloponnese—the locale of ancient Sparta, Mycenae, Jason and his Argonauts—to the island of Corfu, then along the dramatic Dalmatian coast of the former Yugoslavia (as war heated up in Bosnia). By October *Ticonderoga* rounded Italy's toe and reached Antibes, where a new mizzenmast, trucked across France from Southampton, was stepped. From there she sailed on to Gibraltar, the Canaries (where Voit joined the crew) and crossed to Antigua in 18 balmy downwind days.

For the rest of the winter *Ticonderoga*

lazily cruised down island and went up to Antigua in the spring of 1991 for Race Week. Voit again invited Bob Dickson to sail, but the boat's schedule didn't permit her to race in the Classic division; forced to race against modern boats she did poorly. While in Antigua Reardon had some varnishing done. By then he had established a format for keeping *Ticonderoga* in Bristol condition; he called it "blitzing." Every few months he would stop the boat for two weeks, wherever she was, hire a gang from the harbor, and do it all (generally letting the local handymen do the cosmetics, reserving the machinery for himself or a qualified mechanic). In the Caribbean, where the sun is so harmful to varnish, Reardon actually partitioned the cruising season by pre-Christmas and pre-Antigua Race Week blitzes.

Between blitzes Voit would cruise as often

as possible (he averaged eight or nine trips per year, wherever the boat was). He did a couple of long passages, but otherwise he flew to the boat. His friends filled the schedule the rest of the time. As a result, under Voit's stewardship, *Ticonderoga* was "booked" at least twenty-six weeks each year (ultimately to be used, if not abused, as much as in her busiest chartering years).

After the spring 1991 blitz, *Ticonderoga* went to New England for the summer, to Florida in the autumn, then down around Cuba's west end into the Caribbean Tradewinds to Roatan in the Bay Islands of Honduras. This was a new cruising area for *Ticonderoga* and company. It was also the first step of an admirable plan Voit had to bring *Ticonderoga* back to Newport Beach; he wanted to share her with West Coast sailors who hadn't seen her in the two decades since

Bob Johnson's triumphs. From Roatan, *Ticonderoga* sailed down to the aboriginal San Blas Islands off the Panama coast, where Voit joined her for a cruise. The Cuna Indians, a gentle people with their own kings and counsels, occupy the islands, living independently off fishing, farming, and harvesting coconuts. They welcome many visitors (many lamentably off cruise ships) to whom they sell their cheerful, handsewn *molas*. Their reefs and lagoons are not well charted, so *Ticonderoga* had to enter each new anchorage behind a crewman in the dinghy checking depths with a leadline.

From the San Blas Islands *Ticonderoga* transited the Panama Canal and cruised up to Puntarenas on Costa Rica's Gulf of Nicoya, then Acapulco, and on toward Los Angeles. For her return to Newport Beach, Voit had organized a big splash, literally, with fire-boats, fireworks, and a grand yacht club party, timing the opening of the festivities with her arrival. But in Cabo San Lucas, Baja California, *Ticonderoga*'s engine transmission failed. It would have been a terrible letdown, in case the wind died and she couldn't sail into the harbor, if she had to be towed in. So with the help of Voit's brother, Richard, the group arranged for transmission parts to be flown to a California rendezvous for installation. It was well that they did. *Ticonderoga* arrived at Newport in very light air, and she would not have made it into the harbor without her engine. A press boat came out to greet her, as did a great crowd of yachts. *Ticonderoga of Newport* was home.

She remained in Newport Beach all summer. There was a flurry of local newspaper and magazine stories covering her return, nearly all recalling her glory days under Johnson. Otherwise she enjoyed a sedate breather. On one occasion, with Reardon off on a holiday, Voit invited Bob Dickson to skipper her for a couple of days so he could entertain some business acquaintances. Dickson agreed, as usual taking no money, but eagerly accepting a *Ticonderoga* jacket instead. During the first day's outing, however, Dickson noted that Voit was hesitant to handle the boat in the harbor: Reardon was so possessive that Voit had never done it. Dickson gave Voit the helm and he gloried in his brief license to undock and redock his own yacht.

At the end of the summer *Ticonderoga* sailed up to San Francisco for Labor Day then down to San Diego for a fall cruise. The big question for Voit then became: Where do we sail next? As he and Reardon had done in each prior year, they pulled out some charts

With her new mizzenmast, Ticonderoga *cruised southern France.*
(Courtesy of Robert D. Voit)

SAILING TO THE MILLENNIUM

1993 and Beyond

A S *TICONDEROGA* approached Belize City early in May 1993, events were unfolding rapidly up north. Scott Frantz had nonchalantly invited the young woman he was dating, Allison "Icy" Hanley, to fly away with him for a one-day springtime escapade in Central America. He was coy about telling her why they were going to Belize of all places, saying only that he wanted to look at a sailboat there. He *didn't* tell her that he had just agreed to buy that sailboat, or that she was the world's most beloved yacht.

Nor would it have made a great deal of difference if he had told her: Icy Hanley wasn't much of a sailor and she probably wouldn't have recognized the name *Ticonderoga*. Despite her having grown up in Greenwich, Connecticut, a sailors' town, she was normally surrounded by golfers and tennis players. She had sailed a Widgeon only briefly as a child—just long enough to develop a slight fear of heel angles. Her only big-boat experience had been on the J-Class sloop *Shamrock*, whose heel angles and broader

To steer Ti *into the future.*
(Christian Février)

decks she apparently found less intimidating.

But Icy Hanley did guess that something odd was afoot when Scott invited a "chaperone" on this presumably romantic tropical fling: a burly Danish friend, Erik Christensen, who happened to be an expert on wooden boats. The unlikely trio flew to Belize City and were met at the airport by Tom Reardon, who drove them to the boat; he was obviously a bit tentative at first, as one might expect from a captain meeting a new owner, after more than six years of global adventure with another. When the group reached the boat, Frantz was overwhelmed: *Ticonderoga* was in better shape than he had expected. Everything was cosmetically perfect. He again went weak in the knees. Just as important, after his professional, more clinical survey, Erik Christensen was also impressed. He recognized the salient evidence of *Ticonderoga's* splendid reconstruction by Southampton Yacht Services, and her meticulous maintenance since.

Perhaps most important, for the long haul, Icy quickly recognized through her own eyes what Scott saw in *Ticonderoga*; she instinctively shared his aesthetic vision. She

also began to guess that this trip was Scott's subtle way of testing their relationship; thus she found that this classic boat, this *perfect* boat, was already forming a powerful bond between them.

They spent the morning getting to know the young crew. Later in the day Bob Voit flew in. He hadn't planned to go on the sea trial with them, only to secure for himself the emotional assurance that this stranger from Connecticut had the suitable spirit to properly provide for *Ticonderoga*. Like Reardon, Voit was a bit tense as he cautiously checked Frantz out. But the two men talked amiably and Voit got an immediate sense that Frantz was the right man to carry on his caretakership. He went out on the sea trial— as a friend, not an inquisitor. At the end of a radiant sail, under a cloudless sky, the metaphysical baton was passed—only the corporeal paperwork remained to give *Ticonderoga* a new owner and, of prime import, a caretaker altogether equal to the task.

I n the fifty-three years of his life to the day he sold *Ticonderoga*, Bob Voit had owned several large boats. In the thirty-two years of *his*

life to the day he bought *Ticonderoga*, Scott Frantz had never owned a boat larger than a J/24; "Big Ti" was his first big boat. Scott Frantz does not take the middling approach to life; he goes straight for the summit. Literally. By the time he was in his thirties he had climbed Mont Blanc, Rainier, the great peaks of Alaska and Colorado, and (with Icy) Kilimanjaro. And after a 1982 test run, in 1991 he all but conquered that most forbidding of peaks, Everest. Though he was not, by luck of the draw, among the ten climbers who reached the summit, Scott Frantz is a summiteer; he is driven to reach the top in all his undertakings. He appears to have inherited that trait from his parents.

Frantz's mother, Ann Haebler, came from a family involved in brewing, and manufacture of flavors and fragrances. She spent much of her life, however, until her death in 1988, dedicated to charitable work and support of nonprofit institutions. She was also an active participant in the syndicates that campaigned the America's Cup contenders *Weatherly*, *Intrepid*, *Courageous*, and *Enterprise*. As a result, Scott spent some of his formative summers on the sparkling waters off Newport, Rhode Island, chasing 12-Meter yachts. (Only those fortunate to have seen a 12-Meter close up can appreciate the powerful impact that must have had on him.)

Frantz's father, Leroy "Lee" Frantz, Jr., was born to a family involved in banking and dental supplies. *His* father was Commodore of the Larchmont Yacht Club, where he kept a stately motoryacht, *Snow White*, which served as a race committee boat for the club and a lyceum for young Lee to hone his brass-polishing skills. (Unlike the teenage Bob Voit, who found boatwork a grind, Lee Frantz enjoyed it.) And because his father was a benefactor to the yacht club's junior sailing programs, Lee developed an early passion for the sport, which never diminished.

After graduating from Princeton in

Frantz at the helm of the world's most famous ocean racer, and with Mark Whettu on Everest in 1982.

(Top: Christopher Cunningham/Left: Courtesy of L. Scott Frantz)

1949, Lee joined his in-laws' company, Van Ameringen & Haebler. In a decade he was instrumental in turning the company into a major domestic player, then helped pilot a merger with a Dutch firm, creating International Flavors & Fragrances (IFF), which became a dominant power in natural and synthetic food and cosmetic additives. In 1961, IFF went public. Scott was one year old.

Leroy Scott Frantz was born on June 29, 1960. As a boy he developed lifelong obsessions with mountaineering, flying, and scuba diving. His obsession with sailing was launched by a solo voyage he took at the age of five, when his father shoved him off the family's sailboat in a Dyer dinghy, and told him to sail back in time for dinner. Scott engaged in a fierce duel with himself, tacking forty times in a hundred yards. He savored the dinner, as well as his new-found confidence. He then advanced to Blue Jays, Hobie Cats, and Flying Scots, then joined his father on sailing cruisers, most memorably on his 82-foot Rhodes ketch, *Sorrento* (where Scott witnessed some impressive brushes with *Ticonderoga*). By the age of fourteen, Scott put in his first guest appearance on those fabulous Twelves, courtesy of his mother. (In later years he would become a generous contributor to America's Cup defenses and, as a bonus, get to sail on those fabulous Twelves and a few of their swifter successors.)

At Princeton, Scott concentrated on politics and was awarded his Bachelor of Arts degree in 1982. He then went to work for a small consulting firm, Analytic Systems Corp., which had developed powerful investment-oriented computer programs for money managers. Frantz worked for ASC for two years, absorbing considerable market wisdom and corporate savvy. In 1984, succumbing to the 1980s MBA imperative, he enrolled in Dartmouth's Tuck Business School, working concurrently on Wall Street at Donaldson, Lufkin & Jenrette. Later he

(TOP) Icy and Scott Frantz take a turn at the helm. (RIGHT) Ann Haebler Frantz, and Lee Frantz.
(Top: Patricia Lascabannes; Right: Courtesy of L. Scott Frantz)

moved on to Banker's Trust, in its Mergers and Acquisitions department.

The process of playing with businesses for profit absorbed Scott Frantz from the outset; he became a quintessential corporate trader. But the lack of personal freedom in his work didn't thrill him as much; he relished the game but wanted to play it with greater independence. On Christmas Eve 1989 he was working (perhaps *slaving* would be the better word) late in his office, when he was struck hard by the realization that he wasn't even upset by missing the party he had been invited to. The sense of detachment disturbed him; something had to give.

Frantz left Bankers Trust at the age of twenty-nine to create his own firm: a small investment group under the Haebler name. Using his own resources, he built Haebler into an effective blend of venture-capitalist and merchant-banking firm, focusing on the oil and gas industry, computer software, telecommunications, and specialty food imports. In a few years Haebler grew to where Scott knew he could afford the time to dive, climb, and fly when he chose, and to sail a fine yacht of his own.

After the successful test sail in Belize, Reardon headed *Ticonderoga* north to Spencer's in Palm Beach for a haulout and survey. On June 7 she received a glowing report. She sailed up to Connecticut, arriving on June 21 at Stamford's Yacht Haven. Scott greeted her from the wheel of his other favorite waterborne vehicle, a mint-condition 1959 Riva speedboat. Amid friends and family, Scott and Icy rechristened the boat with the traditional champagne, then they took the gang out for a joyous summer afternoon sail on Long Island Sound. The papers were passed and the purchase closed the next day. *Ticonderoga* then participated in the annual Fourth of July celebration in New York

Harbor and Scott brought some more friends in the Riva to watch her. It was a splendid day of sails and spars arrayed against the backdrop of lower Manhattan's glass-and-steel spires, a setting unmatched in the world for its grandeur and drama. After the fireworks, Scott sped the guests home in the Riva; *Ti* sailed back to Stamford.

On July 14, feeling impulsive, Scott at last summoned the courage to take Icy out for a spin alone. But it *wasn't* in *Ticonderoga*. It was in another of his most favored vehicles: a world-champion, Russian-built Sukhoi 29 aerobatic monoplane. The two were flying giddily over Long Island Sound, doing stunts, gazing down on the world when, at a squarely opportune moment— they were upside down—Scott proposed to Icy. Upside down, she accepted. Scott executed a perfect series of victory rolls. In just two months *Ticonderoga*'s catalytic charm had done its work.

Ticonderoga's first cruise was to Fishers Island, where Icy's parents had a summer home, and where the couple had their engagement party. It was there that Icy began seeing with greater clarity the meaning of having a yacht like *Ticonderoga* at one's disposal. Scott had spent his childhood summers on boats; he already knew well their gift of mobility. Icy had spent *her* childhood summers on Fishers Island; she knew best the comforts of fixity. On Fishers Island, with *Ticonderoga* moored nearby, she realized that the promise of mobility could be ever more gratifying—that a free-wandering, well-found yacht can bestow greater autonomy, joy, and enlightenment than even the most familiar, well-found house.

Ticonderoga spent the summer in New England. In Maine, Scott entered her into the Eggemoggin Reach Regatta, her first significant race as *Ticonderoga of Greenwich*. She finished in a bit over three hours and broke the record. And why not? Under ideal conditions she was still "Big Ti." Toward the end of the summer *Ticonderoga* raced in the Opera House Cup off Nantucket, then the Classic Yacht Regatta in Newport. She moved on to

Ticonderoga alongside Neith *in Eggemoggin Reach.*
(Stock Newport/Onne van der Wal)

(*OVERLEAF*) *Thundering along under full sail.*
(Guy Gurney)

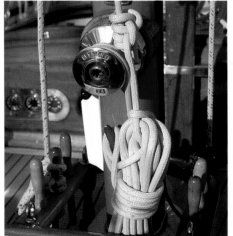

(OPPOSITE) *Drowning the dolphins in Antigua Race Week.* (Christopher Cunningham)

(ABOVE) *The saloon today, and deck details* (Top: Dana Jinkins/Above, left & center: Benjamin Mendlowitz/Right: Patricia Lascabannes)

The Frantzes and friends enjoyed an occasional cruise during the winter of 1994/95, and in April *Ticonderoga* sailed once more among her sister classics in Antigua Race Week. Then, as she had under John Hertz, Bob Johnson, and Bob Voit, she sailed across the Atlantic in search of Mediterranean adventure. With Captain Tom Reardon commanding, she stopped briefly in Bermuda, then the Azores, Gibraltar, and the Mediterranean island of Pantelleria. She then sailed on to the Greek island of Rhodes, once home to one of the world's Seven Great Wonders, the Colossus. There, Icy and Scott joined *Ti* for a summer cruise along the Turkish coast and out into the enigmatic islands of the wine-dark Aegean Sea.

To many a sailor, cruising among the fabled Greek Isles is akin to emigrating to the kingdom of heaven. The islands of the Aegean have a distinctly rugged beauty. They are richly green, redolent with herbs, flowers, and spices in the spring. Then, in the sere heat of summer, they quickly turn to scrubby brown and gray to reveal their geologic underpinnings, gnarled olive trees, dusty

(ABOVE) *Ti in the ancient harbor of Rhodes, Greece.*
(RIGHT) *Captain Tom climbing the cliffs of Keçi Buku, Turkey.*
(Courtesy of L. Scott Frantz)

vineyards, and lots of well-fed goats. The distance between islands is never more than a few hours' sail, and under the bright sapphire skies of a brazen Meltemi north wind the clarity of the air is such that navigation is always by eye. But even when the Meltemi is quiescent, the curtain of sheer Grecian haze that drops gently over the sea barely limits the visibility.

Under any circumstance, by the dual heritage of ancient ruins and contemporary villages on each island, and by the many islands' sporadic placement, each encounter is novel. (To be sure, the Greeks gave us the word *sporadic*, with the same root as *Sporades*, the descriptive name for two major Aegean island groups.) And though the more frequently sailed Caribbean Islands remain more attractively green all year, their colorful Afro-European culture never attains a majesty to equal that of the ancient and modern cultures of the "Cradle of Western Civilization." Besides, where else can you anchor beneath a 2,500-year-old temple, then step ashore to enjoy a home-cooked meal of fresh fish or squid, tasty salad, savory bread, and local resinated wine tapped young from a barrel?

(LEFT) *Scott leaping from a Stromboli cliff, and* (LEFT BELOW) *with Icy on Vulcano.*
(BELOW) *Icy's thirtieth birthday on Ios, Greece.*
(Courtesy of L. Scott Frantz)

For the fitness-conscious Frantzes, their Grecian cruise included daily morning runs, planned so they could look back on *Ticonderoga* from a high vantage point and admire her. And they found other admirers as well. Wherever *Ticonderoga* sailed they met people who knew her: who had sailed on her, read about her, gazed longingly at her (in real life or in many of her famous photos). Often, these were older people who turned misty-eyed as they recognized her. Through these casual meetings the Frantzes discovered that their yacht had brought a great deal of happiness to more people than they had ever imagined.

In their off-the-boat routine, the Frantzes also became obsessed with exploring the undersea caves that are dispersed along the Greek, Turkish and, later, Italian coasts. And they celebrated Icy's thirtieth birthday, anchored off a golden beach on the youth-cult Greek island of Ios, with friends who flew over just for the occasion. Sailing the Greek Islands—so distant in time and spirit from Fishers Island, Monhegan Island or the Virgin Islands—enhanced the Frantzes' sense of well-being, and confirmed that they owned something very special, snug, and familiar.

After *Ticonderoga* left the Aegean, she sailed around Italy, up through the Straits of Messina, between the mythological Scylla and Charybdis, and on to the Aeolian Islands. A dramatic volcanic cluster just 50 miles north of Sicily's Mount Etna, the Aeolian Islands are perhaps best known as home to the Greek god of the wind, Aeolus, who provided that cunning adventurer, Odysseus, with a bag of breeze that, when opened, blew him and his fleet of ships off course for twenty years. Here, amid stunning crags and commanding mythology, Scott, Icy, and their crew indulged in one of their most favored benefits of nautical mobility:

Ticonderoga moored before the bold backdrop of Stromboli in the Aeolian Islands.
(Courtesy of L. Scott Frantz)

The crew at the crest of a living volcano: Vulcano.
(Courtesy of L. Scott Frantz)

cliff climbing. The Aeolian cliffs emerge precipitously from beneath the Tyrrhenian Sea, where the water depth falls sharply to 3,000 feet only a couple of miles offshore. The cliffs are a first-rate challenge to even the most daring climber. The object is to put on good shoes, light clothes, and the right attitude, and climb as close to the summit as courage will permit . . . then plunge headlong into the sea.

On Stromboli, with some of their crew, they attained the island's summit under the eerie light of a full moon, to watch the steam and ash that regularly burst forth every 11 minutes from this still-active volcano. Scott and one of the crew elected to climb around the rim to take photos of the crater, when an

unscheduled eruption forced them to a hasty retreat. Has ever a yacht been used for a more gallant, more invigorating purpose?

From the fairyland of Odysseus, *Ticonderoga* sailed along the spectacular Campania coast, piloted by an Italian-American friend, Clemente, who took the crew to places unheard-of in the guidebooks. First the Frantzes stopped in Sorrento to take a brief spin in a rental car down the spellbinding Amalfi Drive. Then they visited friends on Capri. Next, they anchored off Ventotene, a tiny isle filled with ancient Roman caves, which they explored. They moved next to Ponza to visit the forbidding prison built by Benito Mussolini to dispose of his anti-fascist enemies. Finally, they did a dramatic sail-

by of the tiny village of Circeo, where they lined the deck, waved vigorously, and fired their cannon in honor of Clemente's mother, who lives there.

After her Italian adventures, *Ticonderoga* sailed on to Saint-Tropez, France, for the 1995 *Nioulargue* classic series. Once again, the Frantzes invited a host of friends from home. They rented a charming villa overlooking the sea and the town for their guests. In the evenings, as expected, Saint-Tropez opened its cafes, bars, clubs, shops, winding

(RIGHT) Karenita *sails to the St.-Tropez breakwater at the end of a* Nioulargue *day.* (Patricia Lascabannes)
(OVERLEAF) *The stunning 203-foot topsail schooner* Adix. (Christian Février)

cobblestone streets, and ample heart to this horde of happy sailors and the crews of the nearly three hundred other classic yachts. With her permanent crew of four, a few ringers, and a couple of Antiguan sailors who helped with her offshore deliveries, *Ticonderoga* sailed the *Nioulargue* series with twenty-four people on deck (there seems to be no strict crew limitation in the *Nioulargue*—so long as the food and life jackets are sufficient). Half of the guests were assigned crew positions for each race; the alternates were forced to dedicate their time to frivolity, photography, and catering.

But the 1995 *Nioulargue* was not entirely successful. One race was plagued by light winds; another by a chill, drenching rain. And, despite a sublime international water fight that nearly drained the harbor and made the Armada's defeat look like a clambake, the festive week came to an unplanned halt when an accident resulted in the sinking of a small sloop, killing a crewman. The organizers canceled the remaining races, although some yachtsmen, who had sailed long distances to be in this unforgettable event, entered into friendly match races in tacit honor of the Frenchman who had lost his life in the name of sport.

From France, *Ticonderoga* headed back across the Atlantic via Palma, Gibraltar, and the Canaries, making landfall once more at Antigua. From there she shuttled between St. Barts and the Virgins for the remainder of the winter, returning to Antigua in April for a Reardon-style blitz and Race Week. Again an impetuous gang of the Frantzes' friends flew down to join them. It is this social aspect of *Ticonderoga's* use that so animates the Frantzes, and so effectively closes the circle of the boat's history since Harry and

(CLOCKWISE FROM UPPER LEFT)

Tuiga *sails under* Altair's *lee.* (Christian Février)
Racing: a spectator sport. (Stock Newport/Gary John Norman)
Ticonderoga's *1995* Nioulargue *crew.* (Jack Moffly)
Pen Duick *returns to the harbor.* (Christian Février)

(OVERLEAF) Ticonderoga *in her Antigua mode.*
(Stock Newport/Gary John Norman)

Ruth Noyes took their first grand daysail in August 1936. Yet the Frantzes also see the boat in somewhat different, though complementary terms. Scott, who sought *Ticonderoga* with passion, tries to maintain her to perfection. But he doesn't see her as a museum piece meant only to be admired; even as he knows that she needs to be pampered, he races her fairly hard. Icy, who came relatively late to sailing, sees *Ticonderoga* as a vehicle of pleasure and intimacy. She finds racing exciting, but primarily for its teamwork and camaraderie: nowhere else can she and Scott be so well cloistered with friends, to catch up with them in their mutually busy lives. In either case, the Frantzes have come to agree wholeheartedly with Bob Voit's most earnest of reminiscences: "You can't *possibly* have a bad day on *Ticonderoga.*"

Energy, wind, muscle, seawater, and friends
make the Caribbean day.
(Right: Guy Gurney/Far right & below: Patricia Lascabannes)

In the spring of 1996, *Ticonderoga* again came north, and again made a rather mediocre showing in the Bermuda Race, where she just couldn't get the right combination of breeze strength and angle for one of her classic booming reaches. But, on a more joyful note, two important events loomed large on the horizon: Icy was due to have a baby in July; *Ti* was due to have her sixtieth birthday in August. For the indomitable Icy, pregnancy would mean only a slight curtailment of her own energetic professional schedule: she was completing her Masters program in social work at Columbia University, and working with local educators and Connecticut authorities consulting on substance-abuse policy. The birth on July 10 of eight-pound, two-ounce Christopher Hunter Frantz (named for Scott's brother, who was killed in a helicopter crash) gave a

It isn't all work sailing Ticonderoga, *even for Christopher Hunter (under Icy's attentive gaze).*
(Courtesy of L. Scott Frantz)

new resolve to the couple's life and to their plans for *Ticonderoga.* And it began almost immediately with their taking their four-week-old son to Nantucket in Scott's French-built TBM 700 to attend *Ticonderoga*'s sixtieth birthday party. (To Scott, as many other pilots, flying and sailing share every material aspect, except the obvious one of speed. But, he readily admits he has more fun sailing.) In Nantucket, Christopher Hunter joined an exclusive group of small fry who had enjoyed *Ti*'s comforts over the years: Harry, Pike, and Bradley Noyes (who sailed her often in the 1930s, occasionally with their equestrian sister, Hope); Allan Carlisle III and his brother Robert (who, in the early 1950s, used *Ti*'s cockpit as a playpen); and Margaret and Trevor Mac-Kenzie (who sailed her as diapered infants in the 1970s).

Ticonderoga's birthday, August 10, 1996, coincided with the Nantucket Bucket weekend regatta. In the evening of the Saturday race, Scott invited all the sailors in the harbor for birthday cake and a low-key toast to *Ticonderoga* as she lay with her decks cleaned, her varnish chammied, and her sails neatly furled. Nearly three hundred people showed up at the dock to ask about *Ti*'s glorious history, gaze at her, and accept small souvenirs of the occasion. The miracle of the event was that *Ticonderoga*, after sixty years of life and somewhere around a quarter million miles of sailing, was in truly fine form.

After the party, defiantly shrugging off her sixty-year marker as though those incredible years and her several facelifts had never happened, *Ticonderoga* joined many of her matronly peers in Bristol, Rhode Island, for the 1996 Herreshoff Rendezvous, run by the Herreshoff Museum. This is an annual gathering of yachts designed by Nathanael and Francis Herreshoff, many built by the Herreshoff Manufacturing Company; even modern replicas of Herreshoff-family classics are invited to join the hallowed fleet. It

'Big Ti' faces her 60th birthday without a qualm.
(Guy Gurney)

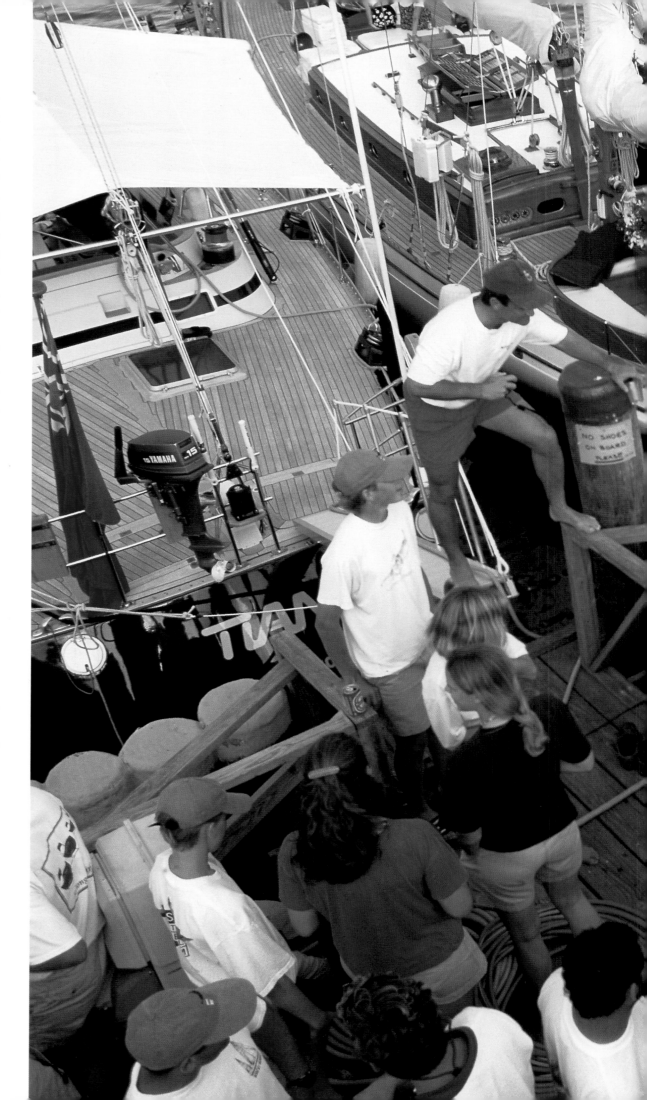

is a rally that bears witness to one major facet of America's astonishing yachting heritage, as driven over more than a century by the Herreshoff family, as well as an informal regatta among owners bent on preserving that heritage in the spirit of play.

For Scott Frantz, however, the highlight of the event was neither the social breeziness nor the historical parade; it was his rematch race with *Radiance*, a new *Ticonderoga* clone constructed of wood over steel frames. *Radiance* had already beaten *Ticonderoga* in the Opera House Cup. With *Ticonderoga* weigh-

ing in at about 18,000 pounds more than *Radiance* and having to race with a crew of inexperienced newcomers, she had every excuse to lose this one also. But she won, and looked all the more radiant for it.

Once the 1996 summer season came to an end, Reardon brought *Ticonderoga* up to another favorite haunt, Wayfarer Marine, in Camden, Maine, for a haulout and work. An earlier survey had found some rot in her cabin top. She also needed a new deep freeze, batteries, chafing gear, some engine work, a bit of paint and varnish (caretakership, they

call it). As had all prior owners, Scott Frantz had already recognized that the assertive combination of *Ticonderoga*'s very woodenness, her relentless aging, and inflation (even at low 1990s rates) made caretakership an expensive proposition. To begin with, when the word *marine* is attached to a product, its price soars: the new freezer, which on the household market might have cost

Cloning is the sincerest form of flattery:
Ticonderoga *and her high-tech sister*, Radiance.
(Guy Gurney)

$2,000, cost five times that much on *Ticonderoga*. (The prior year she needed new working sails—main, mizzen, No. 1 and No. 2 jibs—which were produced for $35,000 by North Sails.) Clearly, *Ticonderoga*'s operating and maintenance overhead in 1996 dollars had risen considerably beyond the $10,000 per month Ken and Fran MacKenzie were humbled by twenty years earlier.

But just as clearly, one can never define the ownership of a classic wooden boat in strictly monetary terms, nor try to justify the cost of maintaining such a boat in anything

but historic terms. The rule of thumb is: if you can afford it, you must have blind passion and an open checkbook; if you can't, then it is best to avoid caretakership altogether. Still, ownership of a museum-quality classic comes with an implicit demand for equilibrium. For the public's sake, it must be a floating open house; but it cannot be open to every tramping foot without some well-meant discipline. Wear and tear must be balanced against history. Such are the strictly orthodox terms of caretakership of a sixty-year-old yacht on the eve of the millennium.

To the Frantzes, *Ticonderoga* is not just a boat; she is an emotional experience. Thus they share a vivid dream: they want to take their child (or children) around the world on *Ti*. They began talking soberly about this while in the Caribbean after meeting a young family cruising on a smaller, humbler boat. The children of that family were profiting from the finest education parental devotion can buy: seeing the world firsthand from the

(OVERLEAF) *No sea is too mountainous for 'Big Ti.'*
(Dan Nerney)

The binnacle; Ti *in the fog.*
(Top: KOS/Right: Dana Jinkins)

deck of their own floating home. The Frantzes want *their* children, in addition to a conventional education ashore, to have that same instruction at sea; to enter other communities and cultures through the wide-open gateways of harbors and roadsteads, not just through the constrictive gateways of textbooks and classrooms. It's a tall order for two vigorous people still solidly anchored in their shoreside community and culture, and committed to highly charged careers. So, perhaps, the *first* time they and their offspring view the world, they will be content to send *Ticonderoga* with her professional crew to distant lands and, like other owners of fine blue-water yachts, join her by way of the well-tested virtues of the Boeing 747 or the DC-10.

The next time, perhaps, Icy, Scott, and their offspring (and no doubt a few willing, venturesome friends), will sail the world together, from port to port, from gateway to gateway, on *Ti's* solid teak deck. Until then, for Icy and Scott Frantz the very few years they have owned her have been, by their own heartfelt calculation, the best of their young lives. And by simple extrapolation, there can be no doubt that the coming years will be ever more rewarding. So long as they are with *Ticonderoga,* and *Ticonderoga* is with them.

*Sailing to the millennium: a bone in her teeth,
her dolphins awash.*
(Left: Billy Black/Above: Patricia Lascabannes)

*T*iconderoga is far from being the largest sailing yacht ever built. At 72 feet on deck (86 feet overall), she is eclipsed by dozens of sailboats. *Ticonderoga* was born a daysailer, albeit an uncommon one that fell off her cradle as she emerged from the womb. She spent her vigorous youth as a loving family's vehicle for amusement. She served her wartime adolescence in an ill-fitting suit of gray. Grown up, she returned to civilian life to provide new pleasures for the wealthy. She was then commanded, as a buoyant young adult, by one dedicated man who in just four intense years built her into an undisputed world champion. Aging but still willing, she retired with her records and trophies intact (if not her original spars, planks and frames), to spend twenty years in the charter grind. Now, in her mature years, as shapely and gleaming as she ever was, *Ticonderoga* is once more a cherished family yacht. The circle is indeed closed.

Yet within *Ticonderoga*'s new planks, frames, and fastenings, there still beats the heart of an ocean racer. Like a retired racehorse on a fast track, once in a great while, when the wind is fresh and free, this great dame, this wooden champion, this most perfect of Francis Herreshoff's creations, can still manage a good, oftimes spectacular, turn of speed. Sometimes she can achieve a first-to-finish; sometimes another record. Give *Ticonderoga* her breeze, in fact, and she may show up some of those precocious modern pretenders to greatness with their Kevlar hulls, carbon-fiber spars, and Mylar sails.

After all, she is—and always *will* be—"Big Ti."

ACKNOWLEDGMENTS

THIS BOOK IS MY SINCERE ATTEMPT to tell the full story of a rare and beautiful yacht. Recreating *Ticonderoga*'s life, like writing any celebrity's biography, required digging into numerous sources to find the essential ingredients of truth. This was an intricate process, because, while few yachts have had more written about them, much of *Ticonderoga*'s published history is the stuff of mythology. This work, therefore, could not have been accomplished without the spirited help of many people and institutions, to whom I remain ever grateful.

I wish to thank first several people who graciously opened their homes, memories, and attics to my restless searchings for their late forebears: John Noble Brown, for reconstructing his handsome father, Waldo H. Brown; Bradley Noyes and Hope Noyes Smith, for bringing to life their beloved father, Harry E. Noyes; Karin Booth Carlisle and Allan Carlisle III, for sharing unfaded memories of their husband and father, Allan P. Carlisle; and Mark Johnson, for bringing his gentle, larger-than-life father, Robert F. Johnson, down to accessible size.

I wish also to thank Mike Anderson, for his unflinching portrayal of John Hertz; friends in the beef-cattle industry for sketching a cameo of Bill Brittain; Baxter Still for confessing the intricacies and disappointments of the yachting life; Robert S. Robe, Brian and Angela Coen, and Peggy Hooker, for recalling *Ticonderoga*'s entry into the charter trade; Fran and Ken MacKenzie, for opening their hearts, baring their souls, and digging into their closets to bring back an unforgettable era; David Edwards, Jan and John Whitney, and Peter Warwick, for recounting their adventures; Robert D. Voit, for inviting me to sail the 1989 *Nioulargue* with him, and for spontaneously expressing the pure poetry and harsh reality of owning *Ticonderoga*; and Tom Reardon, for his insights without limit.

The following people, who sailed (aboard or against) *Ticonderoga* or worked to preserve her, shared spoken, written, or photographic recall of the hell of a storm, the heaven of a first-place finish, or the savor of a *mai-tai:* Skip Allan, Dick Bertram, Peter Bowker, Bob Dickson, Ray Eaton, Dan Elliott, Skip Eveleth, Peter Gerquest, Al Grenier, Bob Hamill, Jr., Billy Letts, Lee Lie-Nielsen, Bill Luders, Frank Mayo, Carleton Mitchell, Alex Pfotenhauer, Frank Rohr, Jill Purdy, George Sustendal, Ray Wallace, and the late Geoffrey Smith.

I am also grateful to these individuals and institutions for providing information, photos or just encouragement: Louis Howland, Bruce King, Prof. Nick Mills, John Munford, and Pat and Jim Roberts; the Hart Collections at MIT, Peabody Museum, Quincy Historical Society, Still Picture Branch of the National Archives, U.S. Coast Guard Historian, Naval Historical Center, Corbis-Bettmann, Hawaii Maritime Center, Herreshoff Museum, *Yachting*, Nova University, Hertz Corp., Center for Cuban Studies, TIME/LIFE, The Disney Company, Southampton Yacht Services, and the Bacardi-Martini Museum. I thank all members of the major yacht clubs in San Diego, Los Angeles, Newport Beach, Honolulu, Miami, and St. Petersburg (with special thanks to Ibbie Jones of St. Pete). And I reserve particular thanks to the photographers credited herein, for their vision, diligence, and focus.

The Mystic Seaport Museum, which has generously published this book, provided invaluable material in my research. For that I first thank Revell Carr, Director, for opening the museum's administrative and archival doors to my unrestricted entry and incessant probing. I enthusiastically acknowledge the assistance of many dedicated Mystic curators and librarians: Doug Stein, Kelly Drake, and Leah Prescott in the Research Library; Georgia York, Marifrances Trivelli, Elizabeth Rafferty, and Phil Budlong in the General Collections; Ellen Stone, Pat Wilbur, and Maria Christenson in Ship's Plans; Peggy Tate Smith, Mary Anne Stets, Judy Beisler, Jennifer Stich, and Claire White-Peterson in Photo Reproduction; and Deborah DiGregorio, Victoria Sharps, Jack MacFadyen, and Julia Doering in the Rosenfeld Collection.

I am deeply grateful to Robin Dutcher-Bayer, copy editor, for her unwavering attention to my cranky writing style. And I am doubly indebted to Joseph Gribbins—sailor, editorial guru, and Director of Publishing for Mystic—for his unfailing encouragement, faithful corrections, and gentle smoothing of my excesses (though I take full responsibility for all excesses and errors that remain).

My profound thanks go to Dana Jinkins and Jill Bobrow of Concepts Publishing for their valued counsel, and John Matthews of Graphic Services who, with Mary Ball, found color where none exists. Above all, I wish to thank Bonnie Atwater, of Atwater Design, who took my chaotic conception of this massive history and, with infinite patience and multifaceted skill, turned it into a work of art and coherence.

Finally, I wish to express my deepest appreciation to Scott and Icy Frantz for choosing me from a large field of authors, and for continuing to support my work in creating this history for the world. Though I know that they would have preferred to publish this book earlier, I trust they are pleased that "Big Ti" will live for many years more, not only on the high seas (through their own good works) but on a prominent shelf in their handsome wood-paneled library.

J.A.S.